To Michael Atkison

Christmas 1991

GEORGE OTTO SIMMS, A BIOGRAPHY

GEORGE OTTO SIMMS
A BIOGRAPHY

Lesley Whiteside

COLIN SMYTHE
Gerrards Cross, 1990

Copyright © 1990 by Lesley Whiteside

All rights reserved

First published in 1990 by Colin Smythe Limited,
Gerrards Cross, Buckinghamshire

British Library Cataloguing in Publication Data

Whiteside, Lesley
  George Otto Simms, a biography
  1. Church of Ireland. Simms, George, 1910–
  I. Title
  283'.092
  ISBN 0–86140–331–2

Printed and bound in Great Britain
at The Camelot Press, Trowbridge, Wiltshire.

CONTENTS

LIST OF ILLUSTRATIONS

FOREWORD

The Most Reverend R. H. A. Eames,
Archbishop of Armagh, Primate of All Ireland

It is a great pleasure to be invited to pen these few words as a Foreword to Lesley Whiteside's biography of Bishop George Simms.

The phrase 'where do I begin?' is often a useful way of saying that you have little or nothing worthwhile to contribute about a person's life or work. In this case the exact opposite is the case. Where does one begin to describe a life of such variety and service?

George Simms has been a part of Irish life for the lifetime of most who will read these pages. He has contributed so much to enrich the lives and experience of members of the Church of Ireland — and of so many of other traditions. As a churchman, scholar, pastor and writer he has set standards of excellence few can emulate. His love for Ireland and her culture, his devotion to the Church of Ireland, his sensitive understanding of Celtic history and his great gifts of expression by spoken or written word, have won him international recognition as a lecturer and writer. His memory is phenomenal and his knowledge of people and events has been rightly described as 'encyclopaedic'.

Allied to such gifts, each of which is sufficient to mark out many a life of achievement, is that particular charm of manner which immediately strikes the right chord of sympathetic understanding in conversation.

Bishop Simms is one of the few who have occupied the position of both Archbishop of Dublin and Archbishop of Armagh. He has brought to such demanding roles a particular contribution of gentleness and spirituality which have given to decision-making and leadership a precious element of sensitivity.

This biography seeks to capture the many facets of a truly remarkable man. I know it will be read and appreciated by so many who have good reason to be thankful for the contribution and influence G. O. Simms has brought to the life of the Church of Ireland and beyond.

See House   Robert Armagh
Armagh

PREFACE AND ACKNOWLEDGEMENTS

This is not an official biography: when I broached the idea with Dr Simms his immediate reaction was 'Who would want to write *my* biopgraphy?' He was, indeed, reluctant to countenance the project, believing that he had done nothing to merit it; however, my argument that a biography might deepen understanding of the Church of Ireland since the establishment of the Irish Free State and that monographs serve as sources for more general histories prevailed. I appreciate that it is not usual to write the biography of someone who is very much alive; my sense of urgency arose from the desire to draw on his encyclopaedic knowledge of the Church of Ireland. As time went on it seemed right to publish it for his eightieth birthday. In the text I have referred to him as 'George' until the point at which he was awarded his Ph.D. After that I refer to him as Dr Simms.

My thanks go first to him for his unfailing co-operation in the research process. (Any quotations which are not accompanied by footnotes are either from our interviews or from his personal papers.) I also want to thank his wife, my husband, Robert, the Ven. R. G. F. Jenkins, the Rev. Dr D. J. P. Hewlett, the Very Rev. J. T. F. Paterson and J. P. T. Lee for reading the draft critically, Dr R. Refaussé and Mrs H. Smith of the Library of the Representative Church Body were most helpful, as was Mrs T. Pope in the Library of Trinity College and Mr J. Vincent in the library of *The Irish Times*. A great number of people provided information and lent papers — so many that I couldn't list them here but I am most grateful. Many thanks also to the Very Rev. J. M. G. Carey, the Ven. R. G. F. Jenkins and the Rev. G. C. Kerr for providing prints.

I wish to thank those who granted permission to quote them and the following for permission to quote from their works: Miss Susan Parkes, to quote from *Kildare Place, The History of The Church of Ireland Training College, 1811–1869*; the Stanford family, to quote from W. B. Stanford's *A Recognised Church*; The Most Rev. H. R. McAdoo, to quote from *No New Church*; The Rt Hon. D. W. Bleakley, to quote from *Peace in Ulster*; and R. D. E. Gallagher and A. S. Worrall, to quote from *Christians in Ulster, 1968–1980*.

My thanks to the following publishers for permission to quote from their publications: to Cassell, to quote from W. M. Abbott's *The Documents of Vatican II*; to Cork University Press, to quote from D. M. Clarke's *Church and State*; to *The Irish Times*, to quote from Michael Viney's *The Five Per Cent*; to Jonathan Cape to quote from Robin Flower's *Poems and Translations*; to Longman, to quote from A. M. Ramsey's *The Gospel and the Catholic Church*; to the McGraw-Hill Book Company to quote from J. B. Simpson & E. M. Story's *The Long Shadows of Lambeth X*; to the O'Brien Press, to quote from Sharon Gmelch's *Irish Life*; to the S. C. M. Press, to quote from A. M. Ramsey's *God, Christ and the World*, William Temple's *Christian Faith and Life*, and Dietrich Bonhoeffer's *The Cost of Discipleship*; to the S.P.C.K., to quote from Alan G. Stephenson's *Anglicanism and the Lambeth Conferences*, and from *Anglican Congress 1963, Report of Proceedings* Eugene R. Fairweather (ed.); and to Unwin Hyman, to quote from Humphrey Carpenter's *W. H. Auden, a Biography*.

Quotations from the Bible that were, for instance, texts for sermons, appear exactly as they were used, mostly from the Authorised Version, but for general reference, the New International Version is quoted.

I

BOYHOOD AND SCHOOL-DAYS

George Otto Simms was born on 4 July 1910, the third and youngest son of Jack and Ottilie Simms of Lifford, Co. Donegal. The Simms' ancestors had arrived in Ireland in the seventeenth century and settled near Castlefin. By the nineteenth century they lived in Strabane, County Tyrone, and ran the Simms Hotel, later the Abercorn Arms. John Francis Arthur Simms, George's father, was brought up in Beechmount, Strabane, but moved to Combermore, just over the bridge in Lifford, on his marriage in 1903. The only one of six children to remain in Strabane, he was a partner in the solicitors' practice of Wilson and Simms and later became the Crown Solicitor for Tyrone.

George's mother, Ottilie Sophie Stange, was an Australian-born German. Her father, Otto Georg Christian Stange had emigrated in the 1870s to Australia, where he was a professor of music, so Ottilie spoke English as well as German from the beginning. While she was still a young girl the family returned to Europe and Ottilie, after a time in a German school, was sent to boarding school in England. Gradually her father emerged as a successful stockbroker, living for part of the year in London. Her mother, however, died in 1892 when Ottilie was thirteen. Three years later her father married an Irish woman whom he had met when she was governess to a German family with whom he was friendly. Jane French was a first cousin of Jack Simms and encouraged him and other Simms relatives to visit her. Thus it was that he and Ottilie came to know and love one another. Otto Stange died in 1901 but Jane remained close to the young couple and later became George's godmother.

In 1903 Jack Simms brought Ottilie as his bride to Combermore. It was an early Victorian country house, set amidst stately limes and beeches and proved to be a pleasant family home. Here George spent a very happy childhood with his older brothers, Gerald and Harry, and younger sister, Dorothea. Writing more than sixty

1

years later he recalled that 'Tall beeches creaking, evergreens whispering and whining, shielded us from the gusts and rushes of the storm as we lay in bed, snug and secure.'[1] The security he felt came partly from the atmosphere of the solid old house but was chiefly afforded by the love within the family. There was no Victorian strictness in the household but a relaxed, affectionate atmosphere, where the children experienced such happiness that they felt only a limited need for outside friends.

George's father walked to his office in Strabane every day. He was widely respected as a kindly solicitor who took a pastoral interest in his clients. (His children had a standing joke about his regular Sunday afternoon visits to 'his widows'.) His ordered conduct of cases in court was aided by a rare sensitivity. Many years afterwards George recorded a famous instance of this: it involved a case during which Jack Simms

used his Irish to extract from a witness who knew little English the desired reaction to convince the judge that her evidence was sound. Apparently the reliability of the woman's eye-witness account was being questioned during cross-examination. Did she or did she not see the incident referred to? The magistrate was becoming impatient and no headway was being made. The woman had interpreted 'Did you see' as 'D'ye see', that is 'Do you understand' and nothing more. My father, perceiving that the two-fold meaning of the English word 'see' was causing the confusion, interposed in Irish 'Did you see him with your own eyes?' (*An bhfaca tú le do shúile féin é?*) whereupon the witness's own eyes brightened with obvious intelligence. She answered convincingly in the affirmative through Irish, and the judge was assured of her credibility.[2]

His sensitivity extended over his professional approach: it was manifest in his concern for 'people' rather than 'cases' and his refusal to handle a case which was in any way tainted.

George inherited much from his father, not only in character but also in his scholarly interests. The walls of the study in Combermore were lined with books, into which the children dipped. Jack Simms was versed in the classics and whenever he was to read the lessons in church he prepared them at home in the Greek original. He had developed his interest in history, especially in the history and doctrine of the Church of Ireland, and frequently lectured on subjects ranging from the life and works of Oliver Goldsmith to Christian citizenship. Invitations came from as far away as Belfast: in 1923, for instance, he was asked by the Bishop of Down to lecture in the Ulster Hall on churchmanship. Within the Church of Ireland at parish level he held every position available to a layman: he was for many years a diocesan and general synodsman, member of the Representative Church Body and diocesan assessor to the Bishop of Derry and Raphoe, a particular proof of the trust reposed in him.

Jack Simms was easy-going and informal with his children to an extent that made their upbringing somewhat unconventional. Their mother was stricter and had a Teutonic preoccupation with system and tidiness but she was sufficiently carefree sometimes to leave the management of the household in order to play tennis with the children. An excellent cook and needlewoman, she also read widely and maintained a cosmopolitan view of events. She had, however, no desire for her children to be seen as different; she did not encourage them to speak German, although the odd word, like 'Oma' for 'Granny' was part of their everyday vocabulary. Likewise her Lutheran upbringing does not appear to have had any influence on them.

Although she was a naturalised British citizen and completely bilingual (she spoke with a London rather than a German accent), the outbreak of the first World War and the forced family estrangements brought her much embarrassment and heartache. Until 1914 comings and goings between Donegal and Germany were constant but then communication inevitably became difficult. On the one hand, her step-mother, Jane Stange, was unable to return to the continent and was obliged to spend the war with the Simmses in Lifford; on the other Jack's twin brother, Monty, was detained in a civilian prison camp in Ruhleben, having been on a business trip to Germany in August 1914. The Simms parents ensured that war-time tensions arising from Ottilie's German origins were concealed from their children, while in the locality she publicly identified herself with the British cause in her work for the Red Cross.

George inherited his mother's fine features and her linguistic facility, but in temperament he was much more his father's son. Ottilie Simms was very reserved and had no ready supply of small talk. She did not suffer fools gladly and acquaintances held her in some awe. One had to know her well to be comfortable with her, while Jack Simms loved to strike up a conversation with anyone he met and had a great gift of friendship, liberally bestowed.

The Simmses were self-contained as a family and made their own fun. There were plenty of trees to climb and they made 'treehouses'; as they grew older they made good use of the Combermore tennis court and also enjoyed playing cricket in the field (George kept the score while Gerald and Harry wielded bat and ball in turn). They helped to pick the fruit in the garden and went on cycling expeditions. Gerald was the one who organised them to go on family picnics, on foot, by bicycle or by train. He was a railway enthusiast and no fewer than three railway companies then ran trains through Strabane; George and Harry accompanied their brother on his forays to spot trains of the Great Northern, Midland and County Donegal railway companies. Dorothea, born in 1913, was very much a little sister to the boys. They called her 'Baby' for many years and generally considered her too young for their more energetic activities.

From an early stage the children were taught to love God and neighbour. The Simmses were active members of the Church of Ireland but, at a time when most Protestants were cautious of crossing the denominational divide, they took no narrow view; the children were encouraged to mix in the community and the youngsters with whom they played tennis and hockey were as likely to be Roman Catholics as Protestants. George recalls that it was Jane Stange who regularly took him visiting local characters and stimulated in him a great interest in people. Thus at an early stage he learned about other Christian traditions and developed a quiet respect for the differing beliefs of his neighbours. His interest in people and the opportunity of serving them was undoubtedly one aspect of his youthful desire for ordination to the Church's ministry.

As a family the Simmses have tended to be more than usually aware of their surroundings. The young George's sense of security seems to have been partly grounded in his sense of Donegal as 'home'. He found 'growing up in the valley . . . a gentle, quiet process' and talks of the rivers flowing through Lifford as 'friendly and companionable'.[3]

Behind Combermore rose a hill. He recalls that as small children they felt that at its top they had reached 'the end of the world'. It was a small world, bounded on the north by Raphoe, on the south by Knockavoe, the 'purple-headed' mountain in Mrs Alexander's hymn, 'All things bright and beautiful', and on the east by the spire of St Columb's Cathedral, Derry.

Lifford was a small town of some 400 inhabitants, nestling in the valley formed by the rivers Finn and Mourne, where they join to form the Foyle. Until 1922 there was only a county boundary between Lifford and Strabane: despite the fact that Lifford was the county town of Donegal it was very much an adjunct to Strabane. The latter was a busy commercial and shopping centre with some 5,000 inhabitants and when Lifford people spoke of 'town' they meant Strabane.

The Simmses attended the parish church of Clonleigh in Lifford; the church is a seventeenth-century building, dedicated to St Lugadius, one of the twelve-man crew who accompanied St Columba to Iona in 563, who was commemorated in an ancient church nearer Derry. Over the wall from Combermore's hayfield was the Prior Endowed School, housed in a pleasant cut-stone building. Founded by the will of Miss Eleanor Prior, the school first opened its doors in September 1880. A. J. Gloster had already been headmaster for twenty-six years when George was enrolled in 1915. His first teacher, Miss Hamilton, took great care in imparting the basic skills to her pupils. Her training in handwriting and spelling stood George in good stead in his later education and it was she who gave him a love of reading aloud. Towards the end of his time at the Prior he received a grounding in Latin from the headmaster. Gloster offered not only Latin and Greek to his older pupils but Hebrew as well; he enjoyed a high reputation as a teacher and many of his pupils later excelled in languages and literature.[4]

Every year the family holidayed by the sea in Donegal; Portnoo was the favourite spot and remains so today. The family awareness of the landscape was fostered by their habit of walking and they walked miles along roads and paths, over moors and mountains, along the sea shore, sharing an interest in all they saw and in everyone they met.[5]

Once George holidayed further along the coast at Glencolumb-kille. Here he revelled in chatting to Irish speakers and listening to their story-telling. From this holiday and the encouragement of his father, himself an enthusiastic Irish speaker, emanated George's love for Irish.

Throughout his life George has never found it difficult to base a radio talk or article on a view of the cliffs from a Portnoo cottage window or the expanse of golden sand across which he has so often walked. These memories are not sentimentalised but are always harnessed to some spiritual insight.

So secure a childhood did George enjoy that he does not appear to have suffered when he left the Prior Endowed School, at the age of nine for preparatory school in England. Gerald had left St Edmund's School, Hindhead, for Winchester College the term before George's arrival in May 1920, so he was the only Irish boy there. It was a long journey for a little boy. In the early years he travelled by Dublin and Holyhead with Gerald and always had a day to enjoy in London en route as compensation for the fatigue of travel.

George now entered a competitive academic world where the prize was entry to one of the great public schools, such as Winchester College. St Edmund's was a relatively new school, having been founded by the Rev. John Morgan-Brown in 1874. Originally sited in Norfolk, it had moved in 1899 to Hindhead in Surrey, on the London to Portsmouth road. Here it operated in a Victorian country house where G. B. Shaw had lived for a time. It had been recommended to Jack Simms by his brother, Nicholas, who was vicar of neighbouring Grayshott.

The school was now run by the founder's son, Cyril Morgan-Brown, with help from his two daughters. It is widely agreed that Morgan-Brown, or 'Ciddy' as he was nicknamed, looked more like an odd-job man than a headmaster[6] but he was a brilliant classicist and George describes him as 'good with little boys'. He could be fierce and had a short temper but George was not oppressed by the headmaster's sternness.[7]

Morgan-Brown emphasised the importance of classics and maths; French and divinity were also given prominence but he considered English, history and geography as one discipline, assuming that boys would acquire a knowledge of English literature without systematic study. If the modern reader is horrified by this disregard of English it should be pointed out that their comprehensive classical training played an enormous part in giving the boys a command of their own language. Its effect was very succinctly explained by W. H. Auden, the poet, who was head boy when George went to St Edmund's.

Anybody who has spent many hours of his youth translating into and out of two languages so syntactically and rhetorically different from his own learns something about his own mother tongue which I do not think can be learned as well in any other way. For instance, it inculcates the habit, whenever one uses a word, of automatically asking: 'What is its exact meaning?'[8]

Herein to some extent lies the origin of the beautifully constructed prose that George writes.

Morgan-Brown provided an excellent library where many of the boys developed a great love of reading. He also organised competitions and played games which were calculated to stimulate their interest. For instance he often made a meal a protracted affair by playing 'fill in the proverb' with the boys.

Discipline was firm but not harsh. As an incentive to good behaviour there was a system of stars and stripes: ten stripes for bad behaviour earned a boy a beating but as stripes could be cancelled by stars for good behaviour few boys suffered it. Ten stars earned a handsome book prize but as the stars were awarded in quarters that involved forty occasions of virtue.

Discipline extended to Sunday letter writing under supervision (with suggestions for news written on the blackboard). Here George began the series of weekly letters which continued as long as he and his mother were apart. Even his earlier letters reveal George's interest in people, his incipient sense of history, his grasp of detail. Often he asked about people round Lifford but, as a typical little boy, paid scant regard to the major political events of the day.

While George was at preparatory school Ireland was going through a tumultuous period. The Easter Rising of 1916 transformed the Irish political scene; 'Home Rule', the great aspiration of nationalists which had seemed on the point of attainment when the First World War broke out, was superseded by the demand for a completely independent republic. With the war in Europe over, Great Britain faced a new war in Ireland as republican guerillas gained ever-increasing support throughout much of the country. By the summer of 1921, when George had just completed his second year at St Edmund's, a truce had been agreed and the republican leaders were invited to Downing Street for a protracted series of peace negotiations.

At last, early in December 1921, an Anglo-Irish Treaty was signed but it was clear from the beginning that the compromise involved in the setting up of the Irish Free State, which remained a dominion within the British Empire and required an oath of allegiance to the King of England, was too much for many republicans to swallow. Civil war broke out in June 1922 and lasted for ten months before the anti-Treaty forces laid down their arms and the new Free State government was able to devote its undivided attention to the task of adapting the country to its newly-acquired independence.

There was, however, a second compromise involved in the Anglo-Irish Treaty which was to have repercussions lasting long after the end of the Civil War. In 1920 the Government of Ireland Act had recognised the strong antipathy to Irish nationalism of the majority in the north-eastern counties by granting home rule to Northern Ireland. The Northern Ireland Parliament, which had been opened in June 1921, was given the option by the Treaty of voting the area under its jurisdiction out of the Irish Free State, and this option was exercised with alacrity. To the Simms family the most practical effect of this partition was the political separation of

P.S. Miss Winnie told me to ask you   St. Edmunds School
to provide me f with a Fancy   Grayshott
Dress for December 18th.   Hindhead
      She said it was important.   Surrey
4th December 1920 Sunday   England.

Dear Mums

        Thank you very much for your letter and the grey
sloucher. On Saturday there was a match against Branksome
and we lost bora change. Branksome got three goals and we
only got one goal. On Tuesday there were new hangings in
the Chapel they look very nice. The old hangings that were
up before the new ones were nearly fifty years old, so
they were quite old were not they? On Friday there was
a half holiday because there was a war memorial put up
for the old boys who were killed in the war. All the Chapel
was decorated with laurel leaves and name of Battles
painted on peices of coulored paper. It was veiled over
with the Union Jack and the unveiling was done by
Feild Marshal Sir William Robertson G.C.B, G.C. MG, K.C.V.O, D.S.O.
On Tuesday I got a letter from Uma. The half-term exam
results were read out the other day. For:——

                 Latin I got 133 out of 200
                 French "   62   "   " 100
                 Geography " 33   "   " 100
                 History "   50   "   " 100
                 Greek   "   61   "   " 100
                 Maths   " 110   "   " 200
                 Total   " 449   "   " 800.   Love from George

Lifford, where Jack Simms had his home, from Strabane, where he worked. County Donegal was part of the Irish Free State; County Tyrone was in Northern Ireland.

A letter to his mother in July 1922 shows how little all this figured in George's mind. It concludes, 'we had the half-term examinations last week. Is the Civil War over yet? What did Mrs Robinson die of?' Despite the frustrations of the border, communications between Lifford and Strabane remained unbroken and his father continued to cycle to the office each day. Clearly his parents' letters sought to stress that normal life continued as far as possible.

While some boys resented the discipline of chapel attendance[9] George enjoyed the opportunity for daily worship and was developing a love of the liturgy and of the psalms for private devotions. The churchmanship in St Edmund's could be described as mildly high; it does not seem to have posed any problems for George, who has always been able to move easily between 'high' and 'low' church, believing in the essential unity of the Anglican communion at large and of all believers in Christ. His experience of the Church of England gave him a breadth of vision, but he was too sensitive a person to return to the Church of Ireland and there manifest practices which were unacceptable.

Every Sunday morning the boys had to learn the collect of the day, a discipline which George never resented. More than sixty years later the Cranmerian phrases roll off his tongue with consummate ease. Some old boys would admit that their greatest zeal was applied to the study of the Church calendar for a red letter saint's day meant a half-holiday. Shrove Tuesday signalled pancakes, while some of the church festivals had their own secular ritual. Ascension Day in particular was eagerly awaited every year for there was always an 'expedition' when a picnic would be packed and the boys would be taken to visit a beauty spot or place of interest.

One of the other highlights of the year was the Michaelmas blackberry outing. The boys set out in 'firms', armed with picnic rations and containers, to pick as many blackberries as they could on the commons and in the fields. They regarded it as a great occasion and the pleasure lasted as long as the housekeeper's jam, carried round by each head of a firm and distributed to members of his team.

Inevitably, sixty years later, it is these highlights of the school year which old boys best remember, but there was organised daily recreation to absorb their energies. There was soccer and cricket, golf on the school course and, in the summer, swimming in an open-air pool. Boys were also encouraged to garden in pairs, an exercise which few seem to have enjoyed.

George joined happily in all these activities but also appreciated the more academic offerings, particularly the Literary Society. With the encouragement of Miss Winnie Morgan-Brown, W. H. Auden and H. Llewellyn Smith had founded the society during their last year in school. Auden was its first president and set it on a course of Shakespeare readings and dramatic productions. George, in his time, was secretary and acted the Clerk of Oxenford in the production of *The Canterbury Tales*.

Academically, George was a bit overshadowed by Gerald and found the work extending. Despite occasional references in his letters to being first in the class (and staying up for supper) some of Morgan-Brown's early reports were somewhat scathing and examination results only moderate. When he left in 1924 he received the gruff concession that 'he ought to make a scholar in time'.[10]

Earlier that year, in correspondence with his father about George's progression to public school, Morgan-Brown had written that George 'seems to regard his mistakes from the point of view of a fatalist, as mysterious dispensations of Providence, against which it is vain to struggle'. In Stoic tradition the headmaster concludes, 'But we will do our best'.[11] One suspects that Morgan-Brown liked to present it as a great effort to prepare the boys for public school and that his opinion of George was higher than he would admit. After all he made him head boy in his last year.

George was not the prototype head boy, who was often an outstanding games player and a 'strong' character, but there is no doubt that the boys respected him. He was popular, for he was even-tempered and full of fun. Although he found English boys different in outlook, he was well integrated and was not prickly about his Irishness. Thus he was not in the least upset when at a Shrove Tuesday pancake party the alphabet song worked its way to:

> U stands for Ulster
> Where Simms has a shack
> With a lot of wee piggies
> In a row at the back.

The respect which the boys had for him was based on something deeper than this: they sensed that he was 'different'. The Rev. Peter Mayhew points this out clearly when he writes: 'At a time when there was a good deal of intolerance among prep. school boys George Simms was an outstanding exception.'[12] George was not what schoolboys then called 'pi' (pious, 'goody-goody') but his quiet caring and understanding of people made him different.

George left St Edmund's for Cheltenham College in 1924: having tried unsuccessfully for a scholarship to Winchester in the previous year when he was a year young for it, he was advised by Morgan-Brown to go for a scholarship to one of the less competitive public schools and thus Cheltenham was chosen.

Founded in 1841, Cheltenham College was the first of the great public schools of the Victorian era. In addition to its academic departments (classical and modern) it had a military department, from which boys proceeded to Woolwich and Sandhurst. The headmaster, H. H. Hardy, was greatly respected by the boys, as his spirituality, his care for the development of the individual and his fostering of a broad intellectual life softened his image as a stern disciplinarian. At Cheltenham George enjoyed 'a series of splendid teachers': particularly he recalls fine classics teaching, in which essay-writing and verse composition, as well as a study of Greek and Latin texts, were exacting but enjoyable ways of developing his critical and literary faculties.

P. H. B. Lyon, later headmaster of Rugby School, had considerable influence on him. A poet himself, and an outstanding schoolmaster, he introduced his pupils to live poets and hung samples of their autographed pieces on the library walls; his classes were stimulating and he encouraged the boys to read widely and to think. Some of George's poetic sense may be derived from Hugh Lyon's tuition, and although he has not written any poetry, that sense is clear in much of his writing and many of his talks and sermons.

Lyon made a big impression on George, particularly as he was his form master at a critical stage. The form master was responsible for activities such as the Ascension Day outing, and any excursion organised by Lyon was enormously enjoyed by the boys.

Cheltenham contributed greatly to George's spiritual development. Since the age of nine he had thought from time to time of ordination. In his own words 'the desire came and went, returning with an insistence that could not easily be ignored. Many people influenced me: no one compelled me.'[13] Among those who influenced him was the chaplain at Cheltenham, the Rev. H. E. Hubbard. Hubbard (later Bishop of Whitby) must have discovered George's sense of vocation when he was preparing him as a fourteen-year old for confirmation. This preparation, shared with the headmaster and the housemaster, was very thorough. A calendar of classes was published in advance and Hubbard wrote short notes for the candidates on various aspects. Clearly the preparation challenged many boys to examine and develop their faith. After confirmation, Hubbard set out to encourage vocations in boys like George. The school was very spiritually orientated and emphasised the importance of careful preparation for and attendance at holy communion, the observance of Lent and of saints' days. It was not a question of compulsion; boys could choose to rise early for communion and to attend Lenten evening services at the cost of fitting in prep at another time. Many boys exercised that choice and a sizeable number went on to ordination. Among these were the Hanson brothers, Richard and Anthony, both theologians, the Mirfield father, W. R. Jarrett-Kerr, a Cowley father, D. N. W. Hemming, and Donald M. Kennedy, a Presbyterian who became a bishop of the Church of North India.

George enjoyed most aspects of life at Cheltenham, with the exception of the Officers' Training Corps. He was not very keen on team games but played a lot of tennis, swam in the school pool and loved walking in the Cotswolds. He appreciated the very good teaching and the well-stocked library. He pursued his studies with an increasing sense of satisfaction, particularly when, in the Upper Sixth, he acquired his own study. Hardy enlisted outside lecturers to talk to the boys on a wide range of subjects, while music flourished under P. J. Taylor, who frequently brought distinguished musicians to give recitals. Drama was also a popular activity and the first full-length play, in 1927, was an ambitious choice, *Arms and the Man*. Thus there was plenty of intellectual stimulus for a boy like George.

On a social level, George was often asked for meals into Cheltenham houses and other boys issued frequent invitations to their homes. There were many lively people in the town, and George fitted in well. As a junior he was orderly ('fag') to Ronald Prain, head of Southwood House. Sir Ronald, later a prominent figure in international mining and President of the College Council, was happy to recall in his biography[14] that his orderly became an archbishop who returned to the College on several occasions to preach in the chapel. The 'fagging' system was by no means harsh in Cheltenham and when George became a prefect he hardly used his orderly. Typically he would have preferred not to have one.

As at his previous school, George was popular with his fellow students. He was no paragon of virtue and had endearing weaknesses like untidiness and forgetfulness. He always forgot something when returning to school; in September 1927 he spent several days 'in exile' in his study as a result of arriving back without his health certificate. His contemporaries liked him for his gentle good humour, but some at least appreciated that there was more to George than that. Sir Patrick Macrory writes: 'I think that every boy with whom he came in contact instinctively recognised his innate goodness',[15] while the Rev. Peter Mayhew, who had proceeded to Cheltenham from St Edmund's with George, says that on leaving school he felt that 'he was the best person I had ever met.'[16] His friends in Lifford had also realised his spiritual qualities from an early stage, to the extent that they often referred to him as 'the bishop'.

II

COLLEGE DAYS

It was always George's intention to seek ordination in the Church of Ireland. Accordingly he opted not for Oxford or Cambridge but for Trinity College, Dublin, where he joined the junior freshman class in January 1929.[1] His brother Harry had read law at Trinity before entering his father's practice. Gerald went to Oxford where he gained a first in both 'Mods' and 'Greats'. After teaching at Radley College for a year he obtained a place in the Indian Civil Service but ultimately became an historian. He lectured in Trinity College, Dublin, for many years, specialising in Jacobite and Williamite Ireland.[2]

Trinity was not only the oldest Irish university, having been founded by Elizabeth I in 1592, but it remained for several decades after the Treaty the automatic choice of almost all those from a Protestant background in the Irish Free State. Besides, it provided the regular route to ordination; its school of divinity was specifically intended to provide a steady flow of ordinands to the Church of Ireland. Only a small number of Church of Ireland clergy received their training anywhere else and when George entered College the overwhelming majority of Anglican clergy in Ireland were Trinity men.

Trinity was, however, no narrow parochial university; it was widely respected on the other side of the Irish Sea where its degrees were considered preferable to those of British 'redbrick' establishments. It also attracted students from British dominions and colonies, as well as some from the U.S.A. It was not a large university, having only about 1,500 students when George became an undergraduate, but it brought quite a cosmopolitan flavour to the centre of Dublin.

George put a lot of pressure on himself academically by sitting 'Schol', the foundation scholarship, in 1930 and by opting for a double moderatorship (two honours degrees taken simultaneously) in classics and ancient history and political science. He succeeded

14

in both and also won the Vice-Chancellor's Latin Medal in 1930 and the Brooke Prize in 1932 on the results of his double moderatorship. He took little pride in this achievement, writing home that W. B. Stanford and A. C. Anderson were the only firsts in classics 'and then a widish gap before the goats trickled in'![3] He absolutely dismisses any suggestion that his success was a mark of brilliance, saying, 'I was a plodder really'.

These academic achievements should not be taken as an indication that George studied ceaselessly: by his own admission, he took his eye off the academic grind while in College, getting involved in a wide range of extra-curricular activities. The tennis, cricket, rugby and rowing clubs occupied much time; he served as junior secretary of the rugby and cricket clubs, regatta secretary, propaganda secretary of the Dublin University Central Athletic Committee (DUCAC) where he represented the women's hockey club.[4] He acted in Trinity Week rags; in 1930 he appeared as a bare-footed nymph, done up in a wig and five yards of butter muslin!

He also worked on the staff of *T.C.D.*, a weekly student miscellany. Originally he wrote 'Campestria', the sports reports, but he became increasingly involved in organising the printing and proof-reading. A succession of illustrious editors, such as W. B. Stanford, D. A. Webb, R. P. McDermott, G. F. Mitchell and R.P.C. and A. T. Hanson, worked with a small but enthusiastic group to produce a publication which was renowned for its sophisticated humour. Irish society and Trinity life were satirised, the Provost alone being spared, while the classical studies and spiritual inclinations of its contributors gave scope for Latin puns and ecclesiastical quips. Many of the students who sat up Monday after Monday putting the magazine together were subsequently ordained; many have seen their later works in print. George was not keen to write poetry or literary prose for *T.C.D.* but does believe that his interest in writing articles began with those he composed for *T.C.D.*

All these activities involved George in the social life of College. Indeed he was a debonair young man who did the round of parties, rugby dances and tennis tournaments. He enjoyed student pranks; on one occasion he and two friends had entertained the Bishop of Tuam, the Right Rev. W. H. Holmes, to lunch in his rooms in No. 9 and then played 'Mrs Mulligan, the Pride of the Coombe', on the accordion as the bishop walked through Front Square with the Regius Professor of Divinity to receive his doctorate of divinity *jure dignitatis*.[5]

During his College days George made real and lasting friendships. Three of his closest friends, with whom he shared academic
and spiritual interests were R. P. McDermott, D. L. Graham and
M. L. Ferrar. McDermott was a scholar in philosophy and won the
Historical Society medal for oratory, and at an early stage George
developed a great respect for his academic acumen.[6] Graham was
a fellow-classicist and a keen rugby player, who won his colours
for Trinity in three successive years.[7] Ferrar read modern
languages and was in line for a first-class degree until serious eye
trouble afflicted him and permanently restricted his academic
studies. He became one of George's most influential friends. Miss
Elizabeth Ferrar, his younger sister, remembers them as a four-
some, some of whom joined the Ferrar family for lunch most
Sundays. These were occasions of good fun and lively conversation: while the other three young men voiced strong opinions and
engaged in polemic arguments George was usually content to
listen.

Douglas Graham recalls that George's rooms 'were always
hospitable and were a favourite place to foregather and talk away
the night, for he was popular with all sorts of students, from heavy
hearties to the pale scholars and aesthetes and besides, with his
phenomenal memory, he knew a great deal about his own interests
and acquaintances and probably more than they about theirs.'[8]
Among the 'heavy hearties' were the Pike brothers. Between them
they spent so much time with him that his rooms were dubbed 'the
aquarium'. George maintained a life-long friendship with them,
particularly with St John, later Bishop of the Gambia and assistant
Bishop of Guildford, Robert (Bobs), Bishop of Meath, and Victor,
Bishop of Sherborne.

The leisurely student life of those days afforded scope for
impromptu hair-brained schemes such as the one recounted by
Douglas Graham: 'One balmy summer night I suddenly said in the
Front Square, "George, let's walk down to Monasterevan,"[9] and
off we went, arriving for breakfast, myself completely worn out
and my feet aching while George was full of talk . . . and skipped
along gaily.'[10]

Despite such impetuous acts and student pranks, happy socialising and late nights, his contemporaries realised that George was a
serious scholar and a deeply spiritual young man. Among
themselves they often referred to him as a saint, without, one
suspects, fully realising the import of their words.

On completion of his double moderatorship George immediately
began work for the divinity testimonium which he was awarded in

1934 and in the same year he won the Berkeley Medal for Greek. In those days Irish candidates for ordination did not reside in a theological college and preparation for the ministry was academically rather than spiritually orientated. George could have lived in the Divinity Hostel in Mountjoy Square, but chose to retain the free rooms in College to which he was entitled as a Foundation Scholar. The training contrasted starkly with that in many English theological colleges, where men received comprehensive pastoral training and benefited from the corporate life based on a strict regime and daily worship.

Most men proceeded to ordination when they obtained the divinity testimonium but, as an academic, George planned to take the theological exhibition first. 'Theo-Ex' as it was commonly called, was a tough assignment; it combined all six parts of the B.D. in one examination, but the B.D. could not be conferred until a thesis was completed.

Faced with the prospect of 'Theo-Ex', George faltered. Aged twenty-four, he saw all sorts of possibilities before him. For a time he considered a career as a librarian: on the other hand he greatly admired Albert Schweitzer and had some thoughts of combining ministry and medicine as he did. He was weary of working for examinations and had become aware how sheltered his life was, and entertained some doubts as to what he had to offer in the ministry.

He had recently spent some time studying at St Deiniol's Library, Hawarden, where he developed an interest in academic librarianship. It was this which led him in September 1934 to apply for a job in the British Museum. He got as far as going for an interview but, on reflection, withdrew his application.

Early in the summer of 1934 he had been approached in relation to the curacy of St Bartholomew's Church, Dublin. The Rev. R. G. F. Jenkins had been curate there for less than two years when he was appointed Warden of the Divinity Hostel. Knowing that this was a blow to the vicar, the Rev. W. C. Simpson, he continued to help in the parish and promptly suggested George as his successor.

Raymond Jenkins had met George when he was acting as an assistant examiner in the divinity school. He clearly remembers being asked if any of the papers had impressed him, and singling out George's as a 'first-class paper, accurate, concise and written in a fine hand'.[11] Jenkins, twelve years George's senior, had cultivated his friendship and had no hesitation in recommending him to Simpson.

Such an appointment would however involve risk on both sides: St Bartholomew's was a church in the tractarian tradition with a daily eucharist and a highly developed liturgy, for which reason it had always been considered necessary to have as curate a priest with some experience. However, Simpson never allowed himself to be restricted by custom or conventions and must have considered that George's gifts would outweigh the disadvantage of waiting a year for him to be ordained deacon.[12]

The risk on George's side, anxiously pointed out by friends, was that he would subsequently find it difficult to be accepted in another parish. This was, indeed, a problem for curates at St Bartholomew's, as there had always been suspicion of its practices. There was even more unease in the 1930s as a result of the vicar being brought to the ecclesiastical courts in 1928 for breaches of the Canons Ecclesiastical of the Church of Ireland. He was found guilty on several counts, which confirmed many members of the Church of Ireland in their suspicions that the parish was ritualistic and 'Romish'.[13]

George's reluctance to consider the post was not based on this problem however. As already suggested, he was happy with 'high' or 'low' church and in his care for things spiritual was indifferent to externals, such as ecclesiastical apparel or terminology as to 'priests' or 'ministers'. In any case Simpson carefully obeyed the Canons after the trial, which removed a potential problem.[14]

George's reluctance emanated from his doubts about his future, and a conviction that as a deacon he would be of little use in the parish. Jenkins waged a continuous campaign for several months to convince George that his faith in God and gift with people could be put to best use in the ordained ministry. George also considered carefully the counsel of Archbishop J. A. F. Gregg, the awesome Archbishop of Dublin, whose concern was to ensure that he was aware of the pitfalls of a curacy in such a controversial parish. However, what probably tipped the scales was the influence of the Temple mission in October 1934.

The mission which William Temple, Archbishop of York, conducted in Trinity, was the highlight and most important event of George's student days. As the secretary of the mission George was deeply involved. Temple was becoming an important figure in world-wide Christianity and as an ecumenist was the inspiration behind much that ultimately found expression in the World Council of Churches in 1948. George was very impressed that at meetings held outside College, Temple was able even then to overcome denominational divisions and to draw out a common Christian concern for human needs.

The archbishop was an inspiring leader; his profound faith,

expressed with clarity and simplicity, his bubbling sense of humour and his concern for people made him a compelling missioner. His talks on Christian faith and life opened intellectual and spiritual windows for George.[15] Their value lay in the flair and insight with which orthodox Christian teaching was offered: there was little that was new to George but the emphases laid by Temple were those that can be seen in George's subsequent ministry. Undergirded by a clearly enunciated doctrine of the incarnation, Temple's talks ranged through the presence of God in history and in our lives, the implications of this in terms of human behaviour and the importance of prayer and sacrament in Christian life. Included were some of his most quotable sayings, frequently heard in ensuing years in George's own addresses, sayings such as 'People are always thinking that conduct is supremely important, and that because prayer helps it, therefore prayer is good. That is true as far as it goes; still truer is it to say that worship is of supreme importance and conduct tests it.'[16]

Particularly relevant to George's stage of maturity was Temple's proclamation: 'If you are quite clear in your acceptance of Jesus Christ as your Saviour and your God, then the mere circumstances of the time constitute a call to the Church's direct service in its ministry which you must face . . . the King is calling, and you must answer.'[17]

This challenge helped to reinforce George's sense of vocation, while Temple's doctrine of the church as 'the means whereby Christ becomes active and carries out His purpose in the world'[18] was enormously influential in his ministry. Again and again, as pastor, teacher, preacher and administrator, as a spiritual leader of the Church of Ireland, and as an ecumenist, George's grasp of Temple's teaching on the church was manifest. His understanding of the Church of Ireland discovering how to be the church by corporately and individually living a life which interprets the being of God to men, his concept of the place of the local church in the Kingdom of God, his stress on the ministry of all believers, the paramount part of prayer and sacrament, his conviction that Christianity is a revelation given in personal encounter with God and not primarily a religion to be defended against 'heresy' or to be debated in academic circles, owed a great deal to Temple.

The significance of Temple's influence on George should not be allowed to obscure the fact that the lunchtime addresses and informal ministry of Temple's mission assistant, the Rev. E. S. Abbott, made as great an impact on him. Abbott, only four years George's senior, was then chaplain to King's College, London, and was one of the outstanding young men in the Church of England. His addresses[19] were more immediate and he was more constantly available to meet students, for he was living in rooms while the archbishop was a guest in the Provost's House. His teaching on the devotional life was readily absorbed by George and his contemplative spirituality made a deep impression. As a result of the mission Temple took an interest in George's career and the two corresponded quite regularly. In 1935 Temple invited him to spend a weekend at Bishopthorpe; George found it 'a great thrill' to listen to the archbishop informally discussing a range of topics. Temple's opinion of George is clearly reflected in a letter of November 1934 in which he wrote 'I must not steal you from the Church of Ireland but I should greatly like to import you into my diocese.'[20]

Many young men might have taken this as an entrée into the wider sphere of the Church of England, but George quietly completed the Theological Exhibition and prepared for ordination in the Church of Ireland. The inspiration afforded by the Temple mission helped George discover the way through his doubts, so that he accepted the curacy at St Bartholomew's, for which he was ordained by Archbishop Gregg on 24 March 1935.

There was an inevitable gulf that day between the quiet and totally inexperienced young deacon and the archbishop before whom he knelt. Gregg, in his early sixties, was approaching the peak of his power: a dominant figure in the Church of Ireland, its statesmanlike defender in the difficult early years of national independence and the guardian of doctrinal orthodoxy and ecclesiastical discipline. Yet, little more than twenty years later, as Archbishops of Dublin and Armagh respectively, the two men were to carry overall responsibility for the affairs of the Church of Ireland.

III

EARLY MINISTRY

The three years of George's curacy in St Bartholomew's were happy and fulfilling. Any curate depends greatly on the training which his rector or vicar gives him, and unorthodox as he was, Simpson taught George a lot. For a start, in common with other ordinands of the time, George had never taken a service before; he learned to do so from Simpson's meticulous ordering of all the services.[1] Simpson also gave him ample opportunity to preach and to develop as a pastor.[2] He did not go in for the formality of staff meetings but told George what was on his mind when they met each day for holy communion at 8.00 a.m., matins at 10.30 a.m. and evensong at 5.30 p.m.

George greatly admired Simpson as a Christian with 'saintly qualities'. He valued his rare brand of evangelical catholicism and the way in which he rescued the term 'evangelical' from party association or narrow interpretation. Simpson was an ecumenist, had a highly-developed social conscience and a broad vision of the church's mission at home and abroad. While many churchmen still considered mission merely in terms of preaching the Word, Simpson's awareness of the servant church convinced him of the urgency of addressing the physical and social conditions of the poor, whether in the crowded streets of East Belfast or in the slums of Calcutta. He was a moving force behind the Rev. N. H. F. Waring's establishment of the Ministry of Healing, as he believed it should be part of the regular work of the church. A proponent of the ministry of all believers, he stressed the role of the laity to an extent which was virtually unheard of in the 1930s.

Simpson's thought-provoking remarks constantly challenged George to examine the internal ordering of the church and its role in society. A. G. Hebert's *Liturgy and Society*,[3] which was published in 1936, also made a great impression on him. In directing Anglican attention to the liturgical movement which had sprung up in the Roman Catholic Church, Hebert spelt out the broad implication of the movement; how its stress on the common faith of the church made it a factor for unity; its belief that the faith is embodied in the liturgy prefaced the restoration of the parish eucharist as the main service; its view of worship as the work of the whole people of God led to liturgical revisions which would make that a reality once more. The influence of Simpson and Hebert in matters liturgical is easy to discern in George's ministry.

As a newly ordained curate George kept a journal in which he wrote parochial information and impressions and details of other assignments, interspersed with self-criticism and more general observations. It is a fascinating and revealing book, which was all-too-soon abandoned due to pressure of work. For instance, in recording a meeting in Dundrum on 9 December 1935 at which he addressed 135 young men and women on the changing world, he mentions that he had been told that he fidgeted too much; in assessing his own effectiveness in communicating a Christian challenge he wrote, 'I find it beastly hard to say anything like that in an attractive manner; sermonising platitudes should be remoulded'.[4]

The journal shows his current preoccupations. While a study of the language of the New Testament was of great interest to him, he continued work on his thesis on Cassian of Marseilles and his influence on Western Christianity, for which he was awarded a B.D. and an Elrington Prize in 1936. He was giving much thought to trends in international society and showing concern about the rise of fascism and the failure of the major democracies to react. Informal jottings like 'Letter writing has gone to pot' and 'My day off and a letter from the vicar telling me to go to Oberbayern for winter sports: but, of course, I won't,' add shading to the picture. Had he maintained a journal throughout his ministry it would have been a rich source of biographical material.

George participated in the full range of parish activities and became very popular. His working day was structured round the daily services; apart from pastoral visiting and classroom teaching he shared the preparation for confirmation, took a large part in the publication of the parish magazine (managing the business side of it), was active in the parish organisations and, although there was no formal hospital chaplaincy, spent a lot of time in the children's wards of the Royal City of Dublin Hospital in Baggot Street.

He had a particular rapport with the young and the elderly. He had no difficulty in talking to the young and getting them to talk to him; he founded a Sunday school and a table tennis club which provided a happy meeting point. He obtained agreement for the removal of some pews at the back of one of the transepts so that the children could sit in an informal circle, showing a happy freedom from the restraints of convention.

Many of the parishioners were elderly; the old ladies in particular loved him for his gentle goodness and listening ear, and so vital was his support for some that they described him as their lifeline. One of his self-styled old ladies was Dr E. F. Badham, principal of St Margaret's Hall in Mespil Road. During his curacy he taught religious education in the school and coached her in New Testament Greek. Subsequently they conducted a lively correspondence in which she constantly sought guidance and information, affectionately addressing him as 'my encyclopaedia'.[5]

The senior girls in St Margaret's Hall were less respectful. They took a delight in testing the mettle of the young curate in the classroom; they were highly amused that one so handsome and boyish in appearance could have such a serious demeanour and frequently posed 'shocking' questions to see how he would react. He also taught at the small school run by the Community of St Mary the Virgin in the Church Home in Pembroke Park and ministered in their home for elderly ladies.

George made quite an impression in Dublin and received many invitations to preach. Three weeks after his ordination he gave the address at a Holy Week service in All Saints' Church, Blackrock; opposite his name in the Preachers' Book the rector, Canon H. B. Dobbs, wrote 'Potential Primate'!

In 1936, although he had only just been ordained priest, he was offered the chaplaincy of St Columba's College, Rathfarnham, near Dublin. St Columba's was the only example of an English-style public school in the Irish Free State. It was a tractarian foundation and laid considerable emphasis on regular worship in its College Chapel. The offer of the chaplaincy was clearly quite an attractive proposition. He consulted Archbishop Temple on this. The Archbishop's chief recommendation was that in his early years of ministry George should seek varied experiences in fairly rapid succession, so he was not dismissive of the job at St Columba's. However, George decided that he had not been ordained long enough to justify a move and in fairness to his vicar remained at St Bartholomew's for another two years.

Archbishop Temple, however, did not let the question of a future appointment drop and immediately commenced discussions with Eric Abbott, who had become Warden (principal) of Lincoln Theological College, as to the possibility of a job there. Abbott was a trainer *par excellence* of ordinands and was discriminating in his choice of colleagues. He urged George to come, on the grounds that 'this theological college demands the very best and . . . we can be content with nothing else'.[6] Although George agreed to visit Lincoln and consider the offer of the chaplaincy, he was reluctant to move. Temple and Abbott laboured hard to persuade him and eventually he agreed to take up the job in February 1938.

Abbott hoped to have George as chaplain for many years, but Temple probably appreciated that George should return to the Church of Ireland before long, and continued his interest in him afterwards. Even during the stresses of wartime he made time to write with open affection: 'I very much want to keep in touch with you.'[7]

George had been very happy in St Bartholomew's and there was widespread regret at his leaving. At his departure Canon Simpson spoke of George's 'Franciscan and mystical temper' and thanked God 'for the glimpses of a character which while still in its youth has reached the deep springs of Christian Revelation'.[8] George never lost contact with the parish. As Archbishop of Dublin he took pleasure in presiding at festal evensong each Easter Day and gladly lent his blessing to the centenary celebrations in 1967. In retirement he has often been a worshipper in the pew, has celebrated the daily eucharist when needed, and in 1988 conducted the parish retreat.

Lincoln Theological College is the modern name of the Scholae Cancellarii founded by Bishop Christopher Wordsworth in 1874.[9] It had been his contention that he was not establishing a new theological college but was reviving the medieval responsibility of the Chancellor for running the theological schools of the diocese, hence the title. The Scholae commenced operation under Chancellor E. W. Benson (later Archbishop of Canterbury) in the former bishop's palace but Bishop Wordsworth provided it with a permanent home when he bought the old County Hospital in 1879. The Bishop's Hostel, as it became known, was situated between the Cathedral and the centre of the city. For a Georgian building it was rather plain but it enjoyed a pleasant view across the Witham valley.

When George joined the staff the Scholae held some forty students and had acquired a high reputation as a liberal-catholic college. In attending to the spiritual development of the ordinands as well as providing lecturers of academic distinction, Abbott followed the policy of Leslie Owen, his predecessor, whose slogan had been 'teaching prayer theologically'. Few future bishops emerged from the Scholae but it was noted for producing a steady supply of faithful parochial clergy.

George's arrival completed a high-powered team of four, with E. L. Mascall as sub-warden and G. B. Bentley, followed by C. F. Evans as tutor, under Abbott's leadership. A. M. Ramsey, the future Archbishop of Canterbury, had been sub-warden from 1930 to 1936 and frequently returned to lecture. George and Michael Ramsey forged a friendship which proved helpful in later years when they worked together as archbishops.

George took a few weeks to settle down; in an early letter to his mother he admitted that 'it is pretty hard work and the change of nationality and temperament does not make it easier'.[10] Soon, however, he felt more at ease. Just a week later he wrote to his father 'The whole atmosphere is very natural and the discipline is good'.[11]

As chaplain George shared in the chapel services, was a pastor to the students and lectured in church history. He also introduced the teaching of Hebrew and gave preliminary talks on the liturgy to enable the students to derive maximum benefit from the highly academic lectures of J. H. Srawley, the Chancellor. Probably he was particularly valued by those men who found Abbott and Mascall daunting; the students joked that he wrote on the blackboard any word which had more than two syllables!

The members of staff worked very much as a team and often gave a series of devotional talks to the students or Lenten courses in neighbouring parishes together. Their technique of dividing a topic like 'They continued steadfastly in the apostles' doctrine' (the warden) 'and fellowship' (sub-warden) 'and in the breaking of bread' (tutor) 'and in prayers' (chaplain) was one which George often employed in his later career.

For George the worship in chapel was an uplifting discipline. A daily celebration and a full range of daily offices provided the framework for a strong and healthy prayer life which had been missing in Trinity College. It was his experience here which enabled him to run schools of prayer, both in Trinity and later in his dioceses.

The staff of Lincoln had close links with Lincoln Cathedral and were licensed by the bishop to officiate throughout the diocese. They maintained good relations with the neighbouring Kelham community, the mother house of the Society of the Sacred Mission. These contacts also provided a stimulus to the standard of liturgical music, for the students sang the services in the Cathedral during the choir's summer holidays and learned plainsong singing from Kelham brother Edwin.

George's quiet contribution to the life of the college was appreciated by staff and student alike. He is remembered by them not for what he said but for what he was. This formed the quintessence of a letter from a former student, asking him to be godfather to a newborn son. Recollecting George's patience with 'all our varied rantings', he wrote 'I never thanked you enough for being you . . . I do now from the bottom of my heart'.[12]

Professor Evans recalls that George was 'modest and self-effacing to a degree I have rarely seen in anyone of his talents'.[13] George, believing that he had far more to learn in Lincoln than to teach, was slow to pronounce on issues but quick to listen and counsel. He was seen as a man in the Abbott spiritual mould.

In the autumn of 1939, the College came under the shadow of war. The ordinands had to decide whether they should continue their training or join the forces and the College set about ordering its life so that its students should match the sacrificial commitment of those who were actively involved in the war. George, never given to expressing strong opinions, said little about the war but had more understanding of the human tragedy than most people in Lincoln. During the 1930s he had paid several visits to Germany, to improve his German and to learn about the country at first hand. Sometimes he had stayed with relatives or friends of his mother but he had also stayed *en pension* with non-English speakers in order to practise the language. George was thus aware of the evils of Nazism but understood why decent young men had been attracted into the youth movement; why opponents of Hitler generally kept quiet; why the Confessional Church was so desperate for international support. Within George's family both sides were represented: there were Lutheran pastors and German servicemen. In Britain and amongst the Anglo-Irish in Ireland many people with German relatives had a difficult time during the war, but George and the Simms family generally were scarcely affected.

There were a few who, in the years after the war, opposed George's preferment on the grounds that he was German or pro-German. Anyone who believed that one could hate Nazism without hating all Germans, who opposed any war of extermination and humiliation and who encouraged the resumption of friendly relations with the defeated nation after the war, laid himself open to such a charge. George quietly proclaimed forgiveness and reconciliation but very few people were foolish enough to construe this in an unfavourable light. The unpopularity of Bishop Bell of Chichester for his outspoken criticism of the Allied conduct of the war shows just how damaging the pro-German label was. Had it not been for this, Bell would have been a serious contender for the archbishopric of Canterbury when Temple died in 1944.[14]

George enjoyed his work at Lincoln and revelled in having ample time to read and study. Having refused an offer of the chaplaincy at Winchester College, he had given no thought to a move until he was approached in the summer of 1939 by Raymond Jenkins about the job of Dean of Residence at Trinity College, Dublin. Jenkins himself was about to vacate the post on his appointment as incumbent of All

Saints', Grangegorman, and realised that George was eminently suited to be his successor. He immediately told Archbishop A. W. Barton, who had succeeded Gregg as Archbishop of Dublin, that this was an ideal opportunity to bring George back to Ireland. The archbishop clearly agreed and realised that there was a danger of losing George to the Church of England.

George's initial reply was negative. At every stage where he was approached about a new job, he needed persuasion: happy in his work and devoid of ambition, he never sought a position to which he was appointed. In the end the prospect of returning to Trinity College in a pastoral capacity won him over. However, he felt bound to stay in Lincoln to serve his notice so he did not take up his new job until January 1940.

His time in Lincoln had been short but very valuable. There he had achieved greater self-discipline, discovered new depths of devotion and acquired a new vision of training for the ordained ministry. There is no doubt that Eric Abbott had a formative influence on George's own ministry. Some of this was related to his approach to theological training, to ecumenism, the ministry of healing, counselling and pastoral work in general: for instance, one of his maxims was that the parish priest should avoid any public commitment to divisive causes within church or state, in order to be equally accessible and acceptable to all his flock; this is not the only tenable approach but it is the one adopted by George.

The force of Abbott's influence, however, stemmed from his spirituality. Speaking at his memorial service in Westminster Abbey on 8 July 1983 the Archbishop of Canterbury, the Most Rev. R. A. K. Runcie, said that Abbott 'was changed from glory to glory by the Spirit of the Lord' throughout his life. It was this that made him such a wonderful teacher of prayer, such a valued counsellor.

Although Abbott was bitterly disappointed at George's departure it did not harm their friendship and they maintained a regular correspondence until Abbott's death. Abbott viewed his correspondence with friends and former students as 'an apostolate of the post'. George has never referred to it in the same way but does the same thing. A short hand-written letter on an anniversary of ordination or marriage, support across the oceans for a missionary abroad, courteous and prompt reply to every letter received, make the recipient feel valued and encouraged. His letter writing, as the Rt Rev. W. J. McCappin, former Bishop of Connor, has said, is part of his 'marvellous gift of nurturing his friendships'.[15]

Another beneficial aspect of his short time in Lincoln was that it enabled him to widen his theological acquaintance and to extend his circle of friends in England. Later in a Church of Ireland given to introspection it was valuable to have a bishop and archbishop who kept in touch with developments in England and overseas and who could produce just the right outside speaker for a clergy conference.

During his curacy in St Bartholomew's George had read a considerable amount of theology and was anxious to be well-informed about the current debate. However, in Lincoln he talked with and listened to some of the leading theologians in the Church of England. They were among a minority of Anglican systematic theologians who were aware of developments in continental theology and were constantly evaluating them. In the thirties writings proliferated from Europe and North America, from Barth, Bonhoeffer, Brunner, Bultmann, Niebuhr and others, attempting a theological reconstruction in the face of the eclipse of nineteenth-century liberal theology. Growing secularism and an ever-increasing awareness of evil in the world spelt doom for a theology based on the optimistic belief that evolution was carrying mankind to ever better things. The aftermath of the First World War and the spread of Nazism and other forms of totalitarianism prompted a rethink of ideas of historical progress and the perfectibility of man.

Barth's proclamation of the falsehood of the 'word of man' ostensibly prefaced a return to orthodoxy, but the theological tenets which he and his school propounded represented so much a reversion to irrational Calvinism that they were in many ways unacceptable to Anglican theologians, whose emphasis on the place of reason and tradition was undiminished. The latter maintained a personal and Christocentric approach to God which was in tune with orthodox belief and which proved more durable and fruitful.[16]

George, of course, read the works of the neo-orthodox movement but his understanding of God and His church, already moulded by Temple, followed the line taken by Michael Ramsey. Ramsey's *The Gospel and the Catholic Church* was very important for George. The preface sets out his basic approach:

The study of the New Testament points to the Death and Resurrection of the Messiah as the central theme of the Gospels and Epistles, and shows that these events were intelligible only to those who shared in them by a more than metaphorical dying and rising again with Christ. It is the contention of this book that in this dying and rising again the very meaning of the church is found, and that the church's outward order expresses its inward meaning by representing the dependence of the members upon the one Body, wherein they die to self.[17]

This approach opened up a fresh perspective on the problems of unity and enabled him with complete consistency to write

the church . . . is the people of God, whose unity of race continues despite the scandal of outward division, and this unity of race has been known to men in every Christian age, and has brought them, through the Passion, a peace which the world has failed to give them. When, through the same Passion, the outward unity is restored, then the world itself shall know that the Father sent the Son.[18]

Ramsey knew that unity discussions failed to make progress because Christians of differing traditions had not realised the inherent oneness of the church and because they argued on premises other than the Gospel. He made unity an urgent and compulsory goal and offered an alternative *modus operandi*. Not being a systematic theologian, George was reluctant to expound at length on a doctrine of the church but it is easy to discern the influence of Ramsey's theology in his later ministry. All in all his Lincoln inheritance was of profound importance for the future.

IV

DEAN OF RESIDENCE

George's appointment to Trinity College, funded by the Representative Church Body, carried the meagre salary of £210.[1] Fortunately the College augmented this by giving him a £50 assistant lecturership in the divinity school[2] and a £40 readership in College Chapel, as well as providing rooms.[3] Raymond Jenkins' dual role as Dean of Residence and Warden of the Divinity Hostel had been split and, much to George's pleasure, the latter post was filled by Michael Ferrar.

Although he was not strictly an incumbent, the Provost being the ordinary of the College Chapel, George found that 'Trinity was a very interesting parish'. As Dean of Residence George was the Anglican chaplain: the Presbyterians and Methodists had part-time chaplains but there was none for the small number of Roman Catholics.[4]

George was content to act as chaplain to any who needed him without any element of proselytism. While his primary concern was for those who lived in rooms in College he wished to exercise a ministry to all, resident and non-resident, staff and student alike. In order to do this it was necessary to establish a wide range of contacts.

Naturally he came to know the divinity students for he lectured many of them and they attended chapel. He also organised their quiet days and retreats. In his twelve years in Trinity College he was pastor to almost every man ordained in the Church of Ireland at the time.[5] Apart from the immediate benefit to them, this was of great value in later days when as bishop and archbishop he met them at the General Synod, on committees and at other church functions. During his years as Dean of Residence George often met with and was consulted by bishops and other senior churchmen. Thus, by the time he became a bishop he had an exceptionally wide personal knowledge of the clergy of the Church of Ireland.

His lecture schedule became increasingly formidable. In the divinity school his courses were St Luke's Gospel, the Epistle to the Romans in Greek, and the Creeds. Soon he was delivering catechetical lectures on Saturday mornings at 9.30. Many lay people attended these, attracted by his ability to open up the intricacies of the course in a way that was always interesting and sometimes exciting.

He began to assist W. B. Stanford by teaching Greek grammar and before long he was lecturing extensively in the classics department, both in Greek and Latin to students taking the pass arts course. During the war staff shortages became acute and there was need for people like George who could fill the gaps. He also lectured the medical students in English; it was quite a taxing job as his classes included many foreigners. (Until the 1960s it was considered necessary for doctors to have a liberal as well as a professional education.) In the process of examining and returning essays to some 150 students each year, George came to know many of them personally. His willingness to help out even extended to examining in Irish and German at matriculation examinations.

By maintaining a constant presence in College, sharing in the life of the common room,[6] dining on Commons, going out to watch matches in College Park, attending society meetings and keeping his rooms (in No. 11) open to all, George's warmth and interest in people established a framework wherein his pastoral gifts could be exercised.

He gives Michael Ferrar the credit 'for having taught me to get to know people in their own areas'; hence he visited them in their rooms and came alongside them in their recreation. The social aspect is only one side of his chaplaincy, however, for he spent countless hours with individuals, counselling them. His approach was a personal one and he was generous with his time. For instance, when, as often happened, a student wished to be prepared for confirmation, George almost always conducted the entire course on a one-to-one basis. It was a rare opportunity for a student to have his questions answered in depth and for George to share his spiritual insights. It is not surprising that several of these candidates were later ordained.

George systematically addressed the needs of incoming freshmen, hoping to make them feel at home in their new surroundings. Working from admissions lists or preferably from correspondence with schools or home rectors, he would invite the freshmen as a group to his rooms and would thereafter amaze them individually by instantly recognising them and using their Christian names. One such freshman, who was to become Bishop of Cashel and Ossory, the Rt Rev. N. V. Willoughby, says 'You felt you were special to him',[7] and that was reassuring for a new student.

Although he felt himself part of the university establishment, unlike an ordinary lecturer George was free to mix with the students. As a matter of principle, however, he always wore a clerical collar, believing that instant identity was helpful with the students. It was highly unusual for students to be on Christian-name terms with lecturers and officially George was called 'Mr Simms' but those who knew him well called him by his Christian name, as did members of the Student Christian Movement (the S.C.M.) for that was the custom with all their office-bearers.

George attended almost every meeting of the S.C.M. and sat on its general council. This gave him the opportunity to travel to England quite frequently during the war and kept him in touch with many friends there. It also involved attendance at the summer conferences, held at venues like the Royal School, Dungannon, and Friends' School, Lisburn.[8] Through the S.C.M. he influenced many non-conformists. For the Rev. Dr R. H. S. Boyd, Director of the Irish School of Ecumenics from 1980 to 1987, George was the source of his understanding of the Anglican tradition and an early ecumenical influence.

The S.C.M. provided some of George's most informal contacts in College. Similarly informal were the breakfasts after early communion on a Sunday which he shared with students who lived in the same block. George expected no 'ceremony' and always kept his own entertaining simple. Frequently he invited small groups of students to his rooms for late-night supper, tea or cocoa and toast but 'never had a bottle to pour nor cigarettes to offer'. In addition to the S.C.M. he also regularly attended the meetings of the Evangelical Union and always welcomed their members at any service or activity organised under the chaplaincy.

Even during the war he maintained quite a succession of 'celebrity' visitors to College and a greater number came in the post-war years. He always invited a selection of students, drawn equally from the ranks of the arts and sciences, to meet such a visitor in his rooms. Sometimes he received a rebuff but many availed themselves of the opportunity to meet well-known men such as Dean Hewlett Johnson, popularly known as 'the red Dean' of Canterbury, V. A. Demant, Bishop Stephen Neill and Frank Laubach, the literacy pioneer.

His other interests in College included an old favourite, the magazine *T.C.D.*, the Social Service Society[9] and the two College missions to Chota Nagpur and Fukien. He even attended rag

meetings, where he encouraged the students in their charitable
fund-raising.

Strictly, students who lived in rooms were obliged to attend
chapel for a fixed number of services each term but the Junior
Dean, whose responsibility it was, applied the rule gently. With
students who did not attend chapel George tried to interest them
in applying Christian standards before attempting to get them
along to worship. He constantly endeavoured to have chapel used
more: to this end he increased the number of services, invited
celebrated preachers and established a book display in the ante-
chapel at which people could browse and borrow titles by the
simple expedient of an entry in a notebook.

Apart from a solid core of the faithful, who attended main services and the Saturday night preparation for holy communion, the
congregation varied somewhat depending on the service. Some
appeared regularly at the mid-week communion, some followed
the Tuesday lunch-hour services, while a few, including
Presbyterian students like Robin Boyd, enjoyed the quietude of
compline[10] at ten o'clock in the evening. One of Dr Boyd's
treasured memories is of George's voice rolling phrases like 'keep
me as the apple of an eye' round the reverberant chapel.

Preaching was an important part of George's chaplaincy, particularly as his 'parish' was a university. The 'university sermon' on
Sundays was a formal theological dissertation usually delivered by
a distinguished preacher from Ireland or Britain. George preached
only once a term and although the Provost and a number of
Fellows were present, he spoke to the students on their level as far
as possible. Students of the time recall that visiting preachers often
failed to overcome the acoustic difficulties of the chapel, while
George's pitch and timing were well-nigh perfect. Each Sunday he
said a prayer after the sermon: many of the students awaited it with
bated breath for they marvelled at the skill with which he chose
from *The Book of Common Prayer* one which drove home the
message of the sermon. His very conduct of the services had a
beneficial influence on the divinity students: without exception
they admired his deft liturgical touch and were encouraged to give
their utmost when it became their responsibility to order the
liturgy.

The Tuesday lunch-hour services were vital to his preaching programme. Week after week the chapel was crowded with a mixture of
staff and students drawn from all denominations. There was
generally one theme for the term; George had a Tuesday calendar
printed, giving the headings for each week, and circulated it

widely. Sometimes the theme was designed to interest the uncommitted student: that for Trinity Term 1947 was 'What Christianity has to say about . . . narrow minds, evil hearts, our future, the money we spend, personal relationships, the futility of spiritual indifference, the necessity of worship', and that for Michaelmas 1950 was 'Religion in College'. A few themes were more academic in tone, such as the series in Hilary term 1950, 'Spiritual biographies of some *Alumni Dublinenses*', men of God who had been Trinity graduates.[11]

The recurrent theme, however, was prayer. Under headings such as 'Ways of Prayer', George saw to it that the students were given teaching on this most vital aspect of the Christian life. The series constituted miniature schools of prayers as they gave guidance on when and how to pray, the balance between private and corporate prayer, the interplay between the component parts — adoration, confession, thanksgiving, supplication, meditation and contemplation. The prominence given to prayer did not surprise the students, who recognised that George's strength as chaplain depended much on his prayer life. He delivered some of the talks himself, but also invited colleagues like Michael Ferrar and churchmen who happened to be visiting Dublin to help.

Prayer also figured largely in the programmes of the two missions which George organised during his chaplaincy. Having been secretary to the Temple mission in 1934 proved very useful in the planning of these. The 1944 mission was led by A. R. Vidler, assisted by Lex Miller.[12] Vidler was an academic, based at St Deiniol's Library, Hawarden. At the time many viewed him with suspicion on account of his radical tendencies but George chose him for his readiness to grapple with the problems of being a Christian in a society torn apart by two world wars within a generation. He had organised a second mission for March 1950, to be led by Bishop Stephen Neill, who had to cancel it due to ill health, so a Franciscan mission headed by Michael Fisher was arranged instead. George had, in fact, left College for Cork by the time it took place in 1952.

George's approach was to teach and preach and live out the Gospel and to leave it to the individual to appropriate it to himself, with the guidance of the Holy Spirit. He was a traditional Anglican in that he never pushed his point hard, never appealed to the emotions, never challenged people in the forthright manner of evangelists such as Billy Graham.

For some students, presentation of the Gospel by word and example was not forceful enough to bring them to the point of commitment. Others mistrusted the pleasant smile and beautifully-turned phrases. Both types might have responded more readily to a more directive pastor and preacher but many ex-students have testified to his influence. For instance, Canon O. A. P. Peare, who now sees that a sermon which George preached at a mission in St Olaf's Church, Waterford, in 1942 was a 'turning point' in his life and who was prepared for confirmation as a T.C.D. student by George, says that 'he played a very large part in my decision to become a priest'.[13] Another student of the forties, Dr J. C. Combe writes 'what a tremendous friend he was to all the students. We absolutely idolised him — he was our hero — our idea of all that a Christian ought to be'.[14]

Despite the happy round of events in Trinity, George was constantly saddened by the tragedy of young men leaving for war, never to return. He joined in the war-time nightwatches to look out for incendiary bombs on the roof of the library and encouraged others to watch and pray with him. Here, as in so many College activities, George was able to build a bridge between the everyday life of the College and the chaplaincy.

The war made travel to Britain extremely difficult and intellectual students and the younger clergy missed the former opportunities to attend English conferences. Such conferences provided valuable stimulus and contact with Christian thought beyond the confines of the Church of Ireland. George initiated an alternative, in Dishopogrove, the residence in Waterford of the Rt Rev. T. A. Harvey, Bishop of Cashel. Peter Harvey was then a student in College and his father readily gave hospitality to the reading parties which George organised.[15] Time was given to sit and read quietly but the parties were important in providing a forum for the participants to develop their ideas. A carefully selected group of young theologians like M. L. Ferrar, R. P. McDermott, D. M. Kennedy and H. R. McAdoo sat amid academics of other disciplines such as E. J. Furlong, lecturer and later Professor of Philosophy at Trinity College, D. A. Webb, lecturer in and later Professor of Botany, W. B. Stanford, Regius Professor of Greek, A. N. Jeffares and Peter Allt, both of whom became well-known Yeats scholars. Invited speakers treated of very relevant topics; in 1943 the subject was church-state relations, examining D. A. Binchy's thesis in his *Church and State in Fascist Italy*.[16] Dr Eric Mascall, known for his Christian social teaching, came from England to deliver a paper to which there was a lively response.

Apart from considering the problems of church-state relations in contemporary fascist states, the topic led naturally to an assessment of relations in Ireland between the state and the churches, both Roman Catholic and Protestant. Several of the participants had already given much thought to the specific position of the Church of Ireland within the Irish state. Some time before, Webb and McDermott had launched a plan for a book on the religion, politics and culture of the Anglo-Irish in contemporary society: their fellow contributors were to be George, Ferrar, Allt and Stanford. The topic for the reading party was particularly apt for them, as it gave them an opportunity to test their views. The book was never finished but Stanford completed his section, which was published as *A Recognised Church, the Church of Ireland in Éire*. His politico-religious treatment was followed by Dr McAdoo's treatise on the subject, *No New Church*.[17] Essentially it was an interpretation of the position of the Church of Ireland in the light of Anglican teaching. The intellectual spokesmen of a rising generation of the Church of Ireland, they articulated their conviction that loyal and enthusiastic citizenship of the new state was perfectly compatible with devout membership of the Church of Ireland. The implications of this new outlook will be examined in the next chapter; suffice to say at this stage that the significance of the Waterford reading parties is evidenced by their attention to issues of such vital importance to the Church of Ireland.

The parties are illustrative of George's involvements outside the narrow confines of Trinity College. It was entirely appropriate that the Dean of Residence should be in the forefront of an effort to foster reappraisals and new developments in theology.

Likewise, as an ecumenist, it was natural that George should avail of every opportunity to establish contacts with Roman Catholics. Openings were rare in the forties but George had friends in such places as All Hallows' College and the Morning Star Hostel, run by the Legion of Mary. The chief point of contact at the time was the Mercier Society. A Roman Catholic initiative, it drew inspiration from the discussions between Cardinal Mercier of Malines and second Viscount Halifax, a leading Anglican layman. The society established informal but pioneering inter-church conversations in Dublin and had as its motto 'Towards a better understanding'. Meetings, held in Ely Place, were addressed by Roman Catholic and Anglican speakers in turn and there was always an opportunity after the paper for discussion.

It is quite remarkable that the Mercier Society existed at all for in Ireland scarcely any progress had been made along the road to church unity. When George was a student the live issue had been that of 'Home Reunion', that is reunion between the Church of

Ireland and the Presbyterian and Methodist Churches in Ireland. The term 'Home Reunion' was borrowed from England and had been coined in the mistaken belief that English Christianity had been unified until people like Knox and Wesley had broken away. During the thirties talks took place with Archbishop Gregg leading the Church of Ireland delegation. A major barrier to Home Reunion was the Church of Ireland insistence that it could be effected only if the non-conformists accepted an episcopally-ordained ministry. The talks were discontinued and were not resumed for some thirty years.

If unity with the non-conformists was difficult, unity with the Roman Catholic Church was perceived as impossible due to its claim to be the one true Church. The conflicting claims of the Church of Ireland and the Roman Catholic Church to be the true successor of the church founded by St Patrick had stood in relief in 1932, the putative fifteen hundredth anniversary of the saint's mission to Ireland. Successive scholars of the divinity school at Trinity College had sought to bolster the claims of the Church of Ireland, pointing to a line of bishops which in many dioceses can be traced back to pre-Reformation times and thence to the early Celtic church. The sterility of such argument can be appreciated in that the Roman Catholic Church could make the same claim but it took a long time for the focus to be transferred to more productive issues.

At the Mercier Society the papers tended to emphasise the differences between Roman Catholic and Anglican theology. A paper on liturgical prayer, read by Michael Ferrar, was something of an exception, in that it succeeded in raising the thoughts of the listeners to a high spiritual level where theological differences became unimportant, as all his listeners could identify with what he was saying. It is no coincidence that of all the Mercier Society addresses he attended it is this paper that George most readily recalls, for Ferrar's approach was very close to his own. In many years of ecumenical endeavour, George's contribution has been more in loving *koinonia* than in hammering out differences or in constructing an actual scheme for unity.[18]

Frank Duff, the founder of the Legion of Mary, Senator Desmond Fitzgerald, a former government minister, the Hanson brothers, Ferrar and George, were among the leading figures of the Mercier Society. As interest grew meetings were transferred to Newman House; sadly, however, Archbishop John Charles McQuaid, the Roman Catholic metropolitan, was uneasy about the rapid growth of an ecumenical society and did not like the idea of

scholars arguing over points of difference in the presence of the
laity so he disbanded it in 1944 and there was no more real dialogue
until the summoning of the second Vatican Council almost twenty
years later. In George's opinion the Mercier Society was
memorable for 'its prophetic touches and wide vision' and important in that, like 'other and much later ventures, it proved that
sharing and rapprochement were possible before all the doctrinal
differences had been sorted out.'[19] Undoubtedly those who were
members became more outward-looking as a result.

Here we must digress to personal matters. Many people were surprised when in June 1941 George's engagement to Mercy Felicia
Gwynn, daughter of Brian James Gwynn and Mary Weldon was
announced; their courtship had been conducted most discreetly and
they had scarcely been seen together. At thirty-one George was
good-looking, charming, clever — in short, a highly eligible
bachelor. As one lady graduate of the forties said, 'he was very
glamorous and half the girls fancied they were in love with him.'
Unless their romantic interest in him was explicitly expressed,
George did not even notice, he treated all the girls in the same
friendly way; sometimes he had to take evasive action. Undoubtedly
he was all the more attracted to Mercy because she showed no
interest in him.

There was a common Donegal background, a shared commitment to the Church of Ireland and there were many family connections: like the Simms family the Gwynns had come to Donegal in
the seventeenth century — they originated in Flintshire. Mercy's
grandfather, the Very Rev. John Gwynn, had been rector of
Tullyaughnish, Ramelton, from 1863 to 1882 and he had married
a daughter of William Smith O'Brien, the Young Ireland leader.
George's sister, Dorothea, had married Brian O'Brien, a second
cousin of Mercy's in 1938, while his elder brother, Harry, had lived
in rooms in College with another of her cousins, Arthur Gwynn.
Arthur's father was Provost E. J. Gwynn and Harry had often enjoyed invitations to the Provost's House. When George had come
to College he was often invited as well and met Mercy at annual
dances there when she was still a teenager.

George readily identified with the Gwynn tradition of combining
service to the church with the academic life. Mercy's grandfather
had left parochial life first to be Archbishop King's Lecturer, and
then Regius Professor of Divinity at Trinity College, while another
uncle, R. M. Gwynn, was Professor of Biblical Greek and later of
Hebrew.[20]

Family connections were not enough to initiate a romance. In

fact Mercy's first recollection of her future husband was unfavourable. When he was a curate at St Bartholomew's he came to
a women's S.C.M. meeting in College to speak on intercession and
Mercy felt he was too good to be true! Elected a scholar in 1937,
she graduated in French and Italian in the following year and went
to Italy to further her studies. When George returned in 1940 as
Dean of Residence, Mercy was back lecturing in Italian.
Their romance began at the S.C.M. conference in Dungannon
that year. Mercy was in charge of the bookstall and George
remembers eavesdropping as she gave rapid critiques of the books
available. What he heard made him want to know her better.
Although he did not intentionally seek an intellectual wife, it was
a natural and intuitive choice. In Mercy he found an ideal companion for life; her intellectual acumen and penetrating examination of any issue, social, religious or political, have always been a
stimulus. Her criticism of draft sermons and articles has consistently
proved useful, as she has a quick eye for inconsistencies and woolly
statements. By temperament and upbringing, having been an only
child in a quiet house, she was self-sufficient and independent —
basic requirements for the wife of such a busy man. In time, when
their children were born, Mercy was content to devote herself to their
upbringing and this was vital as George was a devoted family man
but had to squeeze his time with the children into snatched precious
moments. In all the years of their marriage Mercy has preserved
home as a haven and, without breaking any confidences, George has
constantly sought her considered opinion.

George and Mercy were married in Rathfarnham Parish Church
on 2 September 1941 by Archbishop Barton who was a family
friend. After their marriage they lived in a flat in Morehampton
Road until he was appointed chaplain/secretary of the Church of
Ireland Training College and they moved with their first son,
Nicholas, to live on the premises in Kildare Street. The Church of
Ireland Training College was the sole institution in the twenty-six
counties where young Protestant men and women could train as
national school teachers. Since the foundation of the Irish Free
State it had been experiencing difficulties in maintaining numbers
and meeting its financial commitments so that it faced the danger
of closure. In 1943 when the Rev E. C. Hodges, the principal, was
elected Bishop of Limerick, the governors felt that the College
could not afford to pay a principal and they had the idea of appointing George to do the job without the title. As numbers were so low
it was possible for George to undertake the responsibilities on a
part-time basis, giving the College its due place alongside his

primary role in Trinity College. His knowledge of Irish and his obvious love of the language, combined with his overall academic standing and his facility with students made him a most suitable choice for the position.

For most people it would have proved impossible to do both jobs properly but George was blessed with a superabundance of energy. There were various factors which influenced him in his acceptance of the post: he saw an opportunity to strengthen the links between the two colleges to the benefit of both and of education in the Church of Ireland as a whole; he was pleased at the prospect of living so close to Trinity and of a larger income. Money has never been important to George or Mercy, both choosing to live simply; on the other hand they welcomed an endless succession of visitors so they found it hard to make ends meet on George's small salary in Trinity.

Already in 1942, George had taken on another minor commitment, in order to augment their income. As assistant to the Trench Professor of Holy Scripture at Alexandra College, he conducted worship on Wednesday and Friday mornings and then took the senior religious education class. Somehow he managed to maintain this for the ten years until he left for Cork, which meant that he was in Trinity Chapel for matins at 8.30, hurried back for the Training College service at 9.00, after which he could be seen rushing across St Stephen's Green for his third service in Alexandra College!

In the Training College he was the administrator; he dealt with the Department of Education, looked after the correspondence, prepared for Board and finance committee meetings; he was the manager of the Kildare Place Schools. On the academic side, he himself gave the religious education classes to the students, in the sure conviction that sound scripture teaching by national schoolteachers could provide the backbone of many country parishes. He also shared in the supervision of the students during their teaching practice in the schools. As chaplain, in addition to conducting the service, he acted as pastor to the students.

Mercifully the registrar, Miss E. F. Pearson, and the matron were resident so George was not responsible for the day-to-day running of the College or the supervision of the students. Many of the girls were shy and reticent but he tried to bolster their confidence by sharing with them his conviction that national teachers occupied a vital place in society; moreover he often asked them in during the evening to discuss some topic of relevance to the church universal such as the World Council of Churches. In this way he enabled

them to broaden their horizons. Aware that the girls led a very
sheltered life (the few boys in the College lived out in the Y.M.C.A.
hostel in Rathmines), he encouraged them to take an interest in the
Girls' Friendly Society, to become involved in the neighbouring
parish of St Ann, Dawson Street, and to participate in youth conferences and festivals.

Mercy was scarcely involved in the Training College as they had
two more children, Christopher, born in 1944, and Katharine, born
in 1946, so her hands were full. However, the students enjoyed the
homely atmosphere which resulted from having a family living in
the chaplain's quarters. George also used their proximity to Trinity
College to entertain girl students at home in the evening, something
which he could not do in his Trinity rooms due to the rule that
women had to leave College by 6.00 p.m.

At first there was great resistance in the Training College to a
closer link with Trinity College but George's tact soon eased this.
His diplomacy also enabled him to develop good contacts in the
Department of Education; when controversial issues arose he
always telephoned the relevant official to discuss it before sending
a written reply; when Department officials were engaged in
research he readily made the Training College records available to
them. George thus ensured smooth relations with the Department
which benefited the Training College and also later proved useful
to him as bishop and archbishop.

George guided the Training College through a difficult decade.
As Susan Parkes wrote in her history of the College, 'he gave the
leadership and intellectual stimulus which it needed'.[21] He went a
long way towards reassuring the Department of Education that the
College had a future: when he left for Cork in 1952 the governors,
encouraged by his work, appointed a full-time principal.

In these years, as he calmly recalls, 'the work just grew and
grew.' He adds, 'people thought I did far too many things and did
them superficially.' His engagement diaries reveal to some extent
just how busy he was.[22] In 1941, before he had taken on responsibility for the Training College, he gave the evening Holy Week
addresses in All Saints' Church, Grangegorman, from Sunday to
Thursday and then took the train for Belfast, where he took the
Good Friday three hours' devotions in St John's Church, Malone,
and took part in services through until Easter Day. As was his practice, he preached or took the services in parish churches on most
Sundays outside lecture term. Even on his honeymoon in
September he did duty in Raheny parish.

Also in 1941 he was involved in a three-day school of prayer in Bray in January, gave a talk on St Patrick in Armagh in March, another to the Mothers' Union in Cork in April, contributed to the Greystones week-end for the divinity students in May, gave talks at the S.C.M. summer conference in Dungannon in July and was the conductor of a youth mission in St George's, Dublin, at the end of September. Among other engagements that year was one to celebrate communion in Irish at St Patrick's Cathedral and another to conduct a service in their native language for German refugees.

It was in the forties that his writing began. For an understanding of George it is vital to appreciate that he never initiated any of his writing; he did it only in response to a pressing request and frequently it was a matter of presenting for publication a lecture or series of talks which he had previously given and for which there was a demand in printed form.

Some of his first publications did not even bear his name. In 1943 he was one of a group of clergy who produced *The Country Shepherd*, a guide to pastoral work in country parishes in the Church of Ireland.[23] The first publication which he wrote on his own *For Better, for Worse*, likewise bore no author's name.[24] A short booklet on Christian marriage, which appeared in 1946, it will be considered along with his other writings in a later chapter. On the other hand his address entitled 'Your Faith' to the 1943 youth conference of the dioceses of Dublin, Glendalough and Kildare did appear under his name in *Christ, Youth and the Conflict of Life*, as that publication was a report of the proceedings of the conference and the several addresses were printed as part of it.[25]

George would have one believe that he began his writings on *The Book of Kells* accidentally. As he tells the story, the Provost, E. H. Alton, a Latin scholar known for his work on Ovid, had agreed to prepare an introduction and to collate the text for a complete facsimile edition by a Swiss publisher of Ireland's most famous illustrated gospel book. However, Alton was ageing and his sight was failing so he asked George, as a former pupil, to help. There is no one alive to prove it but it seems probable that Alton had carefully chosen George as a scholar who was likely to make a valuable contribution to the work. Thus he became joint editor with Alton and Peter Meyer. Because of his knowledge of German he also conducted much of the correspondence with Burchardt, the publisher.

What started as a service became part of his life. George, appreciative of the Provost's 'generosity' in inviting him to help, happily worked on collating the text. Rightly, he saw it as a privilege to describe each page[26] and check each Latin word. As he developed his skills as collator, he discovered a sense of fellowship with the scribes and artists. On occasion he gave a talk on the collator's job, pointing out that 'despite all his modern equipment for checking variant versions and deciphering obscurities, [he] must exercise as fine a penelopean patience as was displayed by the monk in his cold and cloistered scriptorium'. He 'must resist the temptation to be rushed; he cultivates a contemplative air. He travels slowly with his eye, syllable upon syllable, line upon line.'[27] Forty years of study of *The Book of Kells* have convinced him that the craftsmen's work was 'little short of worship'. He remarks, 'the personality of a manuscript is revealed long after its first introduction. The parchment must be a constant companion before its character unfolds itself and the secrets of the story filter through'.

Despite the fact that he was often rushing from one place to another, George was by nature a contemplative and was so imbued with the Celtic Christian tradition that he delighted in spending hours in perusal of the text. He received considerable help from his former tutor, Professor A. A. Luce. It was Luce who encouraged him to present his work as a doctoral thesis and he was awarded a Ph.D. in 1950, the same year as the facsimile edition was published.[28] His *Short Description of the Book of Kells* had already been published by the Dublin University Press in 1949;[29] it sold very well and went into several editions and reprints.

As his reputation grew Dr Simms received an increasing number of invitations. In 1949, for instance, he led a mission (through English) in Rotterdam from 27 March to 3 April, in June gave one of his early radio talks, on this occasion on Radio Éireann, on '400 years of *The Book of Common Prayer*' and delivered the founder's day lecture at St Deiniol's Library, Hawarden. From 9 to 26 July he was in Germany under the auspices of the Council of Christian Reconciliation in Europe, which aimed to foster constructive interchange between British and German universities. Taking two students with him to mix socially and contribute to the rapprochement, he delivered three talks in German, on the life and witness of the Church of Ireland, *The Book of Kells*, and training for the ministry. The venture was significant not only because of its ambassadorial nature but because his lecture on *The Book of Kells* was the first of over 400 lectures with which he has been enthralling audiences ever since.

There was no opportunity to relax after the trip to Germany as he had agreed to act as chaplain to the Rossall Conference for the youth of the diocese of Blackburn from 30 July until 5 August. The family didn't have a real holiday that year for Dr Simms did duty in Raheny parish for the rest of August. The hectic schedule outlined above was not completed at the expense of the more regular commitments, for his Irish engagements to preach, to take retreats and quiet days and to give talks were as numerous as ever. The range of his scholarship and the depth of his spirituality was such that the list of subjects on which he spoke constantly expanded. Many of the talks were devotional and in them he gave great prominence to prayer. Already in the forties he was in demand as a speaker on the liturgy, while his forthright and enabling teaching on marriage and personal relationships led to his being a favourite speaker at Mothers' Union meetings and youth guilds. Most of his topics related to practical Christianity but he did not shy away from academic papers such as one to the Dublin Clerical Association on 2 February 1942 on 'The fate of the soul after death'.

Jotted throughout his diaries are meetings (often held in his rooms because they were so central) of various Church of Ireland committees on which he sat. He was secretary of the Anglican and Eastern Churches' Association, a member of the Incorporated Society for Promoting Protestant Schools in Ireland, treasurer of the General Synod Board of Education Examination Committee; he was also the secretary of the Association for the Promotion of Christian Knowledge, commonly known as the A.P.C.K., and strove to make its work more strictly theological. In the post-war years the A.P.C.K. was worried about the cost of producing the hymnal and in 1950 requested the General Synod to consider a reduction in the number of hymns. The Joint Hymnal Committee was charged with examining the issue and the A.P.C.K. was invited to name fifteen members, of whom Dr Simms was one. Soon its brief was extended to the selection of new hymns for the hymnal, which was published in 1960. The committee effected only a conservative revision but it was important as the first item of liturgical revision which was accepted by the General Synod.[30] Dr Simms resigned from the Committee in 1954, so his contribution was limited but he gained experience in the delicate work of revision, to which he returned when Archbishop of Dublin.

To mention all his involvements would be tedious — suffice to say that there was very little going on in the Church of Ireland in which he was not either involved or interested. In the forties he attained a thorough knowledge of the workings of the Church; in this regard his membership of the General Synod from 1941 gave him valuable experience.[31] It is quite amazing that in his frenetic round of activities he found time to act as honorary clerical vicar in Christ Church Cathedral (his chief duty being to sing evensong occasionally and to act as verger over lunchtime), to visit his mother in Donegal (his father had died in February 1941) and to develop many of his friendships.

There was rarely time merely to relax with friends but in his work he had almost daily contact with Michael Ferrar, whose friendship became increasingly important. George's friends have often felt that the relationship was an unequal one in which they were the receivers rather than the givers but, over many years, George consistently sought insight and guidance from Ferrar as he has done from few others.

They were quite unalike; Ferrar had a logical mind, was cautious, introverted and stern. His study and travelling were severely limited by an eye disorder so he concentrated on one job,[32] read selectively and thought deeply. From this combination of character and concentration was distilled a wisdom which was expressed in strong, direct guidance for those who sought it and in clear, enlightened teaching of the faith. George's mind was more intuitive than logical, he read widely and spread his time over a vast range of commitments. As the years passed and preferment came, he often found it difficult to find time to think deeply and always valued Michael's insight into a problem. Sometimes he was told uncomfortable truths, almost always he received strength.

George regarded Ferrar as 'a great teacher of prayer' and exponent of doctrine. After Ferrar's death in 1960 George wrote a memoir to accompany his edition of some of his friend's addresses and papers.[33] In it he explained how 'vagueness about the Church's teaching and naïveté of approach to the Bible stirred Michael to carry out a work not merely of instruction but of prophecy'.[34] George believed that Ferrar's vision made him a notable reformer of the Church of Ireland at a time when 'it was in dire need of a deepening of its spiritual life'.[35]

Writing this in 1961 as Archbishop of Dublin, George's words reveal a lot of what he felt about the Church of Ireland in the forties. Paying tribute to Ferrar's widespread influence, he salutes his desire 'to teach tolerance, to proclaim the whole Faith, to combat narrowness, and to pounce upon the errors of the minimisers and to correct their distortions'.[36] Undoubtedly Ferrar shaped some of George's views but it was his unswerving friendship which led the archbishop to say 'I owe him more than I can ever say'.[37]

Likewise Raymond Jenkins was a very influential friend, whose depth of experience and forthright manner enabled him to give guidance to George on many issues. As they worked together in the forties a very close friendship developed. They shared a catholic-evangelical churchmanship and a profound interest in everything that was going on in the Church of Ireland. Thus it was not surprising that in 1952 when George was elected Bishop of Cork, he chose Raymond Jenkins to be his chaplain at the consecration and that at a later stage, as Archbishop of Dublin, he appointed him archdeacon.

One might well ask how he managed to find time for family or relaxation. Undoubtedly the move to the Training College made it possible to spend more time at home, although much of it was at odd moments during the day. Clearly he could not have lived such a life had Mrs Simms not been so tolerant and self-sufficient. As to recreation, he did play tennis and squash quite frequently and for some years he acted with the Leeson Park Players. In these Trinity years he was surrounded by friends and congenial company. He loved his work and found great happiness in his marriage. His lifestyle was ideal for him and he very specifically states of this period in Trinity 'I never really wanted to go anywhere else; I hadn't any ambitions.'

V

BISHOP OF CORK

Considering Dr Simms' talents it is surprising that he was allowed to remain in Trinity as Dean of Residence for over eleven years. He was approached about the incumbency of parishes both in Ireland and England and about the post of warden of Lincoln Theological College but, as has already been said, he was not ambitious and was extremely happy as he was.

In 1951, however, the Rt Rev. R. T. Hearn, Bishop of Cork, asked him to move there as dean. Hearn was then seventy-six, an elderly bishop presiding over a diocese staffed largely by elderly and conservative clergy. When the aged Dean Babington became incapacitated, the bishop sought a young and lively successor to him at St Fin Barre's Cathedral. It seems certain that Bishop Hearn, in doing this, was consciously importing into the diocese a potential successor to himself. When Dr Simms, who had no idea of this ulterior motive, showed a reluctance to accept the offer, the bishop played his trump card in the form of the primate. Gregg and Hearn had been close friends since their days as curates in Cork at the turn of the century and, no doubt, they shared similar views on Dr Simms' future. Moreover, the other bishops were eager to see Dr Simms promoted, for fear of his being enticed to England again. Gregg succeeded in persuading him to accept the deanery on the grounds that he would have to prepare himself to accept higher office in the Church of Ireland.

Dr Simms was appointed in 1951 but insisted on serving his notice in Trinity College and the Training College, so was not installed until 16 April 1952. He approached the job of dean with his customary vigour. He was soon involved in the multiple facets of the life of the city and in a few short months rescued the cathedral from gloomy isolation. He wanted it to be used to the maximum for worship, to be open throughout the day for prayer and for the inspiration of visitors. Before his arrival the cathedral was closed at lunchtime; he was determined to keep it open and was usually

47

there at that time to show visitors round, relying on Christopher, his second son, to deputise for him when he was unavailable. With great speed he compiled a printed guide to the cathedral,[1] to cater for those who liked to explore at their own pace.

He immediately began to prepare for a clergy conference and a youth gathering at the deanery and an autumn Bible study course, based on the cathedral parish. Initially there was among clergy and people some of the traditional Cork suspicion of a bright young import from Dublin but soon people began to appreciate his friendliness, administrative efficiency and dignified but vital ordering of the liturgy. Younger people in the diocese were talking of him as a 'ray of hope' and 'a breath of fresh air.'

Bishop Hearn died suddenly on 14 July 1952 and, much to his surprise, Dr Simms was elected bishop by an enormous majority on the first vote at the diocesan synod on 2 October. In the weeks approaching the election there was a systematic anti-Simms lobby; his youth (he was forty-two, while the majority of the Irish bishops were in their seventies), and his unproven record as dean (a mere five months)[2] were considerations but there were three other 'charges' against him: that he was high church, pro-German and a 'Sinn Feiner'. Dr Simms' curacy at St Bartholomew's and chaplaincy at Lincoln Theological College were put forward as evidence of high-church tendencies. The pro-German charge has already been explained,[3] the 'Sinn Fein' label is equally far-fetched. For many years after the new Irish state was formed some Protestants remained staunchly Unionist. Even in 1952, after a long period of constitutional government and civic peace, they regarded with suspicion those who cheerfully gave their allegiance to the new state, especially those who, like Dr Simms, were Irish speakers. Although Dr Simms was not outspoken on political issues, his attitude had been carefully noted. Synodsmen were visited and were urged not to consider him for the bishopric but the shallowness of the allegations was shown by the huge vote for him at the synod. From the chair, Archbishop Barton immediately assured him that the bench of bishops would welcome him 'whom we all love'[4] with open arms. His election was widely welcomed and according to Archbishop Barton, 'Dublin received the news . . . with cheers'.[5]

Many in the congregation who attended his consecration in St Fin Barre's Cathedral (and overflowed into Christ Church, whither the service was relayed) on 28 October were hopeful that this young bishop would bring new life to the united dioceses. For convenience he was referred to as Bishop of Cork but Cork is joined to the dioceses of Cloyne and Ross and the area involved stretches from Berehaven to Youghal. The sermon preached by E. S. Abbott, by then Dean of King's College, London, was on the theme of 'The little flock'.[6] It addressed the needs of scattered congregations in a minority situation and encouraged them to look confidently to the future under the leadership of a bishop who was 'holy and humble of heart'. Abbott directed their attention not to their bishop's administrative abilities nor to his academic standing but firmly to his spiritual stature, saying 'All of us believe him to be one of the intimates of Jesus Christ'. There can scarcely be a simpler or more moving recommendation of a new bishop to his people.

In his years as Dean of Residence and chaplain to the Training College Dr Simms had come to know many bishops well. Without attempting a systematic analysis of the individuals he well knew what it was that he admired and could appropriate to his own use. Going back to his student days there was Archbishop Temple, whom he admired greatly. His simplicity and humility were endearing qualities which Dr Simms shared; the young bishop talked to students without condescension just as Temple had to him in 1934 and accorded the same importance to a servant as he did to a dignitary. Moreover Dr Simms identified with Temple's ecumenical zeal, although he could make little progress in the Cork climate of the 1950s.

He admired the primate, Archbishop Gregg, for his integrity and fairness and for his style of chairmanship. From Gregg Dr Simms learned not to have favourites and not to let himself be dominated by one faction or person. However, he knew that Gregg was rather distant and formidable, whereas he set out to be accessible and approachable. (He did not emulate the archbishop in his attitude to clerical attire; Gregg was very particular about his own appearance, gaiters being *de rigueur* for formal occasions, and frequently reprimanded his clergy for lapses from sartorial rectitude. On one occasion George had been extremely fortunate to escape censure: at the S.C.M. conference in Dungannon in 1940, as the weather was fine, he had donned sandals, shorts and an open-necked shirt; when Archbishop Gregg arrived unexpectedly he took one look at George and said 'Ah, John the Baptist!')

Dr Simms was much less formal and was by nature approachable. Whereas Gregg wrote letters it was Dr Simms' custom to telephone when the subject was difficult; 'I didn't want a shock administered', he explains, knowing that he could soften in conversation what might read as cold or stern in a letter. In his approachability he was more like Archbishop Barton. They had worked closely together in Dublin, especially in the Church of Ireland Training College where the archbishop was chairman of the board of governors. Dr Simms admired his practical attitude and pastoral style and set out to emulate them. He was convinced that the bishop's role centres on the exercise of a pastoral ministry and was determined that nothing would deflect him from that.

From observing other bishops Dr Simms had learnt to keep a rein on promises; never to make a promise which he might not be able to honour. This resolution stood him in good stead in Cork and even more in his days as archbishop when he recalls 'everyone wanted you at the same time' and it would have been easy to make shallow promises in every direction.

Prayerful assessment of his role and demeanour as bishop saved him from many of the pitfalls awaiting a young and inexperienced man. However attractive his youthfulness was it could have proved a serious disadvantage. As it was, it certainly made an impression in Cork: when he had arrived as dean, Corkonians had frequently taken him for a new curate; even when he was bishop people who failed to notice the purple stock sometimes made the same mistake!

While the first impression may have been of youthfulness, what made a lasting impression was his spirituality. The Most Rev. H. R. McAdoo, former Archbishop of Dublin, was rector of Bantry when Dr Simms became bishop and then replaced him as Dean of Cork. He recalls that his episcopate 'was like a springtime in the church's life in Cork'[7] and that it had a tremendous spiritual impact.

Given the situation in the 1950s, it was not enough to limit spiritual leadership to the realms of Bible scholarship, prayer and liturgy, it had to extend to establishing a new vital link between the life of faith and Christian citizenship. Dr Simms was eminently equipped to provide such leadership.

The Church of Ireland showed signs of recovering from the lack of confidence and sense of isolation which it felt under the new state but this recovery had not yet begun in Cork. Mention has already been made of the intellectual arguments of Stanford and McAdoo as to the compatibility of Irish Anglicanism with Irish citizenship. An examination of the basic problem and their arguments will serve to demonstrate why Dr Simms' episcopacy marked something of a watershed.

As a result of World War I the Church of Ireland had been drained of young men, while the Treaty led to a flow of emigrants. Many of them were army and government officials but the decline of Church of Ireland members in the twenty-six counties from 249,535 in 1911 to 145,030 in 1936 involved emigration from country areas and the emigrants were often enterprising young men who would otherwise have been a major support to the Church of Ireland.[8]

Church of Ireland members suffered political as well as religious isolation, for theirs had been the church of the establishment, they had associated it with British rule and now associated the new state with Roman Catholicism. While many of their fears were allayed by the stability achieved by an Irish government, developments under the Fianna Fail administration in the 1930s and particularly the recognition of the special position of the Roman Catholic Church in the 1937 Constitution had exacerbated anxieties. Stanford's *A Recognised Church* gave a frank statement of the demoralising aspects of Irish life since independence. In it he presented the issue as he saw it; recognition by the state is no guarantee of the future of the church: 'pressure began despite the efforts of governments and fair-minded citizens to prevent it';[9] political and economic pressure by the exclusion of Church of Ireland members from appointments, by arguments that only a Roman Catholic could be a true Irishman, by the ban on any literature critical of the Roman Catholic Church. It was Stanford's opinion that 'The chief means of expressing public opinion or criticisms in Éire are being progressively tuned to the Gregorian mode.'[10] While he conceded that personal feeling between Protestants and Roman Catholics was generally good, he cited the pressure of Roman Catholic evangelism and of the *Ne Temere* decree regulations on mixed marriages.

His identification of the factors which damaged morale within the Church of Ireland was not just a litany of complaints; it was more an investigation of the reasons why Church of Ireland people were reluctant to enter fully into the life of the nation. In his book he reprinted his address to the Dublin Diocesan Youth Conference in November 1943 'On being a good citizen'. On that occasion he encouraged his listeners to have confidence in their church and in the power of the Holy Spirit to work through even a tiny religious minority. He urged that by everyday witness at their work and in the community and by care in maintaining worship and educating children for life they could maintain their morale. Stanford believed that once the church recovered confidence in its future it could dare to associate itself with Irish life without fearing for its identity. 'I should like our church to take a sympathetic, and active part in building the future of Ireland in freedom.'[11]

Stanford's politico-religious thesis was complemented in 1945 by Dr McAdoo's *No New Church*. This little book was a theologian's interpretation of the essence and contribution of Anglicanism:

his central point was that members of the Church of Ireland, grounded in their faith and convinced of their heritage as part of the ancient Catholic Church, 'looking to the rock whence they are hewn, can make a generous contribution to the spiritual, intellectual and civil life of the country'.[12]

He set out to demolish the argument that a Church of Ireland man should not take part in politics. Drawing a sharp distinction between party politics and politics as referring to 'the ordering of our entire social setting, our laws, our health and social services, our civil and municipal administrations, taxation, and cultural and educational matters' he contended that it was incumbent on Church of Ireland people . . . to make as large a contribution to the national life, not only by active participation in Senate and Dáil but by taking an intelligent interest in all problems, judging the issues by the principles they have inherited'.[13]

While exposing the fallacy of the assumption that knowledge of Irish was a pre-requisite for a good Irishman, he put forward an enthusiastic apology for the Irish language and traced the contribution of the Church of Ireland to its modern development. Dr McAdoo's book concluded with an exhortation to churchmen to explain their faith and to witness to it by their actions in daily life. Encouraging the laity to follow the lead which he and Dr Stanford had given in 'speaking out' he wrote

The policy of saying nothing is fatal, for it begets spiritual and mental apathy, not to mention an inferiority complex. It is a policy from which the Church of Ireland has suffered, and the aim of the present generation . . . must be to achieve articulate-ness.[14]

These works have been quoted at length because of their seminal importance in the process by which the Church of Ireland regained its confidence and resumed a role in Irish society. Dr Simms shared their vision and did a great deal to make it a reality in Cork during his episcopate there but his pronouncements as bishop reveal a somewhat different emphasis. The doctrine of the Church which he had developed through the influence of Temple and Ramsey was so strongly based on the Incarnation that universal consideration of the kingdom of God held priority over everything else and he believed that a religious minority had a right to exist simply because it was serving the kingdom. He tended to look forward to its realisation, rather than backwards to tradition and heritage.

Dr Simms' conviction of the essential unity of the Body of Christ and of a universal Christian citizenship was gently evinced at the civic reception for the diocesan conference held in the City Hall in

Above: the Simms children in 1914. Left to right: G.O.S., Gerald, Dorothea, Harry.
Below: Combermore, Lifford, Co.Donegal, photographed in 1966.

St Edmund's School, Hindhead. Above: the dining hall, showing J.C.Morgan-Brown's portrait (centre), and colour frescoes. Below: the chapel, showing choir and sanctuary.

The chapel, Cheltenham College, looking east. Courtesy, Cheltenham College.

Above Trinity College, Dublin, scholars from the years 1880[(8)], 1890[(9)], 1900[(0)], 1910[(1)], 1920[(2)] and 1930[(3)]. Left to right; *front row,* [3]G.O.Simms, [3]E.C.Allberry, [9]E.J.Young, [9]W.E.Thrift, [8]W.Collen, [8]H.T.Bewley, [8]N.J.D.White, [8]W.O'Neill, [8]W.M.Crook, [3]W.S.E.Hickson, [2]F.W.R.Brambell; *middle row,* [3]E.G.Quin [3]R.W.Reynolds, [3]M.L.Ferrar, [3]T.D.W.Whitfield, [3]C.Duffin, [1]J.C.Dudgeon, [1]G.S.Stevenson, [1]F.laT.Godfrey, [0]C.F.Harvey, [0]T.H.Seale, [0]T.V.Pedan, [3]M.A.Ellison, [3]W.H.Mol, [3]R.W.L.Crosslé. [3]H.O.Duncan; *back row,* [2]J.A.M'Keown, [2]G.C.North, [2]W.Beare, [2]G.A.Duncan, [2]P.Bourke, [2]N.D.Emerson, [2]H.S.North, [2]H.J.L.Armstrong, [2]T.T.Gilbert, [2]W.H.Thrift, [2]W.B.Maginess, [3]E.M.Camier.
Below: Canon W.C.Simpson, with R.G.F.Jenkins and G.O.S., c.1935.

Above: left; E.S.Abbott, Warden of Lincoln Theological College, 1936-45, and later Dean of Westminster; right, the chapel at Lincoln Theological College. Below: Reading party at Bishopsgrove, Waterford, 1942: *front row,* A.N.Jeffares, D.A.Webb, G.O.S., H.R.McAdoo, W.B.B.Magill, W.B.Stanford; *back row,* D.M.Kennedy, G.D.P.Allt, D.P.Lang, F.J.Furlong, W.W.L.Rooke, P.B.Harvey.

The Long Room, Trinity College Library, Dublin. Photo courtesy Trinity College Library.

Above: G.O.S. at the Church of Ireland Training College, Dublin, 1950. *Front row,* Annie Beulagh Moore, Jessie Castles, Vivienne Sherwood, G.O.S., Miss E. Pearson (Lady Registrar), Elizabeth Bonner, Evelyn Hill; *back row,* Emily McCartney, Daphne Free, Irene Shaw, Elizabeth Pearson, Gladys Sloane, Elizabeth Shirley, Sinéad Ludgate. **Below:** G.O.S., on the occasion of his installation as Dean of Cork in April 1952, with the precentor, B.T.W.Nicholson, and the preacher, StJ.S.Pike. The Irish Press.

Clergy refresher course at the Palace, Cork, 1953. *Front row,* J.D.Hutchinson, T.H.B.Royse, H.R.McAdoo, C.F.Evans, G.O.S., R.P.C.Hanson, J.H.Hingston, R.Beresford Poer, D.P.S.Wilson; *second row,* E.P.Mills, A.A.Wilson, A.Gordon, C.G.Gibson, W.W.C.Johnston, C.Allen, B.T.W.Nicholson, G.S.Baker, W.laB.Bourchier, F.Garrett, R.Firebrace, F.T.Armstrong, J.G.Russell; *third row,* J.W.Norcott, W.E.White, A.Cromie, E.Tobias, W.Taylor, F.M.K.Johnston, A.C.Gill, J.W.Macdonald, unknown, J.C.M.Conner, S.R.C.Watts, J.H.B.Talbot, T.F.Smith; *back row* unknown, P.Bury, J.P.Lewis, R.Good, C.Roberts, M.E.Stewart, E.C.L.Dunne, L.Colthurst, G.A. Salter, N.W.McGahey. Photo R.W.Hammond

1953, when he stated that members of the conference were going to 'try to wed their faith to their citizenship, their responsibilities as Christians with their responsibilities to the community, the city, the country, and indeed the world.' Unfortunately he rarely explained the theology behind his pronouncements and actions, so many people failed to understand the implications. However, his entire ordering of the diocese was directed at deepening the understanding of the Christian society and at developing a new and positive self-image for the church. He did not 'hit the headlines' with major, adventurous speeches but his firm leadership is attested to again and again.

First and foremost he aspired to renewal throughout the diocese; renewal for all, lay and clerical, while his responsibility for the clergy was a constant concern. When he became bishop most of them were much older than he but he knew many of them from his time as Dean of Residence. Having three dioceses under his care he had three deans and three archdeacons and one of his first appointments was of Dr McAdoo to succeed him as Dean of Cork. The two 'young fellows', as they were often called, worked very happily together and rejoiced to see the Cathedral congregations grow. Dean McAdoo, at thirty-six, had already established a reputation as a theologian, his churchmanship and political outlook accorded with that of his bishop and he wholeheartedly supported Dr Simms' drive for spiritual education. When the bishop planned clergy conferences or diocesan missions the dean was at hand to assist; likewise when the dean set up a course of Lenten bible classes in the old St Fin Barre's school the bishop readily agreed to lead it. Despite some dismissive predictions the classes proved a great draw — the average attendance was 300!

Although his parochial experience was very limited, Dr Simms had a clear insight into parish life, its difficulties as well as its opportunities. He fostered relations with his clergy by constant availability, informal visits to their homes and at clergy conferences. He never turned down an invitation to preach or attend a parish function unless he had a previous engagement. He always made clergy welcome at the palace and spent hours counselling any who had a problem. He always remembered that he also had a responsibility for clergy wives and families. Often he was well aware that finance constituted a problem for the clergy and that such worries were a hindrance to their work. The income of many rectors was about £500 per annum and Dr Simms constantly sought ways to supplement their income. Realising that the laity are often unrealistic about the financial situation of the clergy, he frequently alluded to it at diocesan synod and council. For instance at the 1954 diocesan synod he spoke of the difficulty of purchasing and maintaining a car, saying 'It is of the utmost importance that the parish clergyman should not have the burden of financial worry.'

One of his early efforts to ensure equitable financial treatment of his clergy aroused considerable suspicion. The Gumbleton Trust had been established in 1920 to augment the stipends of the clergy of the diocese each of whom was accustomed to receive an extra £27 per annum under the scheme. The financial advisers on the diocesan council had convinced Dr Simms that the scheme should be revised to ensure fair distribution but he found he had to smooth ruffled feathers and scotch the rumour that the Gumbleton funds were to be diverted to pay the rates on the palace! Until now the bishop had paid the rates himself: Bishop Hearn and his wife had independent means but Dr Simms relied totally on his salary of £1,700 with no expenses allowance, so to pay the rates at some £400 was too great a burden. Accordingly, at Archbishop Barton's suggestion, the diocese took over the responsibility and gave a lead which was followed by other dioceses in the Republic. By gentle diplomacy Dr Simms won acceptance for both measures and avoided any unpleasantness at the diocesan synod. This misunderstanding arose from lack of trust such as diocesan clergy often feel in relation to a new and youthful bishop. Dr Simms' readiness to ask their opinions and listen to their advice, his openness and compassion gradually overcame it.

Compassion was needed in dealing with the personal problems of individual clergy. As ever his touch was delicate: his method of dealing with one backslider was to visit him at intervals, leaving behind a theological tome, with a request for a considered critique. As bishop Dr Simms did everything he could to rehabilitate the erring. While never condoning what was wrong he avoided being judgmental ('we are so weak ourselves,' he explains). If it were possible to keep the man within the diocese Dr Simms would do so; if circumstances prevented this he laboured to secure a future elsewhere. Not infrequently he accepted clergy who had been obliged to leave another diocese; thus he afforded an opportunity for rehabilitation but inevitably he sometimes had to admit to failure.

Dr Simms used conferences and quiet days to inspire the clergy with new spiritual objectives and to create a close working relationship between him and them. By tradition the clergy conferences for the diocese held each May in the palace were organised by the clergy themselves. Dr Simms regularly provided other in-service training sessions; for instance, in September 1953 the clergy were invited to the palace for a three-day Bible school, at which Professor C. F. Evans spoke on 'How to use the Bible' and Dr R. P. C. Hanson on 'The Bible and Behaviour.'[15] From Professor Evans many of the clergy heard for the first time C. H. Dodd's important thesis on St John's Gospel and took away new information to use in their own preaching and teaching. Lectures were pitched at a high level and in the fifties people used to joke that the clergy of Cork diocese were the best educated in Ireland. They certainly benefited from the intellectual and spiritual stimulation and enjoyed the fellowship which their bishop nurtured.

During Dr Simms' episcopate the morale of his clergy rose and they were inspired to new spiritual endeavour. Moreover each incumbent knew that, no matter how distant his parish, he could rely on his bishop's personal support.

Dr Simms was aware of the criticism that bishops tended to concentrate on the city of Cork to the detriment of the rural parts of the diocese. A bishop born and bred in Dublin might well have experienced uncertainty in mixing with his flock in west Cork, he might have had difficulty in understanding their accents and in finding common ground for conversation. His childhood in Donegal and his love of people led Dr Simms to approach visits to outlying areas with confident anticipation.

Country people of the time were inclined mentally to place their bishop on a pedestal; they did not expect him to be able to discuss farm prices with them, their experience of him was mostly at formal occasions such as episcopal visitations and diocesan synods. Dr Simms was no expert on matters agricultural and his Anglo-Irish voice was as alien to their ears as that of any previous bishop but he overcame many barriers by his friendliness and wonderful gift for remembering names.

Many people have amazing stories about this gift of Dr Simms. Capt. Ray Mills of the Church Army remembers a chance encounter in 1956 when he boarded the Belfast-Enniskillen train at Portadown and found himself sitting opposite a clergyman in a purple stock. Without actually introducing themselves they chatted for the duration of the journey.

It emerged that the bishop was going to fulfil an engagement at Portora Royal School and by subsequently checking the newspaper, Capt. Mills was able to establish that his companion had been the Bishop of Cork. Many years later, when he was a missionary in South America, he wrote to the Archbishop of Armagh to ask to be included in the diocesan prayer list. He mentioned that they once met in a railway carriage and was greatly surprised to receive a handwritten reply from Archbishop Simms, recalling some details of the conversation which they had had twenty years before.

Mrs E. Russell likewise recalls standing on the platform of Heuston Station with Dr Simms some quarter of a century after he had left Cork when they met a group of west Cork farmers, all of whom Dr Simms greeted by name. A bishop with such a gift has a great advantage in gaining acceptance. Cynics have often suggested that Dr Simms could not have remembered thousands of names, correctly attached to the faces without some *aide-memoire*.[16] Stories circulated picturing him driving to a remote parish, drawing in off the road, taking a notebook from his robes case and brushing up on the names, family connections and general circumstances of those whom he would be likely to meet that day. Dr Simms never had such a notebook and never needed one, as can be testified by countless people who met him in most unexpected places and were amazed by his instant greeting of one with whom his acquaintance was slight.

His awareness of the claims of the rural parts of his diocese led him to a degree of decentralisation. He arranged confirmations, which had been centralised, on a local basis, setting the rite firmly in the parish context. There was no question of rushing down from the city for a perfunctory ceremony and rushing away again; after the service he enjoyed the opportunity to mingle with his flock, chatting to all and sundry.

Decentralisation was applied to missions and Bible classes as well. Although he mounted major diocesan missions in the city and held weekly Bible classes in the palace for all who cared to come, he paid due attention to outlying areas. Series of Bible talks in a venue such as Bandon gave him an opportunity to meet with a group several times while, for instance, a mission in Schull in April 1953 meant that he could base operations in west Cork for a week.

While he saw the importance of strengthening parish life he also knew that isolation and parochialism were ever-present dangers, to be countered by broader contacts throughout the diocese. Diocesan missions and conferences had a binding effect and contributed significantly to spiritual renewal. Before a year of his episcopate had passed he had mounted a wonderfully successful diocesan conference in the City Hall. In choosing this location it gave the diocese an opportunity to make a corporate witness in the city and Corkonians marvelled at the large number trooping in and out.

The main theme of the conference was 'What is the Gospel?', the chief speaker being Canon C. E. Raven, Regius Professor of

Divinity at Cambridge. Dr Simms had chosen him as an outspoken lecturer who could relate the Gospel to contemporary problems and supplied a back-up team to speak on moral and industrial issues and on personal relationships. While the focus was on topics of immediate relevance to the people of his diocese, including the thorny question of mixed marriages, the bishop structured the conference to stress the part which the diocese had to play in the Church of Ireland as a whole, within the Anglican Communion and in the world-wide Christian fellowship. The conference schedule was a heavy one, with an early communion service each morning and a lunch-hour service, followed by an evening session. It drew an attendance of 1,500 to 2,000 on five successive nights, well justifying the decision to hold it in the City Hall.

It was significant that this conference was reported in the local press. Dr Simms was determined that openness should be maintained and that Church of Ireland events should be viewed as part of the daily life of Cork and to that end he saw that regular press releases were given and that the press was invited to report, even on the diocesan synod.

Encouraged by the response to the diocesan conference, Dr Simms pressed on to the city parishes mission in October 1954. Again he was deeply involved with the planning and issued a letter urging his people to use this as another opportunity for a new start in the life of the Spirit. At the mission he led by example, sitting among the large congregation as one of them, seeking fresh insights and inspiration in his own spiritual life and joining in the fellowship.

As a bishop Dr Simms was in a position to develop his ideas about fostering vocations. Believing that the Church of Ireland needed to be more active in seeking men for the ministry he instituted vocations conferences at the palace. He acted as chairman and host and the programme included worship, talks given by carefully selected speakers and discussion in small groups. Information about the nature of vocation and ministry was a high priority for Dr Simms deplored the system by which men entered the divinity school as if to an ordinary academic course and proceeded to ordination by way of the divinity testimonium, with the minimum of selection. Vocations conferences were concerned with finding the right men for the ministry. Each participant was given an opportunity to talk about his faith and, if appropriate, his sense of vocation. Ample free time was given for recreation and socialising: this was important as a boy might be the only candidate from his school and locality and might feel isolated or even eccentric.

Dr Simms involved lay people in running the conferences, in order
to avoid excessive ecclesiasticism. He also knew that many of the
participants would not proceed to ordination and was determined
that they should suffer no embarrassment as a result.
These conferences were the model for later national vocations
conferences. Before he left Trinity College for Cork Dr Simms had
been planning a vocations conference for schoolboys in conjunction with the Rt Rev. F. R. Mitchell, Bishop of Kilmore. Translated
to Down and Dromore in 1955, Bishop Mitchell began similar conferences there. This fostering of vocations put heart into the
dioceses involved; spirits rose and a new confidence in the future
emerged. The Church of Ireland in general was not aware of the
serious situation it faced; ordinations in the thirties had run at fifty-
five to sixty a year but in the fifties they rarely exceeded ten. The
bishops were slow to understand that the church would suffer a
crippling shortage of clergy in the eighties and realisation for the
average man in the pew has come only when it has affected his own
parish. The bishops may have been slow to foresee the crisis but
they did take the lead of Bishops Simms and Mitchell on vocations
conferences when they established the Central Advisory Council of
Training for the Ministry (CACTM) in 1961. In this respect their
vision was very important.

On a less formal basis he often had a current or prospective
divinity student to stay and took him with him on his daily round.
Perhaps the personal touch did more than the conferences to persuade the young man that the ministry was a high calling. They all
must have observed his own sense of fulfilment in that calling.

Dr Simms tried to convey at conferences in person what he had
already set out in a persuasive pamphlet. Composed as a letter to
Patrick, a godson, *Into the Ministry*[17] made the important point
that Christ chose 'very ordinary persons' requiring 'willingness
rather than cleverness, faithfulness more than perfection, love in
preference to genius'. While demonstrating that ordinands did not
have to be special people, he did stress that they had a special calling from God to act as 'specialists' in the ministry of all Christian
people. He drew out the traditional Prayer Book definition of the
work involved in that ministry, highlighting reconciliation of the
divided, support of the weak and that unsung role of 'being there'.
'Whatever he does is not the chief point; whose he is, whom he
represents — this is of supreme significance.' His picture of ministry
as 'offering adventure, providing full scope for original methods
and approach with infinite variety of expression', was an idealist's
view but was not divorced from reality for he went on to say that

it 'demanded suffering, patience and utter dependence upon God'.
It is typical of Dr Simms that he did not put his name to the
booklet, nor does his name appear on a follow-up booklet which
he wrote with Bishop Mitchell in 1954. *Which Way?*[18] was a more
formal production which also set out the methods and cost of training for ordination. For some years it acted as a sort of prospectus.

There were many vacant parishes in the diocese when Dr Simms
became bishop. It was a priority to fill these and he had to fill
others as rectors retired. The difficulty of doing this and the conduct of worship in a superfluous number of churches made
diocesan reorganisation urgent and he immediately embarked on
amalgamations. He well knew the hazards of uniting parishes and
closing churches and the bitterness which is often engendered. He
was not prepared to drive a scheme through against implacable
opposition and if he could not persuade the people involved to
accept the idea, he would not proceed.

The difficulties he experienced convinced him that a nation wide
Church of Ireland initiative was required and he was one of the
initiators of a proposal at the 1956 General Synod to appoint a
special commission. The Sparsely Populated Areas Commission
worked for nine years. Originally the Synod and the Representative Church Body expected its work to be finished within three
years but it soon became clear that the size of the task was far
greater than had been anticipated. Nine of its twelve members
served for the full term until its work was finished and its final
report submitted to the General Synod in 1965. Dr Simms was one
of these, as was its chairman, F. L. Jacob.[19] As diocesan treasurer,
Mr Jacob had been closely associated with his bishop in the quest
for amalgamation and reorganisation. Dr Simms held him in high
regard as an administrator and in putting his name forward for this
commission launched him on a course which led to his becoming
one of the senior members of the Representative Church Body.
Thus it happened that one of his most valued associates in Cork
became an official adviser in his days as Archbishop of Dublin and
later as primate. For his part Mr Jacob respected Dr Simms' grasp
of financial questions and his adroitness in chairing committees. He
believes that 'people always behaved better in his presence', that
'his company had a creative effect'.[20] That an administrator
should speak in such terms of a bishop shows how clearly Dr
Simms treated it as an integral part of his ministry.

Under Mr Jacob's chairmanship the commission drew up
schemes for all the rural dioceses of the southern province and for
Armagh, Meath, Tuam and part of Derry in the northern province.

There were two classes of review, one of really sparsely populated areas, the other where numbers were not particularly low but where too many churches were in use in proportion to the needs of the population. In each case the commission first met the diocesan council and then a panel of local commissioners. Great diplomacy and tact was required and Dr Simms displayed these to the full, especially in those early sessions which he chaired. After his translation to Dublin he declined to act in this capacity.

The commission reduced the number of cures in the areas concerned from 344 to 256 and recommended the closure of 144 churches. Its concerns extended to provision for new, economical and easily-run rectories to replace rambling, chilly ones, which were an unacceptable burden to the clergy.

The great advantage of the commission was that it avoided confrontation between a bishop and his people. This was always of the utmost importance to Dr Simms, who wanted to be shepherd of all his flock and took great care not to be identified with any side or faction. Even if a measure was right and necessary he was not keen to adopt it if he risked alienating some of his people, for he believed that he could not minister effectively to anyone who felt alienated. This approach has led to some of the most consistent criticism of him as bishop and more so as archbishop, leaving him open to charges that 'he wanted to please everyone' and 'wouldn't grasp the nettle' and 'wouldn't risk unpopularity by unpopular decisions'. One can discount desire for popularity as the guiding force; Dr Simms consistently had pointed out the pitfalls of seeking popularity to ordinands and had written in one of his ordination pamphlets, 'Banish from your mind the thought of being popular. It would be useless to deny that a clergyman might be sorely tempted to wish to be popular. Such a wish could lead him into social and other activities yielding attractive returns in terms of praise, public approval, influential backing, or material benefit.' He urged the clergy that the respect of the people will only be given to the pastor whom they know as 'a man of God'.[21]

There were numerous instances where his decisions did cause trouble; in many contentious issues there were opposing viewpoints and whatever he did was bound to annoy one of them. Having prayed and thought about it and having sought advice in relevant quarters, he then tried to implement what he believed was best. He was at his most determined when a decision had to be made, but was much less resolute when it was a question of a desirable but not mandatory reform. For example, there was an urgent need for a new city national school and Dr Simms decided that it should be built in a corner of the palace grounds. Many of the clergy were horrified at the choice of site and felt it wrong to encroach on palace property but Dr Simms was convinced that it was right and was determined that the scheme should not be delayed. Likewise his action on Newmarket church showed him at his most resolute. The church had been closed and a proposal was made to convert it into a school. When the glebes committee turned down the idea Dr Simms, preferring this to demolition or leaving it to become a reverential ruin, went to the Representative Body and won his case.

On the other hand proposals were often made at diocesan or General Synod with which he agreed but he would not use his influence to secure their passage. This reticence was rooted in his desire to be acceptable to all, not to be seen to take sides, but also sprang from his conviction that a bishop has no right to impose his authority. Indeed he talked not so much in terms of 'authority' as of responsibility and influence and far from using 'power tactics' he relied on persuasion, consultation, compromise and patience. In this way he usually won his point at diocesan level but such gentle tactics often failed to make headway at General Synod. Many have said that he should have used his position to drive this or that reform through the General Synod but to say that is to fail to understand that such an approach was utterly alien to him. On the other hand there were occasions when strong, clear leadership would have been helpful. Moreover, in later years as archbishop, the pressures were so great that he found it harder to make decisions and this detracted, sometimes seriously, from his effectiveness in administration.

As bishop he sat on the board of many charitable and educational institutions and was involved in the life of the city to a greater extent than his predecessors. His conscientious attendance at meetings was an apprenticeship for his membership of committees after his translation to Dublin. In some cases, such as the chairmanship of the Cork Savings Bank, at which he and his Roman Catholic counterpart served in turn, his participation was restricted to a friendly interest. Where he had more direct responsibility he was very active. He was on the council of the Victoria Hospital. He was *ex officio* chairman of the board of Midleton College and was on the governing bodies of Cork Grammar School, Rochelle and Bandon Grammar School, the four Protestant secondary schools in the diocese.

He was instrumental in moving Cork Grammar School to a new site. This was a brave venture for a new bishop, as it involved delicate negotiations between the local committee, its parent body, the Incorporated Society,[22] and the Department of Education. Functioning in a confined site on a city street, the school required a more spacious location. When Ashton, on the old Blackrock Road, came on the market the local committee was interested but the Incorporated Society felt it would be too expensive. Things changed suddenly when, in a waning property market, the auction failed and there was a chance to buy it at a very reasonable price. Knowing that speed was of the essence, Dr Simms with F. L. Jacob took the initiative; in so doing he came as close as ever he did to driving a scheme through. Having rushed a reluctant Incorporated Society into paying £6,000 for Ashton, with the prospect of another thirty or forty thousand pounds' expenditure to turn it into a school, the bishop took a line which was fraught with pitfalls but proved well justified. The new site was large enough to incorporate the girls from Rochelle in one of the many rationalisation pro-grammes in Protestant education.

He also played a more active role in University College Cork than any of his predecessors. It was very much a Roman Catholic institution where a Church of Ireland bishop, as a member of the governing body, might feel ill at ease but as dean he had already established cordial relations with its President, Alfred O'Rahilly. A hand-written letter sent on the day of Dr Simms' election reveals an open friendliness. It is doubtful if even the redoubtable O'Rahilly would have addressed a new Roman Catholic bishop in such a relaxed fashion.

My Lord,
I am anticipating your title. You remember my asking you if you were too young to be elected? Well, the Holy Ghost — and my prayers! — did the job.
    But I could kick myself for not taking the possibility more seriously and being much more respectful to you!

Dr Simms conscientiously attended meetings of the governing body and frequented the College library on his own academic pur-suits. O'Rahilly retired and the installation of his successor was an occasion when the degree of Church of Ireland separation was manifested: Dr Simms was present at the installation ceremony but did not attend the mass beforehand. Not until his primacy did it become acceptable for a Church of Ireland bishop to attend a special service in a Roman Catholic church or for him to receive a Roman Catholic bishop at a Church of Ireland service. One must remember that in the fifties, the laity did not attend weddings or even funerals in churches of the other persuasion. Before Dr Simms' arrival inter-church relations in Cork had not been good. The Church of Ireland establishment was reluctant to involve itself not only with the Roman Catholic Church but even with the nonconformist churches. For instance, when Gurteen Agricultural College was founded by the Methodist Church in 1947, the diocese of Cork was not prepared to lend open support.

In the main, however, the nub of inter-church relations centred on those between the Church of Ireland and the Roman Catholics. Given the uneasiness felt by members of the Church of Ireland in the Irish state and the unbending conservatism of the Roman Catholic bishop, Dr Cornelius Lucey, the 'ecumenical' climate could not be anything but chilly and civic involvement cautious. On the other hand Dr Simms gave an example of civic involvement and strove constantly to place inter-church relations on a more friendly footing. His lead was taken up enthusiastically by some of the younger people, lay and clerical, who wanted to see Protestants take an active role in promoting a new Ireland.

By the time he left Cork Dr Simms had changed the image of the Church of Ireland in the community. His personality was an important factor: always gracious and hopeful, he was a dignified leader of his people but his dignity was never associated with remoteness or condescension. It was noticed that he treated everyone alike, whether civic dignitaries or the 'shawlies' with whom he chatted in the street.

In building bridges with the majority community in Cork it was a great advantage that Dr Simms and Dean McAdoo were Irish speakers. As Irish-speaking leaders of the Church of Ireland were then quite rare, Corkonians were very impressed to hear them both speak at length in Irish at the Lord Mayor's banquet in their first year in office. In fact it was suggested that their command of the first official language exceeded that of their Roman Catholic counterparts and the civic dignitaries.

Civic occasions presented problems for a Church of Ireland bishop as they often bore nationalistic connotations and were fixed for a Sunday. The traditional attitude of Roman Catholics and Protestants to Sunday observance were very different; Roman Catholics believed that as long as one attended mass one could spend the rest of the day as one wished, whereas Protestants took the commandment to keep the Sabbath holy to preclude many activities, social and sporting.

Civic occasions and many of his community involvements

brought him into contact with Bishop Lucey. They could not be said to have made any real relationship for Bishop Lucey remained remote. On one occasion a drapery dispute was dragging on in the city and Cork Corporation unanimously adopted a resolution that the two bishops should act as mediators; Bishop Lucey acted very speedily on his own to ensure a solution, obviating the necessity for Dr Simms to become involved.

On the other hand, Dr Simms' contribution to the life of the city was valued by many. When he was elected to Dublin Denis Gwynn, Professor of History at U.C.C., wrote an appreciation in the *Cork Examiner*. He stated that 'Public life in Cork will suffer a heavy loss with the impending departure of Bishop Simms. It has been a real acquisition . . . that the young bishop of the Church of Ireland had not only a natural aptitude for public affairs but a personality which won friends and commanded respect on all sides.'[23]

The palace was full of life in those years. Dr and Mrs Simms had two more children, Hilary, born in 1952, and John, born in 1953, and the sight of two prams outside the palace was a source of amazement to the Corkonians. Dr Simms believes that the presence of small children broke down barriers for many visitors, who remembered the formality of former days.

With five young children Mrs Simms was not in a position to accompany her husband often and her involvement was limited to the Mothers' Union Young Wives group, the Girls' Friendly Society, of which she was diocesan president, and the Irish Girl Guides, in which she was area commissioner. However she was always ready to host functions at the palace and to welcome the steady stream of visitors. In addition to clergy and vocations conferences, diocesan organisations were encouraged to arrange meetings there from time to time. The Simmses also permitted the use of the palace by organisations in the city, knowing that such occasions helped foster community relations. For instance, a fund-raising recital held there by the Cork Orchestral Society, of which the bishop was a patron, brought many Corkonians into the home of a Church of Ireland bishop for the first time.

With this open-door policy, Dr and Mrs Simms wisely opted for informal buffets rather than formal dinners. Not only did they make catering easier but they provided better opportunities for socialising and accorded more with the Simmses' desire for simple living. Overnight guests and those who 'dropped in' were entertained in the basement with the family.

It was always the same. Here and in the See House in Dublin Dr Simms anticipated in his lifestyle what the Lambeth Conference of

1968 desired, that bishops 'as leaders and representatives of a servant Church should radically examine the honours paid to them in the course of divine worship, in titles and customary address, and in style of living.'[24]

His dignity did not require bolstering by gratuitous greeting as 'My Lord'; but in the fifties no bishop would have been addressed in less lofty terms. He wrote many of his letters by hand and didn't expect to have a secretary, although it would have been a great asset. When he had arrived in Cork, his only means of transport was a bicycle.

When he was made bishop he bought his first car, a second-hand model whose reliability was suspect. Before long the diocese bought him a new one but within the city he still preferred to walk or cycle because he could have a word with people on the way.

Any Church of Ireland bishop has many duties outside the diocese for he is also a bishop of the church. Dr Simms travelled regularly to Dublin for meetings of the Representative Church Body, the Standing Committee, and the House of Bishops. These took place on three or four days in the third week of the month and country bishops tried as far as possible to schedule other Dublin meetings and commitments for the same days. For Dr Simms there were meetings of the A.P.C.K., the Incorporated Society, the Hymnal Committee, to mention a few of the concerns in which he was involved. An individual bishop might not have any specific task at the General Synod but it was a busy week for all of them. Ecumenical events also figured in his diary; in January 1956, for instance, he chaired Irish Evanston, the conference organised by the United Council of Churches[25] as a follow-up to the Second Assembly of the World Council of Churches in Evanston in 1954.

Dr Simms continued to be in great demand as a preacher, speaker and lecturer. In 1953 for instance, he took a prayer school in Belfast in January, gave the devotional talks at the Castlerock clerical refresher course after Easter, preached in Cambridge in June and in Glasgow and Inverness in September. Invitations to lecture on *The Book of Kells* had become quite frequent. At first he had no slides and his only visual aids were tourist board colour posters. He gave his first lecture in Cork to the University Art Society in U.C.C. by request of Professor Denis Gwynn, who cut pages from a book and mounted them on a epidiascope.

He even found time for some writing, the most demanding of which was his co-editorship of the facsimile edition of *The Book of Durrow*, which was published in 1960.[26] Amidst his heavy schedule the painstaking task of collation proved therapeutic, for it demanded so much concentration that for a time he could forget about his other responsibilities. As he once wrote, 'it is an interesting sideline when vestries get difficult and councils reach an impasse'![27]

His *Irish Times* weekly column 'Thinking Aloud' dates from 1953. It emanated from a men's meeting at Monkstown Church, County Dublin, to which the rector, the Rev. A. H. Butler,[26] had invited Jack White of *The Irish Times* to speak on the church and the media. At the meeting it was pointed out that the Church of Ireland received little attention from the daily press and that an initiative on the part of the Church of Ireland would be appreciated. Some time later White asked the rector to suggest a cleric who could write a regular spiritual column for his paper and Dr Simms' name was put forward. At first its inclusion was spasmodic but it soon became a regular item, appearing on the leader page every Saturday.

One can only marvel that he had the energy to do so much. With that as a vital pre-requisite, the real basis of all that he did as bishop and later as archbishop was his devotional life. The discipline which he had assimilated in Lincoln and the lessons which he had learnt from Temple, Abbott and Ferrar stood him in good stead. Saying matins every morning in St Fin Barre's Cathedral was part of a strict regime of prayer and meditation in which he always managed to sustain a lengthy intercessions list. Even at the busiest times he remembered Temple's dictum 'if you have one minute to pray, spend half a minute preparing' and thus resisted the temptation of busy Christians to bombard God with a list of requests. He personally knew the meaning of that recurring quiet day theme 'Be still and know that I am God' and from regular periods of stillness in God's presence he emerged refreshed and strengthened.

Prayer was not reserved for fixed periods on his knees, for his work, thoughts and prayers were inextricably linked. As he went about his daily duties he prayed; sometimes they were arrow prayers, instant reactions to some piece of bad news, sometimes he thought of a person and prayed for him as he drove along the road, sometimes they were more ordered prayers before a meeting or a hospital visit.

'Keeping close to Christ', as he would put it, gave him a peacefulness which strengthened many and disconcerted others, for people are often disturbed by peace; it contrasts with their own state of mind. Dr Simms admits that he often irritated people by refusing to share their annoyance in difficult circumstances but dismisses any idea that it was an achievement to remain calm by saying that it was largely a matter of temperament. Prayer and temperament combined to produce what has been described by several people as 'a dynamic quietness' and it was this combination which made his episcopacy so significant in Cork. In four years he put new heart into the diocese and he began to prepare it for a more positive future. He emerged as the first of a new generation of bishops and it was increasingly appreciated that his leadership skills could be applied to a sphere greater than a diocese. These years gave him the administrative experience needed and endeared him to his people. When he was elected Archbishop of Dublin there was great sadness at his departure from Cork. The Ven. T. H. F. Royse, archdeacon of Cloyne, encapsulated the feelings of the diocese in his farewell speech, the kernel of which was derived from Daniel 10.2, in saying that George Simms was 'a man greatly beloved'.

VI

ARCHBISHOP OF DUBLIN

When Archbishop Barton announced his retirement in 1956 there
was a groundswell of opinion which favoured Dr Simms as his successor. The see of Dublin is a vital one; as Primate of Ireland[1] and
metropolitan of the southern province the archbishop is in a position to exercise an influence on the faith and worship of the entire
Anglican community in the Republic and, through the location of
his see as much as through the seniority of his office, he has the
most regular contacts with the government and with others who
have political and economic influence. The Archbishop of Dublin
is a national figure, by virtue of his office; he is seen as the
representative of the Church of Ireland (often, indeed, of the entire
minority community) by the people of the Republic as a whole.

Dr Simms was very well known in Dublin and it was felt that
his spirituality, his scholarship, knowledge of Irish, diplomacy
and universal acceptability eminently qualified him for election.
Shortly before the synods of Dublin, Glendalough and Kildare
were due to meet it was rumoured that, on being sounded out, he
had expressed a determination not to accept elevation if elected.
Raymond Jenkins intercepted him on his way through Dublin to an
engagement in Donegal and found, as he expected, that while Dr
Simms was not keen to be considered a candidate, his strong sense
of duty ensured that he would allow his name to go forward and
would assume the responsibility of Dublin if necessary.

Characteristically, he listed the reasons why he shouldn't be
elected — there must be better candidates, he was too young, he
had such a strong affection for Dublin that it could be a temptation
for him — and seems to have given it little further thought until,
while presiding at a diocesan council meeting in Cork, he was informed that he had been chosen as the next Archbishop of
Dublin.[2] In a later interview he admitted that 'my first feelings on
being elected bishop and archbishop were of rather cold dismay'.[3]

The press heralded his appointment in terms such as 'the

68

youngest archbishop of Dublin ever' and 'archbishop like a boy'. At forty-six he was in fact the same age as Gregg had been when he was elected to Dublin. It was true that he looked much younger than his years and this youthfulness often was the first impression which people gained of the Archbishop of Dublin. For instance Archbishop Lord Coggan recalls being 'impressed in seeing so boyish a figure among the primates at the 1958 Lambeth Conference!'[4]

If youthfulness was the first impression it did not carry with it any suggestion of immaturity. The experience of four years as Bishop of Cork had prepared him for the much greater responsibilities of Dublin and he embarked on his new job with a sure touch and sound grasp of the essentials.

Preaching at his enthronement in Christ Church Cathedral on the feast of the Conversion of St Paul, 25 January 1957, he clearly indicated the direction in which he would lead the Church of Ireland. Drawing on the importance of the Damascus road event he stressed the need for repeated fresh vision on the part of the church and continued 'our church allegiance, our beliefs and our way of worship will not hinder but will rather help anything we can contribute in public service, in the field of education, in matters cultural and communal'. Christian citizenship was to be integral to his episcopacy in Dublin, just as it had been in Cork. Now his approach would have greater impact as he worked in a wider sphere. None of his people should have mistaken his concept of Christian citizenship as a doctrine of justification by works for he reiterated the tenet that it was a necessary daily expression of the faith within the believer. 'The life of prayer and worship must be a prior concern for all of us. Where it is organised in our churches on Sundays, on holy days and weekdays, we must rally round and strengthen such witness through worship at every opportunity. Where churches are mostly open and inviting the services become active and strenuous events and a wonderful change comes over the people.'

These were prophetic words but they were uttered in such gentle tones that the hearer could easily miss the point. It often happened with Dr Simms' sermons that many in the congregation came away impressed by the holiness of the preacher but with a rather general message and with no quotable phrases to commit to the memory. Had God given it to him to drive home his theme with forceful words and quotable quotes like those of William Temple his sermons would have been more influential and would have had more power to change lives. Many of Temple's sayings (for example 'I believe in the holy catholic church and sincerely regret that it does not exist') imprinted themselves on people's memories and his prophetic utterances in the Old Testament tone of 'thus saith the Lord' were very powerful. However it was not in Dr Simms' character to be a preacher in the Temple mould.

For those who really listened and who read carefully the printed version of his enthronement sermon the message stood out clearly: regular occupation of a pew on Sunday did not constitute Christianity. For Dr Simms a Christian was a person who lived and moved with God; this involved constant prayer and nurturing of one's faith, both individually and corporately. The importance of the eucharist was implicitly underlined, portrayed as the collective work of a parish, a necessary preliminary to witness in the world. Any idea that the work of the church is the sole prerogative of the ordained clergy was firmly cast aside.

If the Church of Ireland population had taken his sermon to heart how great the transformation would have been. As it was, he set a clear example; even at his most rushed he found time for prayer and meditation. He made a point of praying before going to chair a meeting. (In Dublin there were no fewer than 85 committees or boards of which he was a member and he was chairman of a formidable number of these.) As Bishop of Cork he had said matins in the Cathedral every morning when he was in residence but from the see house in Burlington Road, later in Temple Road, it was not always possible to be in Christ Church Cathedral. However, if he was not there he attended one of his local parish churches. As in Cork, everything that he did was based on a life of prayer.

Dr Simms plunged straight into the responsibilities of his office. Shortly after his enthronement he called on the President and the Lord Mayor, thus entering upon his role as the chief representative of the Church of Ireland in public affairs. Before the end of the month he went to Arklow to institute the Rev. James Poyntz as rector and on to Cork to preside as metropolitan over the election of his successor there.

It was an exciting but wearing year as Dr Simms fulfilled the round of engagements for the first time. The President, Seán T. O'Kelly, held a dinner to welcome him to Dublin, Archbishop McQuaid, the Taoiseach and the diplomatic corps called at the See House and he found himself in great demand from the press. The last posed a problem in that he wanted to establish good communications and to bring the Church of Ireland out of isolation but realised the dangers of being quoted out of context or misquoted. Before long he built up cordial relations with the press by readiness

to give interviews and preparing carefully for them. Wisely he
didn't let himself be rushed; if a reporter unexpectedly rang looking
for his reaction to an item of news, he would tell him to ring back
at a given hour, by which time he would have prepared his reply.
He also appointed a diocesan press officer.

Pastoral concerns were predominant and care of the clergy and
their families was just as much a priority as it had been in Cork.
In this respect he set a standard of episcopal responsibility which
is hard to match: he made a point of getting to know not only his
clergy but their wives and children and maintained a close interest
in them. He dropped into rectories informally, was exquisitely tact-
ful in frequent acts of generosity and was empathetic when problems arose. Understandably, he was a much-loved figure in
clerical households.

On his arrival in Dublin Dr Simms found a body of rectors who
had established lengthy tenures in their parishes. Dr Simms em-
phatically did not believe that lengthy incumbencies were desirable
either for the incumbents or the parishes. In the matter of clerical
mobility he could be at his toughest but he always considered
clergy welfare as well as the needs of his diocese. His forceful persuasion of N. V. Willoughby to move from Delgany to Glenageary
is a fine example, in that he clearly wanted to fill that vacancy with
a suitable incumbent but also felt that after ten years as rector of
Delgany it would enlarge Mr Willoughby's sphere of ministry and
simultaneously provide a fresh start in Delgany. In this instance his
gift for spotting and promoting talent came into play; he was
always desirous of offering new challenges and opportunities to
those in whom he observed qualities of leadership. When he
was anxious for a priest to move to a new parish he was prepared
to devote time to discussing the implications with the man's
wife and to allaying her anxieties. Equally when a priest moved
into his diocese, Dr Simms made a point of calling on his wife.

Typically he used services of institution to build up the
incumbent and his parish, making each occasion unique by his
kindly references to both the former and the new rector, topical
allusions to matters within the parish and by drawing on his amazing memory for apt recollections. There was also a larger number
of curacies in the diocese than in Cork, so Dr Simms had the
pleasure of numerous ordinations.

The upper echelons of the clergy were headed by Archdeacon
John Tobias, who, at seventy-two, was twenty years younger than
Dean E. H. C. Lewis-Crosby. Before long Dr Simms had to choose a

new archdeacon and a new dean. In appointing R. G. F. Jenkins as archdeacon he secured regular advice and support from a trusted friend. There was no suggestion of favouritism in this; it was widely appreciated that the archbishop carried a very heavy workload and was entitled to appoint as archdeacon the man who he felt would be the greatest help to him.

The two men understood each other so well that the mere rise of an eyebrow was enough of a sign. This often smoothed the way at meetings and at the General Synod, where Raymond Jenkins was a clerical secretary. As archdeacon he did everything he could to ease the burdens of his archbishop and recalls this period under Dr Simms as the happiest time of his life. Together they went to enormous trouble to help clergy with problems, one of the most time-consuming demands on a compassionate prelate.

No matter how busy he was, Dr Simms always made time for the individual, to counsel and pray with the troubled, to encourage a student in the choice of career, to listen to someone with a new idea for social enterprise. Callers at the see house were welcomed personally if at all possible, those who rang for an appointment received one promptly. At first he had no secretary but before long, on the initiative of Professor E. J. Furlong, he was given part-time assistance. He never used his secretary to shield him from people; while she looked after his formal correspondence he still wrote a personal letter whenever possible.

Whether counselling a friend or an acquaintance he was always non-directive. He would listen carefully, discuss all aspects of the problem but would not advise what to do. The person often went away feeling disappointed but subsequently realised what he should do and was grateful that the archbishop had enabled him to discern it for himself. On the other hand, some people need directive counselling while others who came to him lacking in experience and understanding would have benefited from advice.

As chief pastor of the diocese he saw occasions such as institutions, ordinations and confirmations as opportunities to meet and talk to the laity as well as the clergy. (While his presence always lent dignity to the occasion he was just as good at ordinary parish gatherings where he happily talked with everyone he met). He never seemed overwhelmed by the large number of confirmations, rather he put it positively, that with twenty-five to thirty a year it meant 'a lot of people to remember'.

Dr Simms realised the importance of his role as preacher and teacher. It has already been suggested that he was not a forceful preacher. Sometimes the beauty of the language distracted listeners from the message — it was easy to be transported by the poetry of his words and the musical resonance of his voice. This quality was, however, a positive advantage when he was reading the Christmas Gospel or any powerful Bible passage at a service; while his recitation of the psalms (often a feature of 'quiet days') could scarcely have been excelled.

During his days in Dublin sermons frequently suffered from hasty preparation. Throughout his ministry his sermons have generally not been heavily theological but have aimed at attaining a correct spiritual emphasis based on sound theology. His simplest sermons have been among his best. For instance, in a sermon on the Good Samaritan his chief point was a striking one — urging people to ask not the question 'If I cross the road and get involved what will happen to me?' but the question 'If I do *not* cross the road to help those in need, what will happen to *them*?'

With such a fecund mind, he was often tempted to stray from his point and there was immediate danger of losing his listeners as he wove and interwove strands of thought. On the other hand he was at his best when he allowed his own spirituality to come to the fore. Although he subscribed to the Anglican principle of self-effacement, not letting the personality of the preacher stand in the way between man and God, sometimes his personal humble faith shone out and had great power upon his listeners.

One of his frequent ordination and ember-tide themes, 'I am among you as one who serves' is memorable for the sharing of his own experience.

None of us dares to think ever at any stage that he is good enough for this kind of work. This is not the point. The point is rather that we are offering our bad characteristics to God as well as what good gifts there may be in us, for His use — and he has a wonderful way of transforming weakness and unworthiness, if we are ready to serve Him in love. What is a clergyman? Nothing and everything. He is nothing in the sense that all he deals with is not his — certainly not of his making. The word of God which he handles, the sacraments which he helps to administer, the people whom he is given to shepherd — none of these is the clergyman's workmanship. He is an instrument used for the worship and the shepherding. He is but a servant. Yet he is everything, for the worship and the shepherding concern the whole of life.'

The time constraints inherent in a broadcast service often produced fine sermons. Also from time to time he gave short religious talks on television or radio and these gave him a much larger audience than his Church of Ireland flock. He received many letters of thanks, mostly from Roman Catholics, expressing the hope that he would be a more frequent contributor and in appreciation of his clarity of diction and the warmth which he projected. On television it was a great help that he kept very still and had no mannerisms to distract the viewer. When Telefís Éireann was launched he gave the epilogue on the second night (New Year's Day, 1962), after which the producer, Shelah Richards, wrote to thank him for his patience amidst the chaos, praising him as the most relaxed man in the studio.

A letter to the Dublin *Evening Mail* of 21 March 1962 recorded the writer's disappointment at the television performances of Irish public figures. Only two exceptions were conceded, President Kennedy (not an Irishman in the strict sense) and the 'golden-voiced' Dr Simms, both of whom 'possess a natural charm which is fascinating and magnetic'.

A couple of years later the Television column of *Focus*, in a critique of a Telefís Éireann programme on marriage and divorce, commented on Dr Simms' forthright contribution, saying 'He has gone from strength to strength on this medium'.[5]

Dr Simms was a careful guardian of the faith. In matters of doctrine and of the conduct of services he was quite strict; although he was in the vanguard of liturgical development he was well aware of the dangers of 'free-for-all' local experimentation and therefore expected clergy to adhere to regulations governing the use of different versions of the Bible and hymnals.

He fostered a churchmanship in which the apostolic faith, Anglican heritage and Church of Ireland tradition were happily welded but his influence would have been greater had he been able to spell this out for the man in the pew, whose perception of such an amalgam was dim. Likewise, as his eclecticism remained unexplained, few, even among the clergy, realised how wide were the influences at work on him.

As guardian of the faith it was desirable that he gave clear leadership on the role of the church in society. One could suggest four possible roles for a minority church: defence of its position, pietism, propagation of the social gospel, cultivation of a positive minority role. The Church of Ireland, since the foundation of the Irish state, has shown no tendency towards a pietistic withdrawal from society and limited enthusiasm for the social gospel. It could not be said that concern for economic policy-making, for the poor, the handicapped and the dislocated, was the motive force within the church, although there were many examples of such concern being translated into action.

The Church of Ireland has concentrated on sustaining the

worshipping community, maintaining its own position and safeguarding its doctrinal integrity rather than on nurturing a special minority role within Irish society. The negative side of this brought an emphasis on what the Church of Ireland was not, rather than on what it was. As Dr Simms said in one of his sermons 'we sometimes forget to ask "what does it mean to be a Christian?", since we are too much preoccupied in finding out if a person be Protestant or otherwise.' There was too little consideration of what it meant to be part of the church universal and little sign of a self-image identified with the servant church.

Dr Simms' concept of the role of the church was broad: the servant church was very important to him and he often spoke about it in sermons and addresses. He had a clear understanding of the creative role which the Church of Ireland could play: it should commit itself to working out the social gospel and to opening discussion of policies which discorded with its understanding of the kingdom of God. In such witness, the church often emerges as a critic of the establishment.

Dr Simms' spoken criticisms were always muted but he sought to give positive leadership on a wide range of issues. Whenever possible he lent his support to practical endeavours, such as education and marriage counselling. In other cases he acted as the spokesman of the bishops in putting forward the viewpoint of the Church of Ireland; on questions of private morality such as divorce, family planning and abortion, on wider political issues such as aid to underdeveloped countries, neutrality and apartheid and, at the broadest, of offering a Christian perspective on life.

Dr Simms' gentle but firm pronouncements did far more than merely defend the position of the Church of Ireland; they enunciated his understanding of the catholic and universal church, of its role as continuing Christ's mission in the world. Here lies a fundamental issue to be faced by all denominations in every country; what it means to be the church. A church is a community in which, individually and corporately, members witness to God's love by their worship and service. As the church is to fulfil God's mission in the world, ministry is the proper activity of all His people. For a long time, however, ministry has been seen almost exclusively as being exercised by the ordained clergy, and lay ministry has been greatly devalued. A report by the Priorities Committee to the Representative Body, published in 1979, stated 'The Church of Ireland is a clergy-dominated church . . . burdened and inhibited by a false distinction between the "sacred" and the "secular", in which theological matters are considered to be the job of the clergy and maintenance and finance that of the laity'.[6]

Long before this report, from the early days of his ministry, Dr Simms realised that this view was both a result and a cause of the church's failure to realise its true self. There was complete harmony between his emphasis on the importance of the ordained ministry and his insistence on the ministry of all believers. The intertwining themes had appeared in his early writings, in his first booklet on ordination, in which he wrote: 'There are many callings . . . and the church is concerned with them all,'[7] and in a guide to clergy on the follow-up of a parish mission, in which he alluded to the need to bridge 'the gap which yawns between clergy and people'[8] by involving the laity in the ministry. Throughout his ministry he never tired of making these points, even when they seemed to pass unnoticed.

Major shifts in the outlook of a nationwide church usually happen slowly and require many sustained influences. Nevertheless, had Dr Simms been able to take as many spiritual initiatives in Dublin as he had in Cork, he would have had the opportunity to steer the Church of Ireland towards a deeper and broader understanding of being the church. Diocesan and city missions such as those he mounted in Cork might have been effective but his extra-diocesan responsibilities precluded such major undertakings. He still managed to give courses of Bible classes, even in distant parts of his diocese like Mountmellick and Wicklow, and frequently led quiet days. In preparing programmes, however, he concentrated on the devotional, where his gifts were paramount, rather than on the sociological, political or theological, in which fields he felt less competent. Likewise, most of his writings during his episcopacy in Dublin were short devotional pieces or informational articles such as Thoughts after Lambeth.[9]

It might seem strange but it is in character that one of the best expressions of his view of the church was in his memoir of Michael Ferrar.[10] Ferrar's sudden death in 1960 was a dreadful blow to Dr Simms. While his friend was in hospital the archbishop visited him every day and his final tribute was written with obvious love and great care in order to capture the essential Ferrar for the reader. He drew out the small characteristics which had endeared Ferrar to those who knew him, such as 'the keen memory for persons and places which is kept green by constant and loving intercession',[11] but he also firmly placed him as a great reformer and teacher of the Church of Ireland. In portraying Ferrar as one committed 'to teach tolerance, to proclaim the whole faith' . . . who 'wanted the church not to be the worshipping community of a particular class, or of a group which shared a common outlook upon policies for world affairs, or a mere organised society of like-minded people, but rather, to be the continuing life of Christ,'[12] he held up his churchmanship as an exemplar for the Church of Ireland.

Dr Simms rarely referred to the theological ferment which was causing such a furore within western christendom in the 1960s. Ever since the eighteenth century enlightenment the Christian faith had been subject to critical questioning but what happened in the 1960s was novel in that the most fundamental questions as to the reality of God were being asked within the church. 'God is dead' theology emanated from an increasingly secular society in which there was doubt as to whether faith in God was possible for 'modern man'. In some ways it was a perversion of the dualism of neo-orthodoxists like Barth and Bultmann; as the weaknesses of attempts to combine a modern secular understanding of the world with a more or less traditional Biblical understanding of God as creator and Lord became increasingly obvious, radical theologians took up the slack. Within the Anglican Communion J. A. T. Robinson's *Honest to God*[13] was disturbing but was far less revolutionary than books like W. Hamilton's *The New Essence of Christianity* or T. J. J. Altizer's *The Gospel of Christian Atheism*[14] which appeared in the U.S.A. in the sixties.

Radical theories were addressed at the time by Anglican theologians with whom Dr Simms identified, notably by Archbishop Ramsey in *God, Christ and the World*.[15] Ramsey's book was written in the belief that it is 'right for the church's pastors to try to grapple with the conflicts concerning belief within and without the church and to encourage right ways of approaching them'.[16] It was vital for the Anglican Communion that the man who became the one hundredth Archbishop of Canterbury in 1961 was a theologian capable of tackling the subject as Ramsey did, with a positive and constructive treatment of contemporary theological trends. Making clear what would once have been considered obvious, that Christian theology was concerned primarily with Christ ('God is Christlike and in him is no un-Christlikeness at all'),[17] he reinstated the doctrine of the incarnation in its proper place. Dr Simms did not, like his Canterbury counterpart, try to grapple with the conflicts. There were two reasons: firstly, Ireland was little affected by the controversy, a fact which is readily understood when one recalls the conservatism of the country at the time; secondly, he was not a systematic theologian and did not find it easy to express himself theologically. His beliefs accorded

closely with those of Ramsey, while his personal inclination was to
take a simple view of the debate, based on his own intimacy with
Jesus Christ. Alister McGrath's later comment on the debate is apt:
'It is remarkably difficult for anyone who has first-hand experience
of the living God to think of him as being "dead" '.[18]

Dr Simms was well aware of theological developments and con-
troversies elsewhere because of his widespread international involvement. It was in the nature of the job in Dublin that almost
every year he attended a major church event of international importance. He played a prominent role in the Lambeth Conferences
held in 1958 and 1968 and when he went to the Anglican Congress
in Toronto in 1963, he undertook with it a heavy preaching and lecturing programme. His attendance at conferences often necessitated
lengthy absence from his diocese, especially in 1968 when he went
to Uppsala in July for the fourth Assembly of the World Council
of Churches and travelled straight from there to London for the
Lambeth Conference. Such a long period away created problems
within the diocese and left him with a dreadful backlog of work on
his return. It also meant that he was unable to take a summer holiday that year. He was very grateful, however, to be able to entrust
confirmations and ordinations to Bishop F. R. Willis, retired
Bishop of Delhi, who had returned to the curacy of All Saints',
Grangegorman, in 1966.

Largely as a result of his active role at Lambeth IX he emerged
as the best known leader of the Church of Ireland in the 1960s and
1970s. He frequently represented his church at special services in
England. Thus he was in Coventry for the consecration of the new
cathedral in 1962 and preached in Westminster Abbey in 1965 during the thanksgiving celebrations of the 900th anniversary of its
founding by Edward the Confessor. Invitations came from across
the Atlantic: Bishop Stephen Bayne of Seattle asked him to preach
and speak in his diocese in 1960. His visit turned into an extensive
six-week tour, as he incorporated a retreat conference in San
Francisco at the invitation of Bishop J. A. Pike and ended at the
Episcopalian Theological School in Harvard. His brief included a
Lambeth follow-up, explaining the traditions of the Church of
Ireland as well as straightforward devotional talks. Even he
admitted the tour was exhausting but was delighted to be returning
with funds for the restoration of Christ Church Cathedral.

Dr Simms was only forty-eight when he attended his first
Lambeth Conference. The theme of Lambeth IX was reconciliation,

a heading which would not lead one to anticipate that its most significant resolutions would be in the areas of family planning and liturgical revision. In a sensitive sphere, where the ordinary lay person needed guidance, the conference came a long way from the reluctant approval given to birth control by the conferences of 1920 and 1930. Its resolutions on the family and responsible parenthood, specifically the statement that family planning was a matter of conscience for the parents, remained for years the Anglican position on the subject.

The strength of the liturgical movement's work for the restoration of the New Testament pattern of weekly communion and for more participation of the laity in worship made it urgent for the Lambeth Conference to face the issue of liturgical revision and this was done by centring the second of the three sections on *The Book of Common Prayer.*

Dr Simms was very surprised to be appointed chairman of the liturgy committee. He may have been a young archbishop at his first Lambeth but he was well known to Archbishop Ramsey of York and several other English bishops; those who knew him were aware of his interest in liturgical matters and probably felt that he possessed the necessary tact to chair a committee at which it would be difficult to obtain agreement.

Their confidence was justified in that the committee achieved a high degree of unanimity in producing resolutions which gained approval at the plenary session. There was a great deal of pressure to complete the report in time, yet the committee did not allow itself to be rushed into hasty conclusions. Dr Simms gently steered his fellow bishops (most of them considerably his senior in years) past the rocks of local susceptibilities and catholic or evangelical tradition towards a report which provided the framework for liturgical revision in the ensuing decades.

His tact was required in winning over those who were opposed to certain changes and in calming ruffled feathers when the Archbishop of Canterbury, Dr Geoffrey Fisher, made an abrupt intervention. Dr Simms drew on the varied experience of all the members to maintain flexibility in stating the principles of prayer book revision.

The secretary of the committee, Bishop L. W. Brown of Uganda, who had been the convenor of the Church of South India committee which had drawn up its holy communion service, made a valuable contribution. Dr Simms' influence was discernible in the prolonged discussion allowed for details such as the doublet 'in love and charity with your neighbour'. His sense of language and his

study of Celtic manuscripts gave him a feeling for words which was
not universally shared. This may have been one of the reasons
why he was teased at this committee for his schoolmasterish ways!
Attention to detail did not hold up the work, as the committee
drew up well-considered guidelines for the revision of the holy
communion, baptism, ordinal, lectionary, psalter, occasional services and ministry to the sick. Dr Simms found it 'very intensive
and rather trying work in thundery weather . . . but interesting'.[19]
Thunder was one of the few things which put him out and there
was more thunder than usual in London that July.

The report was at its most conservative in relation to the ordinal,
as this was inextricably linked with the delicate question of reunion
with other churches; it was highly creative in its attitude to occasional services, believing that the church needed to provide special
services for use in connection with the arts and industry and
science, to parallel harvest services in the agricultural community.
Its largest section was devoted to the structure of the holy communion service and a consideration of the eucharistic sacrifice. Its
handling of the 'unresolved difference among members of the
Anglican Communion' on prayers for the departed shows its
surefootedness. The evangelical tradition, in which the Church of
Ireland stands, holds that as there is no question of spiritual progress after death there is no need for prayers for the departed but
the committee juxtaposes the catholic tradition which sees such
prayers as 'expressions of the love that unites members of Christ's
Body in the communion of saints and contents itself with saying
that 'in view of the fact that our church formularies deliberately
leave room for both these points of view, it may be wise, in future
Prayer Book revision, to provide that prayer for the departed be
permissive and also to provide alternative forms of thankful
commemoration'.[20]

In conclusion the committee pointed out that it was in no way
urging revision on the conference and that the laity for the most
part were opposed to it but it was, nevertheless, already in progress
in many provinces.

It was the chairman's duty to report the findings of his committee
at the plenary session. Archbishop Simms' presentation earned him
one of the few accolades which that grand old man of the church,
Bishop George Bell, was prepared to award for Lambeth 1958.
Shortly before his death he gave a succinct view of the leadership
of the conference. 'Few outstanding figures, Ebor certainly. Dublin
on his own subject also.'[21]

Dr Simms was wholehearted about participating in the Lambeth

Conferences and believed that they were important for unity within Anglicanism. He also believed that when overseas bishops preached in Ireland before and during the Conferences and when Ireland's own bishops returned and reported to their flocks it helped to make the Church of Ireland more aware of being part of a worldwide communion and less frightened of new developments. He returned from Lambeth IX convinced of the desirability of liturgical revision within the Church of Ireland but aware that it might arouse fierce opposition. As a lover of formal liturgical prayer and the flowing phrases of Cranmer, he would have been content simply to use *The Book of Common Prayer* but he believed that the church had to meet the needs of the worshipping people in changing times. Just as he sought to bring an Irish contribution to Lambeth Conferences, he always sought to apply the collective wisdom of each conference to the home situation.

If Dr Simms was wholehearted about participation in the Lambeth Conferences, he was less enthusiastic about their social aspect. While he regarded preaching engagements as a worthwhile extension of the Conference (in 1958 he preached at St Paul's Cathedral and St Margaret's, Westminster, among others), he felt that the numerous receptions intruded unduly on the work time. While he dutifully attended functions hosted by the Queen, the Prime Minister, the Foreign and Colonial Secretaries, and the Lord Mayor, he would have preferred the time to have been devoted to matters spiritual. He was not 'de-skilled' by it all, as were so many overseas bishops, but there was simply too much pomp and circumstance for his liking. Likewise, while the opening and closing services at Westminster Abbey and St Paul's Cathedral were impressive, he appreciated much more the daily eucharist in the parish church and the daily offices in the chapel of Lambeth Palace. His prominence at Lambeth IX opened the way to a wider Anglican role for Dr Simms. Archbishop Ramsey, who became Archbishop of Canterbury in 1961, admired his work and believed that he had a special contribution to make in the ecumenical field.

Although great progress had been made in ecumenism since the first World Missionary Conference in Edinburgh in 1910, the Roman Catholic Church was not involved. It took no part in the developments that led to the setting up of the World Council of Churches and, even at local and national levels, there was little real dialogue between the Roman Catholic Church and other churches. The situation was quickly changed by the advent of Cardinal Roncalli as Pope John XXIII three months after Lambeth IX ended, in October 1958. Pope John's *aggiornamento* was the most unexpected development of the entire century not only within the Roman Catholic Church, but in the whole area of ecumenism. Suddenly there was a thaw in Roman Catholic-Anglican relations; Archbishop Fisher visited Rome and met Pope John, the first such meeting since the Reformation. For the other churches the most exciting thing about the second Vatican Council, summoned by Pope John to meet in September 1962, was its refreshing new approach to the question of Christian unity. The whole issue was approached with an urgency which had previously been markedly lacking and with an openness which went further than many in the Anglican tradition would have believed possible in accepting that some of the blame for disunity lay with the Roman Catholic Church.

The death of Pope John in June 1963 did not, for the moment anyway, check the ecumenical momentum. Under Pope Paul VI the Vatican Council continued its work and the final declaration on Christian unity, agreed before it ended in the autumn of 1965, recognised that 'among those [communions] in which some Catholic traditions and institutions continue to exist, the Anglican communion occupies a special place'.[22]

Pope Paul VI and Archbishop Ramsey met in Rome in March 1966 and expressed a desire for serious dialogue between their churches with a view to re-establishing unity. At the conclusion of their meeting they issued a Common Declaration, acknowledging the 'serious obstacles' that stood in the way and calling for discussions not only of major theological matters but also of 'matters of practical difficulty felt on either side'.[23]

In fulfilment of their wishes, a Joint Preparatory Commission began its work in January 1967. By the following year it had produced preliminary findings positive enough to encourage both churches to agree to enter a full commission. The work of the Anglican-Roman Catholic International Commission, ARCIC for short, will be reviewed in the next chapter. The Irish input was highly significant as Bishop H. R. McAdoo of Ossory was the Anglican co-chairman.

The issue of mixed marriages was one of those 'matters of practical difficulty' referred to in the Common Declaration of 1966. It had become urgent because, on the eve of Archbishop Ramsey's visit, the Pope had issued a new set of rules on marriage[24] in which the only concession on mixed marriage was the ending of excommunication. The question surfaced very quickly when the Preparatory Commission first met at Gazzada in Italy in January 1967. That body recommended the establishment of a special commission on marriage.

Constituted that same year as the Anglican-Roman Catholic International Commission on the Theology of Marriage and its application to mixed marriages, Archbishop Ramsey appointed Dr Simms as the Anglican co-chairman. Archbishop Simms headed an Anglican team comprising one American and one Canadian bishop and an English theologian, Professor the Rev. Canon G. R. Dunstan. The Anglican secretary was Canon J. R. Satterthwaite, succeeded after his appointment as Bishop of Fulham and Gibraltar by Prebendary Henry Cooper, advisor to the Archbishop of Canterbury on Roman Catholic affairs.

The Most Rev. E. L. Unterkoefler, Bishop of Charleston, South Carolina, was the Roman Catholic co-chairman, with one Welsh and one Canadian bishop, and Monsignor Professor P. F. Cremin, an Irish expert on Canon Law, from St Patrick's College, Maynooth.[25] The secretary was Monsignor W. A. Purdy of the Vatican Secretariat for Promoting Christian Unity. He was the son of a mixed marriage and had many personal insights into the problem.

Roman Catholic rules on mixed marriages dated from the nineteenth century when it was stated that they could only take place if a dispensation were issued from Rome and that there would be no dispensation from the obligation to bring up the children in the Roman Catholic faith. These regulations were strengthened by the *Ne Temere* decree of 1908, which was subsequently embodied in the corpus of Canon Law. *Ne Temere*, primarily concerned with conditions for marriage between Roman Catholics, went on to treat of dispensations for mixed marriages. It didn't actually spell out clauses on the upbringing of children but presupposed that a promise had been given to that effect, as the conditions for a dispensation would otherwise not have been fulfilled. The promise was usually but not necessarily given in writing. It was the diocesan bishop who stipulated the conditions, so their rigour varied from diocese to diocese. Mixed marriages had to be conducted by a Roman Catholic priest and the climate was such that there was every discouragement to the participation of an Anglican clergyman.

Not surprisingly, the issue has been a major cause in this century of strained relations between the churches. For a long time the Roman Catholic side felt unable to bend at all, because its position was based on a genuinely-held belief that the Roman Catholic Church was the one true church and that children brought up in any other tradition would not win salvation.

The Commission worked for eight years and met six times bet-

ween April 1968 and June 1975. The first two meetings took place
in 1968, the first at Windsor in April, the second in Rome in
November but, as its work was completed during Dr Simms'
primacy, further consideration of it is postponed until the next
chapter.

To return to developments within the Anglican Communion,
Archbishops McCann and Simms headed the 46-strong Irish
delegation to the Anglican Congress in Toronto in 1963. The Most
Rev. Dr James McCann had been elected Archbishop of Armagh in
succession to Dr Gregg in 1958. Before the Congress began Dr
Simms preached a typically optimistic sermon in Trinity Church,
Broadway, New York. In it he foresaw a greater striving towards
church unity, growing respect for the younger Anglican churches
such as those in African countries, and increased awareness of the
role of the laity.

The keynote address from the Archbishop of Canterbury on
'none liveth to himself; none dieth to himself' pointed to the overall
theme of the church's mission to the world. Discussions, aimed at
achieving a world view of mission on the religious, political and
cultural frontiers, were much influenced by the document which
emanated from the conference of primates and metropolitans, with
the Advisory Council on Missionary Strategy and the Lambeth
Consultative Body, held in Huron College just before the full
Anglican Congress. The document, on Mutual Responsibility and
Interdependence in the Body of Christ (commonly referred to as
M.R.I.), was a challenge to Anglicans to commit themselves to a
better distribution of resources throughout the whole Communion,
more inter-Anglican consultation and, above all, a new realisation
of and obedience to a divine mission.

In his sermon at the opening service Ramsey reiterated the
theme: 'self-consciousness and self-commendation have no place in
Christ . . . we look towards the world, towards one another as
Anglicans, towards other churches, and towards God'.[26] Thus it is
not surprising that there was much talk about the meaning of
Anglicanism and its future as a distinctive Communion. The
M.R.I. document led the delegates to envisage more Anglican
provinces joining in a new united church, thus losing an identi-
fiable Anglican label; some even talked of the total dis-
appearance of Anglicanism. A statement was passed that each
national church must test every part of its life by reference to its
mission and recognise that this would mean 'the death of much that
is familiar about our churches now. It will mean radical changes in
our priorities . . . willingness to forgo many desirable things in

every church. In substance what we are really asking is the rebirth of the Anglican Communion'.[27]

Not all of the proceedings were as controversial; Dr Simms, the only listed Irish speaker, gave a thoughtful but muted address entitled 'Some aspects of the vocation of the Anglican Communion in Ireland'. On his return to Ireland he wrote several accounts of the Congress, in which his presentation was much less radical than the report itself. If he diluted the message it can probably be explained by his personality and style of writing rather than by any desire to detract from it.

An article for the *Sunday Press*[28] gave a general overview for a largely Roman Catholic readership and offered his own definition of Anglicanism: 'it has to be constantly emphasised that Anglicanism denotes something theological, not territorial; it is a religious term to describe a church's way of life, an ethos of worship, a shared doctrinal position, and a fellowship which carries varieties of national customs and characteristics in its bosom'. He quoted the optimistic report to the Congress on progress towards inter-church co-operation achieved at the Vatican Council, under John XXIII and on worldwide examples of joint efforts in mission. He did not add that he had spoken at the Congress about the increasingly cordial relations which the Church of Ireland enjoyed with the Roman Catholic Church and had drawn from it the lesson that the life of an Anglican church in any country must be expressed not in isolation but in relation to the other Christian churches which work there, that the part played by a minority church can be significant.

Accounts written for a Church of Ireland readership explained the workings of the Congress and tried to highlight points of Anglican unity at Toronto. By way of encouragement to the Church of Ireland he mentioned the examples recounted at Toronto of 'strong action taken by minorities'.[29] In implicit exhortation to take a wider view of worship, he described the celebrations of holy communion by the Japanese, Indians and Eskimos, and the varying attempts in different languages and cultures to expresss the meaning of the love of God. He developed the theme of mutual responsibility and expressed the belief that the Irish representatives had returned with 'a new understanding of our own life and witness here at home'.[30] Many of the delegates did have a new vision but their enthusiastic report made little impact on the Church of Ireland.

The next major international gathering which Archbishop Simms attended was the fourth Assembly of the World Council of

Churches in Uppsala in July 1968. A much larger number of churches belonged to the World Council of Churches than at the time
of the third Assembly in 1961; this time there were 705 delegates
from 235 member churches. With advisers, guests, observers,
youth participants, staff and press, the number in attendance came
to 2,500. It was generally believed that the inclusion of Orthodox
delegates and the presence of Roman Catholic theologians constituted a significant advance.

The Irish delegates were Archbishop Simms and Commander
C. A. Herdman, representing the Church of Ireland, the Rev. T.
Carlisle Patterson and the Rev. R. N. Brown, representing the
Presbyterian Church, and the Rev. R. D. E. Gallagher, representing
the Methodist Church. The Anglican episcopal team from Great
Britain was made up of Archbishop Ramsey, who was a vice-
president of the World Council of Churches, and five other
bishops.

The theme of the Assembly was 'Behold, I make all things new'.
Martin Luther King was to have delivered the sermon at the opening service, so it can be assumed that human rights would have
been to the fore from the beginning of the Assembly. He had been
assassinated in Memphis three months before but Dr Simms
reported that his influence was deeply felt for he symbolised many
of the Christian protests that needed to be made against injustice,
poverty, war and racism.[31]

In so saying Dr Simms manifested his concern about these issues;
although one would never label him as a radical, it is noteworthy that such outspoken opponents of racism as Bishop Trevor
Huddleston and Archbishop Desmond Tutu have always felt that
he is at one with them. This accords with his willingness to minister
to German refugees and prisoners of war during World War II and
his determination to pray for the victims on both sides, for his attitudes derive from great resources of compassion and from consideration of human issues.

Perhaps it was partly as a result of Martin Luther King's influence that the Assembly laid less emphasis than formerly on problems of faith and order and more on an outward-looking attitude
through which the churches could work together in the world. One
of the inherent difficulties in such a large assembly is of
affording to a wide range of delegates an opportunity to speak
without unduly straining the patience and endurance of the
listeners. Dr Simms believed, in retrospect, that there had
been far too many speakers but he singled out Martin Niemöller,
famous opponent of Hitler in earlier days, and Willem Visser

t'Hooft, former general secretary of the Council, as outstanding. Much conference time was also devoted to the catholicity of the church and ecumenical ventures, and to the working of the Holy Spirit. Dr Simms was a member of the section which was devoted to liturgy and chaired some of its meetings. He was very pleased that considerable agreement was reached on the recognition of one another's baptism and that a new level of understanding prevailed in discussion of the eucharist. The intercommunion which took place at Uppsala evidenced a tendency to anticipate the life of the one church of the future. The urgency of unity was highlighted by the recognition that Christians were a decreasing minority in the world.

A new relationship with Rome was discernible, not only because Roman Catholic participants were involved for the first time as full members of the Faith and Order Commission and as observers, but because, in the wake of the second Vatican Council, they manifested a new openness. It was very encouraging that one Roman Catholic speaker stated that the difficulties concerning his church's membership of the World Council of Churches were psychological and practical rather than theological. At the beginning of the Assembly a message was received from Pope Paul VI. This also marked an advance but the ecumenical climate had already been cooled by his *Credo* of 30 June, in which he had given a conservative restatement of the traditional Roman Catholic dogmas of papal infallibility, transubstantiation and the immaculate conception of the Virgin Mary. This, following upon the equally conservative set of rules on marriage, led Archbishop Ramsey, at a press conference, to speak out on the damage done. He regretted Pope Paul's stance and stated that the Roman Catholic rules on mixed marriage would have to be altered.

Although Dr Simms agreed with Archbishop Ramsey, he did not focus on this aspect of the Assembly in the regular missives which he sent from Uppsala during the session or in the reports he delivered that autumn. He and Commander Herdman, on their return, sought ways in which the hopeful message of Uppsala could be applied in Ireland and, having enjoyed the fellowship of the other Irish delegates, were eager that the spirit of Uppsala would bear fruit in Church of Ireland, Presbyterian and Methodist talks at home. They also hoped for increased contact with Roman Catholics in Ireland on a more formal basis, whether through the Irish Council of Churches or some other way. Their hope to see action in Ireland spring from the work at Uppsala was nurtured by the wide publicity given to the Assembly in Irish newspapers. John

Horgan, Seán Mac Réamoínn and Christopher O'Donnell were felt to be participators in as well as reporters at the Assembly and they demonstrated an understanding of the Protestant churches as they strove to convey the message of Uppsala to their Irish readers.

Another point which Dr Simms emphasised was that Uppsala's respect for minorities showed people in Ireland that a minority has a contribution to make and a witness to bear in the Christian fellowship at large. This, of course, was one of the archbishop's consistent themes; he had made the point in Toronto in 1963 and when Michael Viney was researching articles on Irish Protestants for *The Irish Times* in 1965 Dr Simms had told him 'I don't think of [my people] as a minority — and I hope they see themselves as part of a world-wide communion. . . After all, Christians in the world at large are in a minority.'[32]

At the conclusion of the Assembly Dr Simms hastened to London for the Lambeth Conference. Lambeth X was a very different conference from its predecessor: it was affected by the fresh approach to the church's mission voiced at the Toronto Congress, by the ecumenical advances of the decade and by the impact of the newly phrased, disturbing theological exploration of the fundamentals of the faith which rocked the church in the sixties.

Lambeth X was quite different in its structure as well. For the first time suffragan and assistant bishops were invited, so that the number of bishops attending rose from about 300 in 1958 to 462. Using an idea which prevailed at the Vatican Council, observers from other churches were invited to attend and Anglican consultants were invited to write an introductory paper to each of the thirty-three topics under consideration. Observers and consultants together brought an extra 100 participants to the Conference, which could no longer be accommodated in the library of Lambeth Palace. The 1968 Conference was held at Church House, Westminster.

The responsibility for these changes largely rested with the steering committee of which Archbishop Simms was a member. The other members were Bishops Stopford of London, Mortimer of Exeter, Eley of Gibraltar, Bayne, former Anglican executive officer, then vice-president of the executive council of the Protestant Episcopal Church of the U.S.A., and Dean, Bishop of Cariboo, his successor, also episcopal secretary to the Conference. Clearly they acted with the encouragement of the Archbishop of Canterbury and their desire was to set up a conference which was more truly representative of the Anglican Communion and which could draw inspiration from an ecumenical input and from the expertise of non-episcopal theologians and experts.

Early in the Conference another innovation occurred, when it was decided to admit the press and the public to the plenary sessions, bringing the Conference into line with other modern assemblies. Much of the work was done at committee level and in order to give individual bishops an opportunity to speak the steering committee established thirty-three sub-committees, each to deal with one aspect of the three main subjects, the renewal of the church in faith, in ministry and in unity.

Another new departure came in the form of a formal message from Pope Paul, the first from a pontiff to Anglican bishops. This was delivered by Archbishop Willebrands of the Secretariat for Promoting Christian Unity who, as a symbol of respect, kissed the Archbishop of Canterbury's ring as he reached the podium. The effect of the Pope's gesture was, however, diminished by the renewed prohibition of all artificial methods of birth control in his recently issued encyclical *Humanae Vitae*. The Lambeth Conference, anxious not to damage the new friendly relations between the two churches, issued a mild resolution to the effect that 'it could not agree that all methods of conception control other than abstinence . . . are contrary to the "order established by God" '[33] and reaffirmed the conclusion of Lambeth IX that family planning was a matter for the individual consciences of a married couple. The resolution was largely based on Archbishop Ramsey's own statement: it showed that although he was deeply committed to nurturing dialogue with Rome, he was yet again dismayed at papal intransigence on this matter.

Archbishop Ramsey was the dominant figure at Lambeth X. The three extempore speeches and the many brief interventions which he made in the course of the Conference were lucid, significant and highly influential. Dr Simms was greatly impressed by his leadership of the Conference.

One of the criticisms of Lambeth X was that, despite the growing numbers of overseas bishops attending, it was still English-dominated and, as a result, over-conservative. This was not entirely fair as the steering committee was half English, half overseas, and the three main sections of the Conference were headed by Archbishops Clark of Canada, Coggan of York and de Mel of India. Conservatism certainly prevailed in the section on faith, from law and order topics through to the thirty-nine articles. For instance, a draft declaring that 'the Christian commitment is generally to the maintenance of law and order' raised many objections from bishops who lived in areas where the government was oppressive. They would have substituted 'justice' but the conservatives were only prepared to amend the wording to 'a just law and order'.[34]

The Church of England also proved conservative on the question of the ordination of women, one of the contentious issues in the section on ministry. Lambeth VIII in 1948 had rejected the ordination to the priesthood of the first woman, Florence Li Tim Oi, by Bishop Hall of Hong Kong and South China in 1944. Now, however, it became a big issue and the chairman of the ministry section, Archbishop Coggan, was very keen to press forward to the ordination of women to the diaconate. After much heated discussion the Conference made hesitant steps towards this but was clearly fearful of some provinces going ahead without prior consensus in the entire Communion. That is exactly what happened within the next twenty years, as many provinces have proceeded to ordain women priests and others, notably the Church of England, have been very slow to admit them to the diaconate. The non-committal resolution that 'the theological arguments as at present presented for and against the ordination of women to the priesthood are inconclusive'[35] did not have much effect.

Even close friends were uncertain as to Dr Simms' attitude: at one time Raymond Jenkins set a mock examination paper for Elizabeth Ferrar on which one of the questions read, 'What is George's view about the admission of women to ordination?' In fact he saw no theological objection but felt that it would not be helpful to make his views known. In an appraisal of the Lambeth Conference, written for the *Church Observer*, he resolutely avoided any bias and yet his account makes certain things clear. In writing 'At the plenary session many bishops would vote in principle for a resolution if they thought its implementation might help in another part of the world, even if it did not seem to be immediately applicable to their own dioceses', one can discern his care for the unity of the Anglican Communion. Of the debate he wrote 'The sincerity of the debating is patent to all. . . The suffering involved, even when contrary opinions are expressed with clarity and charity, bears a fine Christian witness. The bishops were able to disagree without being disagreeable.'[36]

If the sections on faith and ministry produced conservative reports, that on unity produced what was widely viewed as the most radical report ever produced at a Lambeth Conference. Unity had figured large on the Lambeth agenda since 1888 but it was now approached with new zeal. Archbishop Simms, a very serious ecumenist, spoke four times on the subject. He happily concurred with the first resolution (44), that each bishop should ask himself how seriously he took the suggestion of the 1952 Lund Conference on Faith and Order that we should do together everything which conscience does not compel us to do separately, that ecumenical life at local level should have priority while efforts were directed towards the creation of a genuinely universal council of all Christians. While Dr Simms agreed with this he well knew that more could be attempted in countries like India and Pakistan, where united churches were in being or were about to be inaugurated, than in Ireland.

Resolutions 45 and 47 constituted a radical step forward, following lines suggested by Archbishop Ramsey. They stated that all baptised persons would be welcome to receive holy communion in Anglican churches in order to meet special pastoral needs, that Anglicans could receive at altars of other churches on occasion, that intercommunion was acceptable between churches where unity negotiations had reached a certain stage. Dr Simms spoke in support, suggesting that intercommunion might be an aid towards the goal of unity without examination of orders. No specific mention was made of the Roman Catholic Church but some bishops subsequently interpreted the resolutions as applying there as well.

On relations with Rome the draft report was sensational. It read 'We believe that a considerable majority of Anglicans would be prepared to accept the Pope as having a primacy of love, implying both honour and service, in a renewed and reunited Church.'[37] Dr Simms knew that few Irish Anglicans would countenance the idea: the Irish bishops, particularly in the northern province, would have received a very hostile reception on their return if they had agreed to that! In debate the Archbishop of Canterbury suggested that this section should be scrapped and the final version was considerably watered down. It said that the Conference recognised the papacy 'as a historic reality whose developing role requires deep reflection and joint study by all concerned for the unity of the whole Body of Christ'.[38] The final resolution was a much closer reflection of the thinking of the Church of Ireland.

The Conference went on to lend its wholehearted support to a permanent joint commission and to the Anglican Centre in Rome. Some of the debates on unity raised a lot of heat but none as much as that on the Anglican-Methodist talks in England. The trouble arose over the draft resolution (51) that 'the Conference welcomes the proposals for Anglican-Methodist unity in Great Britain and believes that the proposed Service of Reconciliation is theologically adequate to achieve its declared intentions of reconciling the two churches and integrating their ministries'.[39]

There was considerable opposition within the Church of England, both in high church and evangelical circles, to the unity scheme and some bishops, led by Easthaugh of Peterborough, felt that the Conference was being swayed by overseas bishops who were giving glib answers without sufficient consideration of the issues. Something of an impasse was reached and the steering committee met to consider a compromise. Next day on behalf of the committee Archbishop Simms put a new proposal to the Conference. 'This Conference welcomes the progress made since 1952 towards unity between the Church of England and the Methodist Church in Great Britain along the issues recommended by the Lambeth Conference of 1958, and hopes that the churches will be able to proceed to full communion and eventually to organic union.'

This was weak and non-committal and not surprisingly proved unacceptable. Bishop Hamilton of Jarrow then proposed a resolution which was a slightly watered-down version of the one originally proposed and the Conference was invited to choose. In a disorderly debate Archbishop de Mel stood up and called Archbishop Simms' proposal 'a toothless, bloodless, colourless thing.' De Mel had great experience in ecumenical matters and had witnessed the successful negotiation of denominational hurdles to form united churches in South India, North India, Pakistan and Ceylon. The steering committee's over-cautious proposal made him angry and his description of it was quite accurate. Unfortunately, his tone was sharp and he turned to sarcasm as he continued, 'A little more of this behaviour and the Anglican Communion will get such a magnificent reputation for double-talk that we will become utterly disreputable.' His outburst was sufficient to secure an overwhelming majority for Bishop Hamilton's proposed resolution but it also led to a sense of revulsion. Bishop Trevor Huddleston (recently returned from Tanzania, soon to take up responsibility as Bishop of Stepney) denounced the speech as 'utterly unChristian.'[40] Some bishops were reluctant to attend the final eucharist in St Paul's Cathedral because de Mel was to be the preacher, and Bishop Easthaugh subsequently took the *Church Times* to task for praising the speech. In a letter to the paper he said it was 'not a speech which should be heard in any civilised assembly, let alone an assembly of Christians. It was a torrent of abuse, insult and hysteria'.[41]

It was a sad incident: Dr Simms refused to take offence, excusing de Mel on the grounds that in his enthusiasm he did not understand the slowness of progress in England and that his attack was not intended to be personal. Nor did he allow it to sour their relationship and he had de Mel to stay when he was Archbishop of Armagh. On the other hand many bishops interpreted it as a personal attack on a gentle and lovable bishop and their abhorrence of its tone obscured the fact that they had disagreed with the Simms proposal.

It could be argued that the steering committee was being realistic in recognising the difficulties facing the Church of England over the unity scheme and in its reluctance to allow the Lambeth Conference to influence the outcome. As it turned out the scheme was defeated by the Church of England the following year. Yet the Conference aspired to giving leadership within the Anglican Communion and unity between Anglicans and Methodists in Great Britain posed small problems compared with those which have been successfully overcome in other countries.

Throughout the Conference Dr Simms sent detailed reports for the *Church of Ireland Gazette*. In these and in subsequent writings and speeches he ranged widely over the proceedings and sought to convey something which could easily be effaced, the spirit of the Conference. He liked to recall the frequency with which the bishops took Christ's washing of the disciples' feet as a corporate meditation, in order to reinforce their concept of 'the servant church' as a movement *in* the world but not *of* the world. For him it was important that 'talking gave place to concentrated waiting on the Spirit before decisions were made and resolutions framed.' It was a spiritual experience which he built into his ongoing ministry in Ireland. With hindsight his compassion for the 'delegates who were undergoing affliction and were deeply implicated in the problems of the world' seems prophetic; in saying that their presence 'demonstrated almost physically the meaning of the cross and the deep influence of that most excellent Christian virtue called charity'[42] he anticipated a feeling which some delegates expressed about him when he attended the Lambeth Conference of 1978, a primate worn and aged by all the sorrows of the conflict in Northern Ireland but radiating the same charity as ever. For the moment, however, the Northern troubles were unforeseen.

On his return from Lambeth he was invited to give a lecture on the conference at the Jesuit Institute, Milltown Park, Dublin. He gave a careful and non-judgmental report on its proceedings, quoting Archbishop Ramsey's opening address in full. This broad review made it clear how closely he was in accord with Michael Ramsey. It was much deeper than a shared churchmanship; he shared his eschatological view of the Anglican Communion, that it should look to the future with prophetic anticipation of a new way and not just depend on its history and tradition. Likewise, before his Roman Catholic audience he stated his agreement with Archbishop Ramsey that, while unity is given to Christians once for all in Christ, its full realisation takes centuries to achieve, a veritable counsel of creative patience! The large audience at the lecture asked many questions afterwards and it was his experience that Irish Roman Catholics showed more interest in Lambeth X than did members of the Church of Ireland. It saddened him that there was not more interest among his own flock, for these were questions of great relevance.

The Lambeth Conferences and all his outside contacts were valuable in that they enabled Dr Simms to keep in touch with other parts of the Anglican Communion and with Christendom at large and to share the benefits with his people in Ireland. A further international responsibility arose from his attendance at the World Council of Churches Assembly at Uppsala. At that meeting he was elected to the central committee and this necessitated his attendance at a twelve-day meeting in Canterbury in 1969. Dr Simms undertook one other major foreign trip during his time as Archbishop of Dublin. At the invitation of *Church Illustrated* he led a pilgrimage to the Holy Land in 1964. As this was his first visit he confessed to 'not knowing much about the Holy Land' but that mattered little as guides were employed to take his fifty-strong party round. He saw his role as one of nurturing a sense of devotion and fellowship; he celebrated holy communion every day on the roof of a house or in a borrowed room or church. The Holy Land was sadly commercialised but the profound scholarship and spiritual depth of their leader enabled the pilgrims to capture the atmosphere of the gospel. Dr Simms, who was accompanied by his wife, enjoyed himself richly. With glee he wrote home to Raymond Jenkins 'I try out bits of Hebrew on the guides and bus drivers and occasionally I can get them to understand what I am saying'![43]

As has been seen, much of Dr Simms' international involvement was in the ecumenical sphere. Obviously he was eager to use his experience to foster inter-church relations in Ireland but during his years in Dublin it was more a matter of courtesies rather than serious dialogue as far as the Roman Catholics were concerned. Despite all his encouragement, prayer and hopefulness it took a long time to create an ecumenical climate. Seizing every encouraging sign on the Roman Catholic side, he preached repeatedly at Christ Church Cathedral and elsewhere on the new relationships between divided Christians. In every press interview he found something positive to say, no matter how difficult the circumstances. One of the barriers to progress was the conservatism of Archbishop McQuaid. On a personal level the two archbishops developed a good relationship and Dr McQuaid was soon at ease with Mrs Simms, forgetting his shyness as he earnestly discussed issues of social concern with her. Nevertheless he would not have countenanced any ecumenical gestures in his diocese had he not been compelled to implement the new Vatican policy. He was at the peak of his power in 1961 when the Patrician year brought an outbreak of triumphalism. In the same year his pre-Council submissions to the Vatican expressed the hope that it would bolster the powers of a bishop within his diocese and foster devotion to the Virgin Mary. His attitude offered little hope for ecumenical advance. When the Archbishop of Canterbury, Dr Geoffrey Fisher, came to Dublin that year for a meeting of the British Council of Churches, no arrangement was made for him to meet Archbishop McQuaid. Later in the year Michael Ramsey, as Archbishop-elect of Canterbury, visited Dublin for a mission in Trinity College and he was received by Archbishop McQuaid, but it would have been premature to attempt ecumenical dialogue on the occasion of a courtesy call.

Soon after his arrival in Rome for the second Vatican Council, Archbishop McQuaid found that he was at variance with its mood. Realising that he was in the minority and unable to change his own attitudes he kept his counsel; as a loyal churchman he endeavoured to implement the reforms of Vatican II but the changes came in form, not in spirit. For example, in 1964 he instructed his people to pray during the Church Unity Week but this advance was diminished by asking them to pray that Christians separated in doctrine and discipline from the Roman Catholic Church might rejoin the one true church of Christ.

In Unity Week 1965 he allowed Monsignor P. F. Cremin, Professor of Moral Theology at St Patrick's College, Maynooth, and his advisor at Vatican II, to deliver four talks in Trinity College without interference but usually his ecumenical gestures were clumsy. Most unfortunate of all was the so-called 'empty chair meeting' in the Mansion House in January 1966. Sponsored by the recently-founded Centre for Religious Studies and Information, the meeting was intended as a highlight of Church Unity Week.

Radio Éireann decided to broadcast the proceedings live. The press generated expectations of a great occasion and a real step forward, and a huge crowd filled the room on the night. Archbishop Simms had been invited but had received no information about the arrangements for the meeting and was uneasy. Wearing an ordinary suit with his episcopal stock under an overcoat, he arrived at the Mansion House to find that nobody knew where he was to sit. He was eventually seated along with President de Valera and other important guests in the front rows while Archbishop McQuaid, the Papal Nuncio, and Fr Roland Burke Savage and Monsignor Arthur Ryan, the lecturer from Belfast, appeared on the platform in full canonicals. Far from fulfilling expectations, Monsignor Ryan delivered a defensive Roman Catholic orientated lecture on the Vatican Council's Decree on Ecumenism and the prayers were led by the Papal Nuncio, to the disappointment of many who were expecting the two archbishops to lead them. Moreover there was an empty chair on the platform, which the press assumed had been intended for Archbishop Simms. They made a large issue of it, blaming Archbishop McQuaid, and were joined in this by many Roman Catholics who felt angry and were impelled by their shame to greater ecumenical effort.

An article in the St Louis Review, an American Roman Catholic journal, of 11 March 1966 well illustrates Roman Catholic dismay over the incident. In it John Horgan, then religious affairs correspondent of the Irish Times and one of the most respected journalists of the time, suggested that 'ecumenism is running the risk of becoming Ireland's No. 1 bloodsport'. He pointed out that the meeting was a Roman Catholic take-over and for that reason 'a great many people felt that they had been cheated.' Amid the welter of misunderstanding he had been unable to obtain a satisfactory explanation of the empty chair incident but said that 'countless annoyed and embarrassed Catholics throughout the country are now looking for a convenient scapegoat'. That scapegoat was Archbishop McQuaid, who became something of an anti-celebrity in the international press. Horgan was probably correct in suggesting that the 'lavish pre-publicity received was responsible for the more wary Catholic attitude' on the night, given the fact that Archbishop McQuaid's 'extreme caution in ecumenical matters is reinforced almost to the point of calcification by his theologically formal mind and a marked personal shyness.' Other Roman Catholic views were less kindly stated.[44] Many could not help contrasting the forbidding character of their own archbishop with the gentle graciousness of the Church of Ireland archbishop. Dr

Simms was very popular with Dublin Roman Catholics and many eagerly listened to his devotional talks on radio and television. The slights which caused this furore were not noticed by Dr Simms. He found the atmosphere uncomfortable and the lack of a welcome somewhat disappointing but he did not take offence. He did not expect to sit on the platform and would have been reluctant to take a seat there if no other Protestant leaders were included. His lead was followed by Church of Ireland people generally who were bemused by the row and wished it at an end.

Notwithstanding the difficulties, the ecumenical climate did improve, as is evidenced by the altered Roman Catholic attitude to the visit of the Archbishop of Canterbury in 1967. When Archbishop Ramsey came to Dublin for the centenary of St Bartholomew's Church, an inter-church reception was mounted at the airport, to which both the Roman Catholic primate, Cardinal William Conway, and Archbishop McQuaid sent representatives. He called on Dr McQuaid, visited St Patrick's College, Maynooth, and drew a large audience for his lecture at the Royal Dublin Society on 'Rome and Canterbury'.[45] On this visit he was sufficiently encouraged to speak of a new spirit of ecumenism in Ireland.

Apart from special occasions, progress in the ecumenical sphere was slow. There was a number of Roman Catholic theologians who turned their attention to the ecumenical movement. Foremost among them was the Rev. Michael Hurley, S.J., who was determined to make unity and joint mission a high priority for the Roman Catholic Church. During the sixties he established contacts with Protestant clergy, north and south, and informed himself of the finer points of the tradition and theology of the Protestant churches. He met indifference, if not hostility, in many quarters but, undeterred, he forged ahead until in 1970 he established the Irish School of Ecumenics.

Unofficial regular contacts between Roman Catholic and Protestant clergy and laity were established in the 1960s in the inter-denominational conferences at Glenstal, County Limerick, and Greenhills, Drogheda. These allowed for free discussion of theological issues but the Roman Catholic side did not want to discuss such thorny questions as marriage and education, issues which had to be addressed if ecumenical dialogue was to become meaningful. Asked about barriers to church unity for an article in the *Sunday Independent* of 21 January 1968, Dr Simms was reported as saying that 'it was something to have had unofficial conversations, but it was not very easy to see how it could become official.' It was only after his translation to Armagh that the

troubles in the North brought such a sense of urgency that the
Ballymascanlon inter-denominational conferences were started and
formal discussions between leaders of the different churches began.
When Dr Simms became Archbishop of Dublin there was
scarcely any enthusiasm for ecumenism among his own flock.
Their growing commitment to it during the sixties is a powerful
testimony to Dr Simms' leadership but the path was not smooth.
In 1966 the House of Bishops found it necessary to issue a pamphlet
on the doctrines and position of the Church of Ireland, to allay
grassroot fears of a 'Romeward trend'. These anxieties arose
because of the ecumenical impetus in the Anglican Communion at
large and in the World Council of Churches and the bishops had
to reassure the people that unity discussions conducted in other
countries could not be binding in Ireland.

Apart from differences of doctrine and religious practice, the big-
gest barrier to ecumenical progress in Ireland was the Roman
Catholic position on mixed marriages. The difficulties involved were
experienced between Protestants and Roman Catholics in every
country but were the more keenly felt in Ireland because of the enormous disparity in numbers. In some instances entire Church of
Ireland families disappeared as all the sons and daughters either con-
tracted mixed marriages or preferred to remain single, rather than
face the problems of marrying a Roman Catholic. Until recent years
a mixed marriage almost inevitably meant that the children were
brought up as Roman Catholics so the Church of Ireland found its
numbers decimated because of the policy of the Roman Catholic
Church. There were all sorts of unpleasant connotations. For instance, if a Church of Ireland woman married a Roman Catholic and
was later widowed, was she obliged to honour the promise to bring
up the children as Roman Catholics? It could be argued that as the
Roman Catholic Church allowed for the dispensation of vows where
there was notable difficulty in keeping the vow and that, as the promise given by the Church of Ireland partner was not as formal as a
vow, she should be relieved of her obligation. However in such an
event, the Roman Catholic in-laws often wanted to take responsibility for the children, in order to ensure a Roman Catholic upbringing.
Faced with this prospect, the widow might even flee the state with her
children.

In Ireland most Roman Catholic bishops applied the rules on
mixed marriages with maximum strictness. In the Dublin archdiocese Archbishop McQuaid usually insisted that the ceremony
should take place before 9.00 a.m. in the sacristy, turning what
should have been a joyful occasion into a 'furtive ritual'.[46]

At an international level Dr Simms earnestly hoped for progress on this difficult question. At home, seeing no advantage in confrontation, he made firm but charitable statements of the Church of Ireland position when occasion demanded it and worked quietly behind the scenes to help the Church of Ireland partner in difficult situations relating to a mixed marriage. He was always saddened by the tragic tensions affecting the individual family and the frequent legacy of bitterness. He also knew what the Roman Catholic authorities never wished to acknowledge, that the rule on mixed marriages posed a veritable threat to the survival of the Church of Ireland community.

There has been a great deal of misunderstanding about the relative positions of Roman Catholics and members of the Church of Ireland and other Protestant churches on questions of marriage and private morality. It arose because the law of the Irish state had in the twenties and thirties absorbed so much of the social teaching of the Roman Catholic Church. The natural corollary of this was the recognition in the 1937 Constitution of the special position of the Roman Catholic Church as the guardian of the faith professed by the great majority of the citizens. As Article 44 also embodied the guarantee of religious freedom given in the 1922 Constitution and further recognised the Church of Ireland and other religious denominations existing in Ireland in 1937, Church of Ireland people made few objections to the Constitution but when they saw that it provided the basis for new, conservative interpretations of the law, there was widespread unease. Relations were at a low ebb in the early fifties as a result of the Tilson case, in which the Protestant partner in a mixed marriage found that the courts supported the Roman Catholic rules on the upbringing of children. This discovery prompted *The Irish Times* to assert that 'it is difficult to avoid the impression that the philosophy underlying Irish jurisprudence is tending, slowly but surely to be informed by the principles of the Roman Catholic Church'.[47]

In more recent debates on matters such as divorce, contraception and abortion, the Protestant churches have sometimes been portrayed as permissive because they do not agree that the law of the land should adhere to the teaching of majority church. This arrogant and offensive denial of their integrity ignores the sincerity of the Protestant position and seeks to identify religious pluralism with an absence of moral principle. The Protestant position is a conservative one: the sanctity of marriage is unquestioned and divorce and abortion cause as much dismay as in the Roman Catholic Church. However, religious pluralism and tolerance implies non-discriminatory treatment of all citizens irrespective of their religious beliefs (or lack of them) and this principle is violated when a state enacts laws which are binding on the conscience of only a section of the people.

In recognising the role of the Roman Catholic Church in Ireland as the guardian of the faith, Eamon de Valera, the architect of the Constitution, sought not a tool of intolerance but a support for the moral fibre of the country yet, as Desmond Clarke explains,

intolerance is a characteristic part of the ideological framework of the majority church in Ireland. It is consistent with its beliefs about infallibility, and it feeds on its fear of moral contamination if adult citizens are exposed to alternative belief systems which might challenge the hold of the churches on the minds of the citizens. An insular people, taught by a majority 'infallible' church, and cultivated for many decades by an explicit government policy of fostering a nationalist ideal of religious and cultural homogeneity, is hardly likely to provide a paradigm of political and religious tolerance.[48]

Infallibility implies freedom from error in matters of faith and morals; those who framed Ireland's restrictive laws had no doubts on this score, nor did they realise that changed circumstances would make a nonsense of them. Article 41 of the Constitution introduced a ban on divorce and declared a bigamist any one who had obtained a civil divorce elsewhere and had remarried. In time the government had to acknowledge the fact that one can legislate against divorce but one cannot legislate against the breakdown of marriages: the number of non-Christians, Protestants and, indeed, Roman Catholics, who obtained a divorce in England or abroad, remarried and continued to live in Ireland posed unpalatable alternatives; either the government would enforce the law and be regarded as oppressive, or it would ignore its evasion and allow it to appear ridiculous.

The Roman Catholic Church did not help matters by extending the grounds for annulment. It was (and is) always a matter of astonishment to Protestants that although a couple remained married in the eyes of the state and although they had been married by a Roman Catholic priest and might have several children, the Roman Catholic Church could declare that their marriage was invalid and that they were both free to marry!

As already stated the Protestant attitude was conservative and far from welcoming divorce. Most of his flock thoroughly approved of Dr Simms' pronouncements on the subject. During the late sixties, when there was talk of removing the constitutional ban on divorce, Dr Simms repeatedly reiterated the Anglican belief in the indissolubility of marriage. Wont to quote Sir Edwyn Hoskyns' saying that 'marriage is difficult and dangerous at the beginning, in the middle and at the end' he always stressed the principles stated in *The Book of Common Prayer*. For him the words 'those whom God has joined together let no man put asunder' were crucial, yet he readily admitted that non-believers were not bound by such promises and that marital breakdown did occur despite the best counselling. Unlike his Roman Catholic counterparts he did not find the issue clearcut; he was extremely reluctant to consider divorce and yet his belief in pluralism suggested that a negative clause on divorce in the Constitution was undesirable.

For Dr Simms and his Church of Ireland flock the question of family planning was more straightforward. After the Lambeth Conference's approval of birth control in 1958, few continued to entertain doubts. The importation and sale of contraceptives was however banned by Irish law from 1925 until the Supreme Court ruling on the McGee case effectively ended it in 1973 by declaring the ban unconstitutional. Mr Justice Walsh's judgment that 'the private morality of the citizens does not justify intervention by the state into the activities of those citizens unless and until the common good requires it',[49] was an important new departure. For years the position had been farcical, as married couples risked discovery when importing contraceptives or used the easier expedient of getting a sympathetic doctor to prescribe the contraceptive pill 'for health reasons'. By no means all of these couples were Protestants or non-believers. The issue of abortion scarcely surfaced in the sixties but the position of the two churches was very close: both totally rejected it as a method of birth control but within the Church of Ireland there was gradual acceptance of it in cases of undeniable medical necessity.

The misunderstanding of the Protestant position on these issues did not help the ecumenical climate during Archbishop Simms' years in Dublin. Considering the difficulties which prevailed it is amazing that any significant progress was made. Undoubtedly much of the credit was due to Dr Simms himself. On his appointment to Armagh *The Times* of London opined that 'he has been responsible for the marked degree of togetherness prevailing between his church and the Roman Catholics'.[50]

He used his tact and friendliness to break down barriers and build up trust. The way he did it was illuminated by Fr Michael Hurley in a letter to *The Irish Times* on the occasion of the Archbishop's retirement in 1980.[51] It applies as much to his ecumenical endeavour in Dublin as to that of his primacy; 'He has opened the hearts of many of us to the goodness of the Anglican and Protestant traditions. And, having a way with words as well as with people, he has also opened our minds to the spiritual riches of these traditions.' Rightly Fr Hurley realised that his love of *The Book of Kells* and of all things Irish had played a large part in bringing about an important change of attitudes. The Church of Ireland was no longer seen as an alien English intrusion, and this was a notable gain for inter-church relations at home. Dr McAdoo summed up his ecumenical work comprehensively when he said 'he shed the light of his countenance on every effort to bring people together'.[52]

It should not be forgotten that there was another side of the ecumenical endeavour, rapprochement with the other Protestant churches. Although relations were quite friendly there had been no formal unity discussions since the failure of reunion negotiations in the 1930s. Under the auspices of the Irish Council of Churches[53] attempts were made to bring the Protestant churches towards unity; there were a few experiments in the sharing of churches and in joint housing schemes but real dialogue only recommenced in the sixties. By 1964 there were three separate sets of discussions; Church of Ireland-Presbyterian, Church of Ireland-Methodist and Presbyterian-Methodist. Despite immediate and highly vocal opposition from within the ranks there was enough support in each church to ensure the continuation of the talks but the intricacies of three separate negotiating structures would have proved fatal had not they merged in 1968 into tripartite discussions. As this happened only a year before Dr Simms' translation to Armagh, consideration of their progress belongs in the next chapter.

While Archbishop Simms' primary concerns were always as pastor of his people and as guardian of the faith, inevitably administration took up a great deal of his time. Central church administration, at Representative Body and Standing Committee, continued much as before, except that as Archbishop of Dublin his profile and responsibility was somewhat greater, especially as so much of the administration of the Church of Ireland is Dublin-based. Within the actual diocese, administration was not greatly different from that in Cork. His four years' administrative experience in Cork and his mastery of the rules of synod were of great use as archbishop. He knew how to steer a debate, he never sought to impose his will, every contribution he made was towards keeping people working together in the service of the church. Some synodsmen complained that one never knew what the archbishop felt about a given topic but those who worked closely with him knew very well without any need for him to spell it out. 'Do you think so?' in reply to a statement was quickly taken as evidence that he disagreed, while a seemingly casual question 'Isn't there something in the rules which allows . . .?' was seen as his preferred course of action. He employed the same approach at committee meetings, as he was always keen to get people to think things out for themselves. Inevitably many people failed to appreciate this type of leadership, finding it too subtle and indirect for their liking.

One of his first difficulties in his new diocese was the closure of churches. The findings of the City and Town Parishes Commission led to unions of parishes and closure of churches both in Dublin city and in the country areas of his three dioceses. Dr Simms was well aware of the unhappiness caused and yearned to ease the pain. In his address at the diocesan synod of 1960 he spoke about it and was genuine in sympathising with those who were enduring difficulties. 'I wish I could comfort them during the times of readjustment' he said but went on to direct them to look for fresh opportunities and new life.

Whenever possible he injected a positive note by closing a church with a great service of thanksgiving; sometimes consensus was reached by his patient chairmanship — sitting for hours hoping to allow the opposition to talk out its objections and come around to acceptance. Once it was impossible to avoid unpleasantness: when the archbishop prepared to implement the Commission's recommendation that Carysfort Church should close a group of parishioners contested it in the High Court. Their appeal, on the grounds that it was a trustee church, was ruled invalid because it had been handed over to the diocese. Dr Simms relied on his legal advisers and endeavoured not to become embroiled in the wrangling.

It was the profusion of committees that made the job of administration in Dublin much more onerous than that in Cork. Education, hospital and social concern committees filled many hours each week. Protestant secondary education, well-serviced in Cork, was nevertheless to a large extent Dublin-based and Dr Simms was an *ex officio* member of many school boards. His time as archbishop coincided with a period of amalgamations, closures and moves to new suburban sites. It was his sad duty to preside over the death-throes of some schools, while all his reserves of kindly diplomacy were required to smooth amalgamations such as those of Morgan's School and Mercer's School with The King's Hospital.

His interest and experience in education and his friendly contacts with the Department of Education were very valuable in these years. Dr Kenneth Milne was secretary to the General Synod Board of Education from 1963 until 1977, throughout which time Dr Simms was chairman. The secretary's job was to plot the course of education as it affected the Church of Ireland community. At a time of unprecedented change his responsibility was great and he valued Dr Simms' oversight. Dr Milne gives a clear insight into the archbishop's style as administrator:

Dr Simms was well aware of the groundswell of change and was well able to master the minutiae of developments. Briefing him took very little time — apart from the delays caused by one's own attempts to answer his supplementary questions, or to fill the gaps that he (invariably) found in one's presentation. In general, once he had satisfied himself about policies, whether to do with reorganising the secondary school system, or the national schools, or introducing innovations in religious education, or initiating specialist youth work, he then left one to it. Always available with advice and always prepared to facilitate, he never *directed* in any authoritarian manner.[54]

On the other hand Dr Milne found that the archbishop was ready to intervene personally when appropriate; for instance he rose to speak at the General Synod of 1965 when an advisory committee recommendation to amalgamate small national schools was in danger of defeat and his strong appeal 'for the sake of the children' helped secure its acceptance.

These were occasions when he realised that he had a particular contribution to make and so took the initiative. He was *ex officio* manager of the Church of Ireland Training College, an institution which, very naturally, was particularly close to his heart. He preached enthusiastically in the College Chapel at the thanksgiving service on the occasion of the 150th anniversary of the foundation of the Kildare Place Society but realised that the site was no longer suitable. Accordingly he was in the forefront in finding a new site, and securing government funding. In 1963 the Kildare Place site was sold and Rathmines Castle was purchased. Dr Simms devoted a lot of time to overseeing the move to Rathmines in co-operation with the principal, Canon R. J. Ross. The new College, incorporating its own national school and Coláiste Moibhí, the Church of Ireland's Irish-speaking secondary school, was opened in March 1969. As Susan Parkes says in her history of the Training College 'to all who attended the opening ceremony that day, the new buildings symbolised the achievement of long years and the hope for the future'.[55] Dr Simms would accept little credit for the achievement but his knowledgeable encouragement and unfailing support were important. The establishment of a modern well-equipped College accorded closely with his vision for the Church of Ireland as a community which confidently played its part in the country. The presence not only of the Minister for Education, Brian Lenihan, but also of President de Valera and of the Taoiseach, Jack Lynch, was an indication of how good relations were with the government and Dr Simms paid tribute to the government's 'most generous treatment and consideration' in the project.

The sixties saw many educational changes in his diocese. In 1967 a radical scheme was put forward by Donogh O'Malley, Mr Lenihan's predecessor as Minister for Education. His idea was that Trinity College and University College would merge in a new University of Dublin, thus avoiding duplication and saving money. Dr Simms was careful not to react negatively to the suggestion, although many Church of Ireland hackles rose instantly. Speaking at the diocesan synod in October 1968 the archbishop pointed out the historical links between Trinity College and the Church of Ireland, the importance of the divinity school in training ordinands, of the school of education in giving the professional qualifications for teachers in Protestant secondary schools and of the link with the Training College. 'Without any wish to promote exclusiveness or cling to a past that is gone' he stated his belief in the importance of retaining student choice of college — 'choice so that a student may opt . . . for the college to which he wishes to belong in order to pursue his studies'.

Some feared that he would not press the Church of Ireland case hard enough if the amalgamation went through — for instance Terence de Vere White, writing in the *Sunday Telegraph* of 7 July 1968, posed the question whether the Minister for Education would put both archbishops of Dublin on the governing body of the new university, and concluded that 'if he does the representatives of University College . . . with few exceptions will be afraid to utter and Dr Simms . . . is so given to courtesy that he will bow himself out of counteracting influence'. In the face of fierce opposition from both colleges the scheme was dropped in favour of co-operation and amalgamation of certain schools, so the fears of government action were not fulfilled.

Nevertheless, within a few years of the removal of the Roman Catholic ban in 1970, Trinity College had changed utterly from the university which Dr Simms knew as student and Dean of Residence. Students' choice of college was largely unimpaired, the Church of Ireland links with the school of education were maintained but the intimate atmosphere and the Church of Ireland ambience evaporated. Roman Catholics now shared the use of the chapel while the divinity school was transformed into a non-denominational school of Hebrew, biblical and theological studies, with specific Anglican preparation of ordinands being passed in 1980 to the newly-constituted Theological College. In the context of these developments the wisdom of Dr Simms' address to synod in 1968 is apparent. There was indeed no point in clinging to a past that was gone, one could only welcome the new and enlarged role of the College and hope to guarantee the future of links which were vital for the Church of Ireland.

Away from the educational field, Dr Simms sat on the board of several city hospitals and preserved a special relationship with the Adelaide as the only hospital under Protestant management. He was a patron or committee member of many other organisations, including the Sunday School Society, the Irish College of Preachers, the Mission to the Adult Deaf and Dumb, the Hibernian Church Missionary Society, the Church's Ministry of Healing, to name a few. Some only required attendance at an annual meeting, others involved a considerable amount of work. As patron of the Association for the Relief of Distressed Protestants (later to become Protestant Aid), he took a particular interest in its homes for the elderly and made the annual radio appeal on its behalf.

Dr Simms had been a member of Cumann Gaelach na hEaglaise (The Irish Guild of the Church) since his student days in Trinity College. As early as 1934 he had been a member of the literary committee and he became a patron while Bishop of Cork. Its status within the Church of Ireland was enhanced by the fact that, for the first time, the Archbishop of Dublin frequently presided at its services in Irish.

In the administrative routine an archbishop mostly carries on where his predecessor has left off but there is always scope for initiative and each man makes his individual contribution. This depends partly on the circumstances and challenges of the time, partly on his interests and sympathies.

Both Archbishop and Mrs Simms were keenly interested in social issues. One of the committees on which Mrs Simms served was the Church of Ireland Social Service Society. Its chief concerns were unmarried parents and unwanted children, unhappy families and unjust social conditions. In time Miss Beatrice Odlum, the social worker/secretary of the Society discerned a need for a marriage counselling service and found that one of the committee, the Rev. M. A. Handy, already had the same idea.

They found ready acceptance from Archbishop Simms, who had previously shown his interest in the Social Service by appealing to the Representative Body for funding for its work and whose care to promote Christian marriage was well-known. The Church of Ireland Marriage Counselling Service was established in 1962, with Archbishop Simms as its president. In many ways it was modelled on the National Marriage Guidance Council in England but it did not have official assistance from the parent body in the early years. The archbishop was one of the three selectors at the first conference in 1962 to choose counsellors for training. Like the N.M.G.C. the service provided preventative and remedial services, ranging from courses in schools, through marriage preparation courses to individual counselling of one or both partners of a marriage in trouble.

Archbishop Simms' encouragement was vital for the establishment of the service and his authority was essential for its acceptance within the Church of Ireland. In the early days he took every opportunity to promote the M.C.S. as a *bona fide* agency; at Synod and other gatherings, he encouraged his clergy to make referrals to the M.C.S., he also managed to produce funding from time to time. At first the M.C.S. was a service funded by the Church of Ireland, provided by Church of Ireland counsellors for members of the Church of Ireland. Soon it broadened its scope, abandoned its Church of Ireland title and began to work under the auspices of the Dublin Council of Churches.

Dr Simms continued as president until his appointment to Armagh but his departure led to a noted diminution of support from the Church of Ireland. In the early seventies the M.C.S. ceased to have any religious affiliation and acquired a national identity quite separate from the churches.[56] It thus developed rapidly in a direction which Dr Simms had not foreseen. Even if it ceased to function as one of the church's social services it continued to fulfil his basic wish, that marital counselling should be provided professionally by trained lay counsellors, over and above the help which parochial clergy can offer.

Another special interest of Dr Simms was the work of the Ministry of Healing. He set aside the week-end of the annual festival in order to take part in the special service and to chair the public meeting. He often used the opportunity to draw attention to this neglected aspect of the church's ministry and, as a resolute intercessor, to encourage other intercessors in their daily commitment.

Much administrative work was carried out on behalf of the

whole Church of Ireland. As archbishop he sat on the divinity
school council, presided over the Hostel and sought to establish
close contacts with the ordinands. One of his priorities was the
establishment of national selection conferences, an expansion of the
diocesan conferences which he and Bishop Mitchell had run in their
dioceses of Cork and Down. The first conference of what became
known as C.A.C.T.M. (Central Advisory Council of Training for
the Ministry) took place in 1961 and its structure owed much to Dr
Simms' planning.

While Michael Ferrar was Warden of the Divinity Hostel he and
the archbishop were planning to move the Hostel from Mountjoy
Square and were looking for a new site. After Ferrar's death Dr
Simms oversaw the appointment of J. S. Brown as Warden and
continued the search with him. The new Hostel in Braemor Park
was opened in 1963. Many were sad at the idea of abandoning
Mountjoy Square (some felt that, apart from tradition, it was good
for the students to see the rough side of life in inner-city Dublin)
but Dr Simms subscribed to the view that a new hostel with single
study rooms in a more salubrious area was required and it would
provide the basis of a proper theological college, a hope which was
finally realised in 1980. He also influenced the move of the
Representative Body to Church House, Rathmines, and its library
to Braemor Park, in convenient proximity to the new Hostel. In
central administration, at the level of the Representative Body, the
Standing Committee and the Finance Committee, Archbishop
Simms enjoyed the support of leading members, who recognised
his administrative ability and trusted his judgment. Two of the
members of the Representative Body had worked with him in
Cork: F. L. Jacob (formerly his diocesan treasurer) and J. L. B.
Deane (his assessor). He had already earned their respect for, as Mr
Jacob put it, he was 'extraordinarily adroit at handling committees'
and 'you didn't have to explain complicated financial questions to
him'.[57]

In general terms Mr Deane sums up his standing in succinct
terms: 'Quite simply George always got his own way.'[58] He never
tried to rush a discussion or dictate to others but his gentle steering
of debate and members' respect for him was such that his opinion
generally prevailed. It was not that he expected to get his own way;
on the contrary, at diocesan and national level he always behaved
as a constitutional bishop and was most careful not to appropriate
to himself what should be done by synod, Representative Body or
council.

At General Synod he generally did not speak on a contentious subject lest he should be identified with one faction; if he wanted to have a proposal put forward he would ask a suitable synodsman to make it; rarely did he speak directly to a motion, though his support for Sir Cecil Stafford King-Harman's proposal in 1959 to establish episcopal electoral colleges was a notable exception. The bill owed much to Dr Simms' initiative. He was convinced that the existing procedure was unsound, so he worked towards a system which would be fair and effective and would correctly make the election of a bishop a concern for the whole church and not just for an individual diocese.

The existing system of election by diocesan synod[59] was to be replaced by an electoral college consisting of six clerical and twelve lay representatives of the vacant see, two clerical and two lay representatives from each of the other dioceses of the province and three bishops nominated by the House of Bishops, only one of whom might be from the same province.

The bill allowed for a flexible procedure in the hands of the metropolitan, specifying informal discussion before any proposal of candidates, with prayer and discussion alternating as progress was made towards a decision. Any number of rounds could be allowed by the president until a two-thirds majority (voting by orders) was attained. If the president concluded that the college was not going to reach a decision he would then refer the choice to the House of Bishops.[60]

Dr Simms, who was to second the bill, sat quietly while it came under attack as undemocratic, a slur on the diocesan synods, a system with an inherent capacity for forcing a bishop on an unwilling diocese. Then he rose and explained why he supported the measure in tones which made his hopes quite clear. Sir Cecil believed that the archbishop's decision to reserve his speech was 'the turning point: it produced a completely different atmosphere throughout the Synod at the vital moment. In war the timing of the counter attack has always been the most difficult decision of the whole battle and you judged it to perfection'.[61]

The Synod duly passed the bill and it happened that the first two elections were held in the southern province under Dr Simms' presidency. This afforded him the opportunity to establish the atmosphere he considered desirable. Pleased with the new structure he wrote an article, 'The Appointment of a Bishop', for the *Church of England Newspaper*.[62] Starting from the premise that

It is notoriously difficult in a human gathering to maintain a high standard of integrity and wisdom in the delicate and sensitive surroundings of an election, [he states his belief that] a good tradition in this respect has already begun. Furthermore, it is reasonable to suppose that in the less manageable and more rigidly formal setting of a diocesan synod, where discussion was precluded in the synod hall, much ill-informed and very probably inaccurate description of candidates picked up unofficially before the date of election brought just that feeling of uncertainty and uneasiness which stirred the General Synod to seek out a fresh method.

Under his skilful presidency there was general satisfaction that time was given for acquiring meaningful information, for such prayer and discussion as was necessary to discern the will of God and to translate that into a wise choice. He knew that rushing an election was disastrous, while a timely adjournment could afford an opportunity for a fresh approach.

If the episcopal college is a reform attributable to Archbishop Simms, there were also instances when he was not the prime mover but acted in response to the initiative of a pressure group. For instance, although the 1958 Lambeth Conference had stimulated his long-standing interest in liturgy, he took no formal steps to expedite liturgical revision within the Church of Ireland until the mid-Belfast deanery approached the Standing Committee on the subject. The House of Bishops decided to introduce legislation and Dr Simms gladly took responsibility for proposing the bill to establish a standing advisory committee at the General Synod of 1962.

His carefully-worded bill aroused no controversy, perhaps because members who acceded to it did not realise that it might lead to a very different new prayer book. There was some opposition to the suggested list of members of the committee as the 'low church/evangelical' side, anxious about the prospect of liturgical revision, believed that it was inadequately represented. The *Church of Ireland Gazette* report of 25 May 1962 shows how effective was the archbishop's approach:

At the end of the first day the members of the synod, though welcoming the proposal, were not so happy about the composition of the Committee, one member saying 'Give us more laymen,' and another 'Give us more Northerners'. The Synod rose before a conclusion was reached, and when, on the next morning, members looked at their Order Papers, they found a much larger Advisory Committee was being suggested, that it was to be required to report to the Synod annually instead of only when the occasion arose and that not all the committee were members of the General Synod. These had been the points of contention the previous evening, and where there had previously been hesitation, skilful handling of the matter by the Archbishop now convinced the house.

Dr Simms acted as chairman of the Liturgical Advisory Committee from its inception in 1962 until his retirement in 1980, during which time he attended virtually every meeting.[63] From the beginning he knew that he faced a delicate task: the moving force for liturgical revision was a small number of clergy but there was no widespread recognition of its desirability. The Church of Ireland remained a highly conservative church in which the post-Disestablishment Canons were a disincentive to liturgical development.

For twenty years or so there had been some interest in the liturgical movement, most of it channelled after 1952 into the Irish Parish and People Movement.[64] The Irish organisation was closely modelled on the Parish and People Movement founded in England in 1949, in which the leadership of Henry de Candole, Bishop of Knaresborough, and Kenneth Packard, and the liturgical scholarship of A. G. Hebert and Gregory Dix were vitally important.[65] The thrust of the Irish movement, exemplified by Michael Ferrar's conducting of devotional 'Days with the Prayer Book', was to help people use *The Book of Common Prayer* to the full, rather than to initiate revision. Eight of its members were appointed to the Liturgical Advisory Committee in 1962 and their study of matters liturgical immediately proved useful.[66]

Much of the early work of the committee was exploratory: liturgical developments in other parts of the Anglican Communion and in other churches were studied, with close reference to the recommendation of the 1958 Lambeth Conference. In this regard it was highly significant that Archbishop Simms had been chairman of the liturgy section at Lambeth.

Initially a conservative revision of *The Book of Common Prayer* was envisaged. Writing for the pre-Lambeth number of *Pan-Anglican* in 1968, Dr Simms referred to the 1967 draft holy communion service as 'a conservative revision in comparison with other such draft services in the Anglican Communion. Undoubtedly the Church of Ireland is reluctant to change its order of service'.[67] Gradually however the Committee came to realise that a more radical revision, incorporating the fundamental principles of the world-wide liturgical movement and written in modern English, was needed in order to provide for meaningful worship in the late twentieth century, but where this was not acceptable *The Book of Common Prayer* would remain available for use.

The decision constituted a watershed and cleared the way for the holy communion rite of 1972, which was, with minor amendments, adopted for *The Alternative Prayer Book* of 1984. The shape of that service was determined by the decision to adapt *The Book of*

Common Prayer tradition of morning prayer followed by holy communion, incorporating old testament, psalmody and canticle into the new communion rite.

As chairman, the archbishop was slow to reveal his own preferences, allowed the expression of all opinions and was meticulously fair. He was capable of presenting the differences in churchmanship which frequently surfaced in the positive light of Anglican comprehensiveness and thus led the Committee towards constructive compromises. Being sensitive to members' prejudices, he was skilful at getting them to voice their criticisms; with a delicate touch he could produce a quotation, perhaps from the Bible or an ancient liturgy, perhaps from an Anglican Congress or an Assembly of the World Council of Churches, which would cause the Committee members to pause for thought or which steered them on a new path. Equally, his gift of proffering a well-turned phrase often would bring agreement over a much-debated point.

Archbishop Simms' method of dealing with criticism by encouraging its expression paralleled and may have influenced the approach of the Committee. Critics who represented a definite viewpoint within the Church of Ireland were co-opted, the annual reports to the Synod were open to debate, questionnaires were sent to the parishes, forms of service were issued for use on a trial basis; widespread discussion was fostered in the same way as Dr Simms encouraged it at Committee meetings.

Although much work remained to be done during Dr Simms' primacy, when he left Dublin in 1969 the Liturgical Advisory Committee was on course for a revision which was comprehensive enough to reflect international liturgical developments and local enough to suit the Church of Ireland.[68]

The 1965 General Synod established an Advisory Committee on Administration to examine the administration of the Church of Ireland and recommend such changes and reforms as it might consider advisable. It was a five-man committee, comprising Dr Simms, Canon E. P. M. Elliott and three prominent laymen, M. F. E. Dobbin, V. G. Bridges and R. C. Gibson. The Representative Body appointed J. G. Briggs as secretary and Dr Simms agreed to act as chairman. Although he suggested at the start that the chairmanship should rotate, the other members wished to have him in the chair and so they embarked on a thorough review of central administration, representation at General Synod, diocesan administration, staffing of cathedrals and parishes and clerical stipends.

Having met nearly every other weekend in Dublin or at

Murlough House in County Down, it worked under considerable pressure to produce for the 1967 Synod a hundred-page report with numerous appendices offering statistical analyses to back up its points. The foreword is an important piece of writing for it shows that the members of the committee were up-to-date with contemporary Anglican theology and shared the thinking of the Lambeth Conference of 1958 and the Anglican Congress held in Toronto in 1963.

The foreword states 'The church's mission is the mission of Christ to the world in every area of human concern, . . . to bring people to be the church, to realise that being or becoming a member of the church is to share her common life.' To achieve this understanding requires 'the elimination of what is meaningless, and the removal of sheer redundancy and unnecessary routine in the church's organised life, in order that there may be a fresh appraisal of what is, through the power of the Holy Spirit, living and personal, truthful and sacred'.[69]

The primary theme of the Toronto Congress had been the church's mission to the world. It had taken a global view of the church's needs and had laid considerable emphasis on the need for renewal. Archbishop Simms and Mr Dobbin had been among the forty-six Irish delegates and shared the vision of the Congress. So large did mission figure in their minds that the committee wanted the mission division to occupy a central position in a new administrative structure, under the control of an executive officer who would also be the secretary of the General Synod. Renewal was the aspiration of the Administration report, a document which firmly directed the church away from its preoccupation with the past, towards planning for the future. 'Only if the church is more interested in what it is to become than what it has been, will it seek continuous renewal.'[70]

The emphasis on mission and renewal at Toronto had been accompanied by deep reflection on the share of the laity in ministry.[71] Dr Simms was in full accord with the Administration report's words on the 'full share' of the laity 'not only in the worship, life and government of the church, but also in the church's witness to Christ through public affairs and everyday concerns'.[72] A section of the report explored specific areas in which lay ministry, scarcely existent, should be nurtured.

Congress resolutions and committee reports both require more widespread acceptance if their recommendations are to be implemented. The Administration 1967 report far exceeded the vision of the General Synod and failed overall to win acceptance. It demanded a radical rethinking of the role and ordering of the church, for which the Church of Ireland was unprepared.

Some of the report's ideas found favour and were the basis of new legislation at General Synod, while some were glossed over. These included such vital recommendations as the lightening of a bishop's administrative duties in order to enhance his pastoral relationships with his clergy and people. Two decades later this is an ever more urgent area for reform. Considering that the original idea had been an examination of central administration, it is somewhat surprising that its recommendations in this sphere were largely ignored.

A few of its proposals, however, were greeted in the Synod with such hostility that the image of the report was tarnished.

What caused the opposition was largely the question of clerical tenure. Recognising that in many areas the traditional one-incumbent-per-parish pattern had broken down, it suggested a system which was considered revolutionary. It provided for different kinds of parochial unit: the traditional parish for a settled community, the pastorate for an area where the traditional community had broken down due to population movement, where the work of the church needed to be done through a larger unit than the existing parish. The pastorate would be a team ministry, served by a rector, vicar(s) and/or curate(s). The third kind of parochial unit envisaged was the chaplaincy, which would operate in areas which were unable to sustain either of the other types of unit but in which tourist influxes or other circumstances sometimes exceeded the needs of the permanent local community. The chaplaincy would be served by a rector or vicar with the help of a curate or priests released for a short period each year from parishes and pastorates. Believing that the system for appointing an incumbent gave too much influence to the individual parish, made movement between parishes and dioceses too difficult and detracted from an awareness of the needs of the Church of Ireland as a whole, the Committee put forward a detailed clerical mobility scheme in which an approximate time-scale existed for progress from the first curacy through to a rectory. Incumbents would be expected to move at regular intervals (like Methodist ministers) and parishes would have a more limited role to play in appointments. The message was driven home in forceful terms:

> To perpetuate the existing system would be disastrous. It was designed to suit circumstances that no longer exist throughout the country: it does not allow the church to make the best use of the gifts and energies of her clergy: and it serves to increase the rigidity of her pastoral organisation.

The present system cannot be satisfactorily patched up. . . . Makeshifts
will not do.[73]

Clergy mobility was closely linked to a revised scheme of diocesan
organisation on the basis that there were too many cathedrals and accompanying dignitaries and that it was impossible to enjoy 'the fuller
life of worship and witness that a cathedral normally should present
to a diocese'.[74] Excluding St Patrick's Cathedral the Committee
wanted there to be only one cathedral with one chapter and one archdeacon in each diocese or united diocese.

Exception to the last regulation was advised for Dublin and Glendalough because of the 'particularly heavy representational duties'
of the archbishop. Given that 'an archdeacon is intended to be the
bishop's assistant in administrative matters and his usefulness in
this respect depends partly upon the extent to which the bishop is
prepared to delegate authority to him', the Committee believed that
the archdeacon should be appointed by the bishop whom he was
to serve but that he should hold office for five years only.
Dignitaries moving from one diocese to another in accordance with
the mobility scheme might lose the dignity they held and the Committee remarked that in this respect there would be 'a noteworthy
contrast between the clergy and other professions. This could well
encourage a detached attitude to matters of rank and status'.[75]

The Committee believed that it was achieving something for the
clergy by offering a more just and flexible set-up but its efforts were
not appreciated. Some of the clergy were very upset and felt their
position was threatened. The report was criticised, sometimes in
bitter words as 'left-wing', 'undemocratic' or 'uncaring'. None of
these labels fitted: care for the welfare of the clergy was apparent
in every section which related to them, in seeking a manageable
parochial unit and work-load, a rectory which was easy and
economical to run, in questioning the practice of using it as
part-home, part-office, in recommending a new and equitable pay
structure, a life assurance scheme, and adequate provision for
retirement and for clergy widows and orphans. Had the recommendations been implemented, the church's care of the clergy would
have been significantly improved. Some of the provisions have
been put into practice over the years, with benefit.

Consideration of church buildings was integral to this scheme of
reorganisation at diocesan and parochial level. The committee's
recommendations were based on those of the Sparsely Populated
Areas Commission and the City and Town Parishes Commission
and gave priority to spiritual considerations. Under the title 'A

tendency to put churches before the Church' the report opined that

the rather rigid territorial pastoral system that we have inherited . . . can
. . . foster such a fierce local loyalty, usually centred on its church
buildings, that the mission of the church there and elsewhere is positively
obstructed. This is sometimes the case even when all pastoral justification
for retaining a church has gone. For such a superficial and mistaken idea
of stewardship the church as a whole pays dearly; all too often her sense
of mission is imprisoned — in a church.[76]

The question remains: was the report too radical? Rather it seems
to have outpaced progress within the Church of Ireland and may
have underestimated the resistance to change. It also suffered from
its presentation in forceful, sometimes stark language. All the Committee members favoured a report which addressed the subject in
direct terms but in the process of condensing it and in the hurry to
get it completed, it became terse. There was some feeling that the
report required an amount of rewriting to ensure acceptability at
the General Synod: Canon Elliott recalls the advice of one prominent Dublin layman after studying the report: 'Get George to
rewrite it and you'll get it through the Synod.'[77] The archbishop,
however, made no bid to rewrite it, the report was presented as it
stood and it was not favourably received.

Dr Simms played an active role as chairman and his comments
and suggestions were always taken seriously. He did not, however,
figure prominently in the actual wording of the report, the terseness
of which is most unlike his style. There are only two sections in
which the archbishop's input is unmistakable, once when the
phrase 'little flock'[78] is used for the people in a sparsely-populated
diocese, a borrowing from Eric Abbott's inspirational sermon
on the occasion of his consecration as Bishop of Cork in 1952,
and secondly with reference to the proposed removal of west
Glendalough and Kildare from the Dublin diocese as part of the
diocesan reorganisation. A rider was added: 'the Archbishop of
Dublin wishes to record that his acceptance of these particular proposals, as being ultimately in the best interests of the church, in no
way implies a lessening of his personal concern and affection, as
their present Father in God, for the clergy and people of Glendalough and Kildare'.[79] The statements of spiritual objectives are
couched in terms such as the archbishop used but the more urgent
attempts to drive home the point are much more forthright than
any of his pronouncements, yet he did not try to use his chairmanship to promote a more cautious report. His consciousness of grassroot feelings must have made him aware that the report would not

The bishops in session at the 1958 Lambeth Conference. G.O.S. is seventh in the front row on the left. Dr Geoffrey Fisher, Archbishop of Canterbury, at the table centre right.

Above: G.O.S. proceeding to St Fin Barre's Cathedral, Cork, for his consecration as bishop, on 28 October 1952, preceded by T. Perrott (verger), and followed by J.H.Hingston and R.G.F.Jenkins. Below: A family group at the Palace, Cork, December 1956. *Seated:* Hilary, Katherine, John; *standing,* Nicholas, G.O.S., M.F.S., Christopher.

Above: G.O.S. and Harry Simms at Portnoo, Co.Donegal, 1957. Below: Opening of Booterstown National School, Co.Dublin, March 1957. Lt Col. Brennan, An Taoiseach, Eamonn de Valera, R.H.Bertram, E.M.Batement, G.O.S. Photo, Irish Times.

M.F.S. in New York as Girls' Friendly Society World President in 1960.

Archbishop Ramsey's visit to Dublin in 1967. Left to right: the Archbishop of Canterbury, G.O.S., J.Andrew, Archbishop McQuaid, J.M.G.Carey.

Above: At the Anglican Congress in Toronto, 1963. G.O.S. in conversation with Bishop W.H.Gray of Connecticut. On extreme right is Dr A.M.Ramsey, Archbishop of Canterbury, with Archbishop James McCann of Armagh next to him. Below: the two Archbishops of **Dublin**, G.O.S. and Dr J.C.McQuaid.

Above: Rededication of All Saints' Church, Grangegorman, May 1968. Below: The Palace, Armagh, 1976. Photo, Richard Scott.

Above: the See House, Armagh, in 1976. Photo, Richard Scott. Below: Peace campaign press conference at the Palace, Armagh, in 1974. Rev. Harold Sloan (Methodist President), Cardinal Cornway, Dr A.J.Weir (Clerk of the Presbyterian Assembly), G.O.S., Rt Rev. Temple Lundie (Presbyterian Moderator).

be well-received, yet his optimistic nature and his constant readiness for God to intervene made him accede to the report as it developed. Perhaps the language of the report was immaterial. Undoubtedly the church is conservative and synodical government makes the process of reform slow and difficult. *Administration 1967* is by no means the only report which failed in its objectives; cynics often question the function of reports, wondering if they are not more intended to allay trouble than to expedite reform! Dr Simms shared the hope of his fellow committee-members that the report would be considered as a whole, accepted in principle, and systematically implemented. Some of its proposals were gradually implemented — the number of dioceses was reduced, synods were amalgamated in certain areas, unneeded churches were closed, non-stipendiary ministry developed, composition of nomination boards was altered to reduce local influence, team ministries came into operation in a few places, some stipendiary improvements were made, new compact rectories were built, the appointment of youth officers was sanctioned, but these have been piecemeal reforms, often dictated by financial rather than spiritual consideration. No large-scale reorganisation has been attempted and the envisaged renewal has not taken place.

All the surviving members of the Committee are adamant that Dr Simms could have done no more at Synod to secure acceptance of the report. Even his considerable influence was ineffective and any attempt to win over the opposition might have led to an even more emotional reaction. Sad as he was about the reception of the report, Dr Simms accepted it as the rough which accompanies the smooth in democratic government, steadfastly refused to be downcast or embittered and did not let it upset his work as archbishop. On the rare occasions when he found himself in the centre of bitter controversy he adhered to the highest Christian standards of charity; no enemies were ever made, no grudges held. At subsequent synods he often referred to the report and affirmed its value in gentle, encouraging tones.

When Archbishop McCann announced his retirement in 1969 it was almost unthinkable that anyone other than George Simms would become primate. Always prepared to face up to his responsibilities, he was nevertheless daunted as all his ministry had been in the South, except for his short spell in Lincoln, and he knew how difficult it would be to preach the Gospel and gain acceptance in the North.

An additional factor in the worry about taking on the primacy was the increasingly disturbed state of Northern Ireland. During the mid-sixties hopeful signs had appeared that the traditional suspicion and hostility between the Protestant and Catholic communities were beginning to be overcome. An improved political atmosphere was created by the willingness of Captain Terence O'Neill, who became Prime Minister of Northern Ireland in 1963, to cross the community divide, bringing to an end four decades during which Roman Catholics had the distinct impression that governments regarded them as second-class citizens. With economic conditions improving steadily, people from both communities could look forward to increased prosperity in a peaceful and progressive Northern Ireland. In addition, cross-border relations began to thaw for the first time when the Taoiseach, Seán Lemass, travelled to Belfast in 1965 to meet Captain O'Neill.

These hopeful signs proved a false dawn. Politicians from the Catholic side became increasingly impatient; O'Neill's goodwill was all very well but they needed positive action to end discrimination in local government, housing and employment. In 1968 the Northern Ireland Civil Rights Association was founded and a series of marches and demonstrations began. A more extreme attitude had also begun to make itself felt on the Protestant side. Many traditional Unionists had been uneasy about O'Neill's policy and his leadership came under increasing pressure. The most vocal of his opponents, the Rev. Ian Paisley, Moderator of the Free Presbyterian Church, had already become notorious as the archenemy of ecumenism, leading protests against any contacts between the reformed churches and Rome. He drummed up such strongly anti-Catholic hostility that several of the civil rights marches and rallies ended in disorder and bloodshed. He entered the political arena and effectively ruined any chance O'Neill might have had of holding the middle ground of Unionism. In April 1969 the Prime Minister resigned and the primatial election two and a half months later took place against a background of community mistrust and political uncertainty.

Already, in January 1969, the leaders of the four main Irish churches, recognising the extremely dangerous situation which was developing in Northern Ireland, had taken a significant step towards presenting a united response to communal disturbances. Meeting together officially for the very first time, the four leaders decided to set up an *ad hoc* committee to advise them on the developing situation. This committee, which had two Roman Catholic members, one each from the Church of Ireland, Presbyterian Church and Methodist Church and one nominee of

the Irish Council of Churches, had a valuable function in counter-
ing the simplistic impression that was beginning to gain credence
internationally: that it was the churches, not just the communities,
that were at each other's throats.

A letter to Raymond Jenkins shortly before the primatial election
on 17 July reveals Dr Simms' state of mind.[80] 'I am afraid things
look more and more as if I'll have to let myself be considered
on Thursday — I am fearfully torn . . . we must just pray that
the right decision in all the difficult circumstances is made —
problems bristle in it all — the house, the disturbances, and the
paucity of Northern bishops, all add up to a complex that is
unenviable.'

Yet when he realised that he was the unanimous choice of his
fellow bishops he accepted with good grace. He didn't pretend to
look forward to his translation ('it's not something anyone would
seek') but humbly said that 'I have the feeling of being sent to serve
and will do my best'. Identifying a need for greater understanding
of the problems in the North he continued, 'getting to know the
people and getting to hear the other side requires patience and commitment which I am afraid can never be satisfactorily mine'.

In farewell he said 'Dublin has been wonderful to me, and I've been
tremendously happy here'.[81] Dublin was sad to see him go and tributes
poured in from all sides. He had indeed been happy, as had his wife and
family. When they came to Dublin their youngest child was only three.
When they left for Armagh the three eldest were grown up, Hilary was
in Alexandra College and John was at St Columba's College. As the
children had grown more independent Mrs Simms had become involved in a number of organisations in Dublin. Never keen to be in the
limelight, she had worked quietly behind the scenes where possible.
Mention has already been made of her work for the Church of Ireland
Social Service Society; she was also involved with the Protestant Child
Care Association and the Magdalen Home. Always committed to practical ecumenical endeavour, she tried to establish a Dublin Housing Aid
Society in conjunction with the Countess of Wicklow, Daithi Hanly
and others. What they envisaged was a parallel to Father Eamonn
Casey's[82] Catholic Housing Aid in London. With a broad ecumenical
base, it set up an advisory office and bought one or two half-way
houses but it eventually failed and its work was taken over by the
Roman Catholic archdiocese. The work was not wasted, in that it
opened the way for another agency; it was, however, significant that
the wife of the Church of Ireland Archbishop of Dublin was involved.
She was also a member of the Government Advisory Committee on
Itinerancy and her work in this field was recognised when she was

invited to speak about it at a Catholic Social Study Conference. Shortly after coming to Dublin Mrs Simms was appointed all-Ireland president of the Girls' Friendly Society. As Dublin was due to host the next meeting of the international council she became international president for a time. Most of all she enjoyed the international aspect of the Society and, as a pacifist, was enthused by the idea of international friendship. She was also a member of the Anti-Apartheid Movement but didn't join in their marches until her husband retired, lest she should put him in an embarrassing position.

Her most important role continued to be in support of the archbishop. A great number of visitors were received at the See House; formal visitors, like members of the diplomatic corps, who were entertained to tea, distinguished churchmen who stayed with the Simmses while preaching or speaking in Dublin, a host of friends, academics, clergy, some of whom joined in the family meal. Mrs Simms accompanied her husband to many formal dinners in Dublin. As Archbishop McQuaid rarely attended these, Dr Simms was usually the chief clerical guest of honour and Mrs Simms often sat beside the Taoiseach of the day.

Mrs Simms followed the political scene with interest and on one occasion took an initiative of her own. In 1965 there was quite a fanfare for the visit of Seán Lemass to Stormont to talk with the Prime Minister of Northern Ireland, Captain Terence O'Neill. A couple of years later when Mr Lynch became Taoiseach, Mrs Simms arranged a private lunch at the See House for Mrs Lynch and Mrs O'Neill, who was in Dublin for a Mothers' Union meeting. Nobody knew about it, least of all the press, and she felt she had achieved something.

Apart from occasions when his wife was expected to attend, Mrs Simms did not accompany her husband to many functions. She rarely went with him on trips abroad but she did go to the Lambeth Conference in 1958 and was very embarrassed to find herself prominently placed as his wife. At forty-three she felt very young in such a gathering. Clearly she felt her role was as home-maker and she did not get deflected from her purpose. She would never interfere in the archbishop's concerns but always took an interest in anything he shared with her. His strict rule of confidentiality extended to her but he was grateful that she would read a vast amount of printed material that appeared in his post and digest it for him. It was a great help in keeping abreast of new thinking.

In normal times an archbishop being translated from Dublin to Armagh could have looked forward to a lighter workload. The burden in Dublin had become very great, although Dr Simms was reluctant to admit it. Press photographs of the sixties often reveal a tiredness he could not hide.

During Dr Simms' episcopate there was some discussion about the need for an auxiliary bishop in Dublin. Nothing came of this but for some years Dr Simms was able to avail of the help of Bishop Willis. Unlike his English counterparts, the Archbishop of Dublin did not enjoy the services of a private or domestic chaplain. Such an appointment would have relieved him of a great burden of routine and preparatory work but Dr Simms never complained, even in the early years when he didn't have a secretary either. The increased pace of life, sharp challenges to the faith, frequent and distant travel abroad, and greater Church of Ireland involvement in Irish life placed greater pressure on Dr Simms than on his predecessors. His extraordinary physical stamina and overall resilience meant that he could cope but his very energy made it difficult for his successors. Despite the fact that tenure of the see broke the health of Archbishops Buchanan and McAdoo, the problem has still not been addressed; even allowing for resistance to change, the absence of real debate is probably partly a legacy of the Simms energy. When concerned people told him he was overworked and needed an auxiliary bishop, full-time archdeacon or domestic chaplain he shrugged it off, assuring them that he was all right.

When Dr Simms left Dublin there was great sadness in the diocese. The morale of the Church of Ireland was higher than at any time since 1922 and its people were now truly integrated into Irish society. The improvement in the ecumenical climate was largely attributable to Dr Simms, who was a well-known and much admired public figure. His years as archbishop were fruitful and fulfilling; he was about to enter the most difficult phase of his ministry.

VII

ARCHBISHOP OF ARMAGH

Dr Simms never knew a normal primacy. Even before he had taken up residence in Armagh the situation in Northern Ireland deteriorated so much that he found himself embroiled. Tensions had been rising since the Orangemen's traditional demonstrations on 12 July and the Apprentice Boys' march in Derry on 12 August sparked off riots there. In West Belfast Roman Catholics took to the streets in sympathy and when the police were sent in, they were followed by Protestant mobs who burned down a large number of houses in which Roman Catholics lived. The first deaths of the Northern 'troubles' occurred that night. The next day, 15 August, British troops were sent in to restore peace. The intervention of the army, at first welcomed by the Roman Catholic population, led to much deeper involvement by the British government in Northern Ireland. Northern Ireland affairs fell within the sphere of the Home Secretary; no previous incumbent had felt it necessary to visit the province but Mr James Callaghan came within a fortnight, in the vain hope of restoring peace. He aimed to achieve reforms which would remove Roman Catholic grievances and lead to a return to 'normality' under the Stormont government.

When the violence erupted in Belfast Dr Simms was at a meeting of the Central Committee of the World Council of Churches in Canterbury. In the first anxious days he kept in touch with advisers by telephone but soon decided that he should absent himself from Canterbury and fly to Belfast. Initially he hoped to return to Canterbury but that proved impossible. He preached in St Anne's Cathedral, Belfast, on Sunday 17 August, on the theme 'Father, forgive' and in the evening spoke in four churches in the worst affected areas. He met with other leaders of the Protestant churches on 18 August and attended the first session of the community conference summoned by the government to meet at Stormont on the following day. During that week he made his first television broadcasts on the Northern situation and issued a pastoral letter to be read in all churches in Northern Ireland on Sunday 24 August. That day he preached in the Cathedral and all five city churches in Derry, in an effort to bring calm there. On 27 August he and the other church leaders met with Mr Callaghan for the first time. He relied heavily for guidance on Canon E. P. M. Elliott, the Church of Ireland member of the *ad hoc* committee appointed in the spring of 1969 to keep the church leaders informed on the developing situation.[1] The committee met almost daily during the latter half of August, so no one in the Church of Ireland was better placed to advise the primate than Canon Elliott. Dr Simms stayed with the Elliotts during three difficult weeks; at that time their warm hospitality and the canon's local knowledge were a great support for him. Together the two men walked the riot-torn streets each evening, seeking a deeper understanding of the conflict, and speaking to Protestant and Roman Catholic alike of peace and reconciliation.

The primate's presence in the streets of Belfast in those weeks was later instanced by David Bleakley in his *Peace in Ulster* to show that the Northern conflict was not a religious war.[2] He started his chapter 'No Holy War' as follows:

Belfast . . . an evening in August 1969. The barricades were up and tension was high in the working-class district. Into the maze of shipyard streets came the Archbishop of Armagh, Primate of All Ireland, on one of his meet the people walkabouts. As he turned into Seaforde Street, Roman Catholic heartland of East Belfast, the people surged out in their hundreds to greet him.

Bleakley recorded the hastily prepared tea and the relaxation of tension, highlighting the significance of the occasion;

this Primate was Dr George Simms, a leader of the Protestant community and head of the Church of Ireland; he was being received in the centre of St Matthew's Catholic parish; and all at a time when communal violence was near at hand.[3]

Bleakley's point was that no-one who knew Dr Simms and understood the religious situation in Northern Ireland should be surprised at his presence in Roman Catholic areas of Belfast, nor at the welcome he received. Although his was not as much a household name in the North as it was in the Republic, Roman Catholics welcomed him for his warmth and caring. He did not recognise 'no-go' areas, he neither expected nor received hostility. In fact throughout his years in Armagh the hostility he encountered was rarely from Roman Catholics, but rather from extreme Protestants.

Dr Simms' presence was all the more important in the early

stages of the conflict because three of the Northern bishops were on the point of retirement and the fourth, Bishop A. A. Buchanan of Clogher, was translated to Dublin in September. For some time the primate was the only bishop really active in the North and then, with four new bishops, there was a period of settling in during which his leadership was particularly necessary.

It was important for the witness of the Church of Ireland in the new-found tragic situation that the primate left an international gathering to be there. There was general identification within the church with the active role he took in promoting peace and reconciliation. His approach accorded with that taken by the Bishop of Down and Dromore for instance. Age and infirmity made it impossible for Bishop Mitchell to walk the streets or to engage in whistle-stop preaching tours of his dioceses but he summoned his clergy to return from holiday to their parishes and held a special meeting of the diocesan council on 20 August to consider the situation. From that meeting emanated a resolution to be read in every church on the following Sunday, expressing the same positive message as did the primate. Bishop Buchanan was also out on the streets fulfilling the same role until his departure for Dublin.

During those weeks the archbishop was in frequent demand for radio and television interviews at short notice and he began to experience the inherent difficulties. In Dublin he had rarely had to make an instant response to a complex question; in the highly-charged atmosphere of Northern Ireland, where it soon happened that almost every day some act of aggression or atrocity was committed, he was expected to give instant replies to a barrage of questions. Even when he was in residence in the palace he had no clerical secretary to parry the first line of questions, unlike the Roman Catholic primate, Cardinal Conway. One thing he did was to initiate a Church of Ireland Information Centre, based in St Anne's Cathedral, to enable the Church of Ireland to cope with mass-media communication.

Although he absolutely refused to assume the quasi-political role which seemed to offer itself, he could not avoid some political involvement and that inevitably meant that what he said was always wrong in some people's eyes. In every pronouncement, however, he weighed his words carefully for fear of hurting anyone. His first concern was always to proclaim the Gospel and so he talked repeatedly about peacemaking, reconciliation and love. These themes were reiterated wherever he spoke; on radio and television, to the press, in sermons, at synods and other meetings. Preaching at his enthronement on 26 September 1969, on the text 'They continued steadfastly' (Acts 2.42), by implication he directed much of his sermon towards Christian mission in Northern Ireland. Pointing to the ideal of the 'servant church', he expressed hope for the 'removal of ambiguities, misunderstanding and mere slogans, as Church of Ireland members attain a greater understanding of their own beliefs, of service and of relations with other churches.' One of the criticisms of his primacy was that he talked of peace rather than justice, but here, at the beginning he stated 'it will be our aim and endeavour . . . to explore new ways . . . of proclaiming the essentials of the Gospel of love and justice'.

On his arrival in Armagh he found that a programme of conferences throughout the diocese had already been drawn up to mark the centenary of Disestablishment. He agreed to be speaker at all five meetings: thus he gained an opportunity to meet his people and to exchange views with them. Likewise, in his presidential address to his first diocesan synod in October 1969 he said 'The importance of expressing opinion that is balanced, free from self-interest, free from fear, but rather informed and tested by the faith of our church, expressed in the Bible and biblically spelt out in *The Book of Common Prayer*, can scarcely be exaggerated in these troubled days'.

One might ask what was the reaction of the Church of Ireland people in the diocese and more generally in Northern Ireland to their new archbishop? Many who appreciated his stature in the church were very pleased at his appointment. The more closely they were involved with the life of the church, the more they valued his qualities. On the other hand a great number were highly suspicious, viewing him as an Irish-speaking Republican. The presence of representatives of the President and Cardinal Conway at his enthronement did not cause universal pleasure. For many years primates had come from the South but in the new troubles in Northern Ireland, the appointment of a 'Southerner', albeit from Donegal, suggested an outsider interfering in internal affairs.

Some of what he said did not go down well. When he pointed out that there was need for repentance on both sides, that Protestants in the North shared the responsibility for the troubles, many grumbled in disapproval. At those first conferences around his diocese he faced thorny questions about the Orange order and 'the Romeward trend' of the ecumenical movement. His answer invariably was that 'in the new climate' it would be good if the Orange order would re-express the language of its charter in positive, fresh terms to reflect changes in attitudes of Roman Catholics since Vatican II and if it would detach itself from identity with any one political party. He always reassured his audience that 'the Romeward trend' of the ecumenical movement was illusory and that there was nothing to fear. Despite the fact that his answers displeased some, the meetings were harmonious. A few hard-liners came with the intention of barracking but kept their peace. They may have disliked his opinions but they could not take exception to the love, warmth and gentleness with which he expressed them. His sheer goodness was the key to his acceptance in the North. Gradually too, they realised that he was going to be supportive of the government and that was reassuring. On the other hand he was criticised for this by those, mostly in the Republic, who believed that the government offered too little too late. It was a very delicate balance; Christianity teaches support for legitimate authority, but on social and human issues the church frequently has to criticise that authority, without undermining it. Canon Elliott at a very early stage recognised the conundrum: 'If you're a strong leader you antagonise, if you seek to be conciliatory and fair, you're "weak" '.[4] Certainly he always tried to be conciliatory and fair and was often deemed weak. Canon John Barry writes 'Some would say he lacked decisiveness — "steel" — maybe so — but "steel" is not something I ever wanted in him.'[5] What many people sought was 'a strong leader' of the Protestant community. Unlike Ian Paisley, George Simms never wished to assume that role, for he knew that he would be sucked into the political maelstrom. He did wish to be a strong spiritual leader of the Church of Ireland but his task was made vastly more difficult by the fact that many were so imbued with the bitterness of strife that they would not listen to him.

One of his problems was that he didn't speak the same language as his Northern listeners. His classical turn of phrase, his Anglo-Irish accent, his way of couching unpalatable truths in gentle terms, were in stark contrast to the direct Northern way of 'calling a spade a spade'. In some situations in the seventies it was almost impossible to say anything, so tragic and complex had the issues become, yet there were many times when it would have been helpful if Dr Simms had been able to express himself in terms more assimilable by his people. He was aware of this handicap and was grateful that some of his clergy, notably his last archdeacon, F. W. Gowing, had a flair for expressing the mind of the church on quasi-political matters in words with which the man in the pew readily identified. In the long run, Dr Simms' insistence on peace and reconcilation was influential to a degree but the Christian life he led was more influential than anything he said.

He quickly won acceptance among the clergy and those of the

laity who came into personal contact with him but made little headway with those who did not. The degree of acceptance was attested by a standing ovation which he received at the 1971 diocesan synod. J. A. Anderson, pre-empting a challenge to the archbishop, read a statement on behalf of the lay members, setting out their appreciation of his leadership of the Church of Ireland. Recalling the primate's visits in the autumn of 1969 to rectors and parishioners who had suffered violence and intimidation he said, 'Your presence on those occasions was much appreciated and acted as a wonderful tonic.' He urged critics to remember how difficult it was to be primate of a divided island, to issue a statement which was acceptable to people on both sides of the border. Recognising that the archbishop always brought his saintliness of character to bear on solving problems, he finally thanked him for his 'magnificent leadership and understanding of the many complexities'.[6] That the speaker was an Orangeman, as was the seconder, and that the house rose for a standing ovation, testifies to their love and respect for him.

On Dr Simms' appointment to Armagh *The Irish Times* had stated that he 'has the making of an influential catalyst', a 'bridge-builder'.[7] The archbishop was indeed in a unique position to develop relations between the Roman Catholic and the Protestant churches because of his widespread contacts with members of all churches, and his understanding of their traditions. It was known that he was a person through whom approaches could be made, in whose house meetings could take place, who would support any constructive ideas. The leaders of the four main churches had first met together in January 1969, at the instigation of the Irish Council of Churches, when they established the *ad hoc* committee. As the situation worsened their meetings become so regular that the advisory committee became unnecessary. It was remarkable that they managed to reach consensus, for a 'them' and 'us' outlook prevailed in society amidst the constant turmoil and it took a great deal of courage to maintain impartiality.[8] During Dr Simms' primacy their meetings became so frequent that the entire inter-church scene at the top level was transformed. He played a vital role by his encouragement of the other leaders: the Methodist and Presbyterian leaders changed every year, which led to repeated interruptions of momentum, and progress was seriously slowed by the death of Cardinal Conway in 1977. In providing an element of continuity, Dr Simms was able to maintain a positive atmosphere at the meetings.

Cardinal Conway and Archbishop Simms became very close. In

the early stages their mutual understanding was aided by the fact that the cardinal did not drive a car and accepted Dr Simms' offer of a lift to meetings. Such journeys proved a good way of getting to know each other to a degree which was unheard of previously for the two primates. The cardinal, having grown up in West Belfast, understood the attitudes of working-class Roman Catholics. A former Professor of Moral Theology and Canon Law at St Patrick's College, Maynooth, he had as Archbishop of Armagh taken part in the later stages of the second Vatican Council. Inspired by the ecumenical spirit of the Council and by his relationship with Dr Simms, he developed a new warmth towards other denominations and his approach to joint initiatives in the years that followed was positive if cautious.

When the four leaders had issued their first joint request to the Irish people to pray and work for peace, on New Year's Day, 1968, they were afraid actually to meet lest they cause an uproar among their own adherents and had negotiated by telephone, letter and personal emissary. Before the end of 1969 not only were they meeting frequently to discuss the Northern crisis, but they had held two informal meetings on the theological differences which separated their churches. This represented a major breakthrough and initially the very fact of their meeting for informal discussion was more important than anything they said. It was probably easier for Dr Simms to enter such dialogue than for any of the other leaders, given his international ecumenical experience and the '*via media*' stance of his church. In claiming to be both catholic and reformed it had distanced itself both from the long-held claims of the Roman Catholic Church to be the one true church and from the anti-Roman bias of the non-conformists. Also, as a sizeable proportion of Church of Ireland members lived in the Republic the consensus in his church was somewhat more broad-minded than in the non-conformist churches, whose membership was concentrated in north-east Ulster.

In 1970 the four leaders guided the individual churches to appoint a Joint Group on Social Questions. The group operated by setting up working parties to report on such matters as drug abuse, pollution and housing. Its most significant report in terms of the troubled situation was *Violence in Ireland, a Report to the Churches*,[9] Published in 1976 after fourteen difficult plenary sessions it was an unanimously agreed document drawn up under the joint chairmanship of Bishop C. B. Daly, then Bishop of Ardagh and Clonmacnoise, and the Rev. Dr R. D. E. Gallagher. Unfortunately its many valuable observations and recommendations were not translated speedily into action by the churches. The Joint Group's reports suffered in the same way as did the leaders' joint statement and appeals. First, the churches trusted too much in their efficacy and secondly were slow to develop other, practical, methods of addressing the problem.

In their treatise on the troubles, *Christians in Ulster 1968–1980*, Eric Gallagher and Stanley Worrall dwell on this point.[10] The one a prominent Methodist minister, the other the Methodist lay headmaster of the Methodist College, Belfast, they were both closely involved in the traumatic events of those years and sought to give a Christian perspective on them.

The concluding chapter attempts an evaluation of the role of the churches in the conflict; it explains the dilemma which they faced. Joint statements were not merely a device of the churches, but were

initially expected and sought by the professional communicators and the politicians. They seemed to think that the churches could work miracles of which the secular world was incapable. In this expectation they were exaggerating the religious element of the conflict; they thought that, if Roman Catholic and Protestant churchmen said the same thing, there would be nothing left to fight about. . . Today, however, there is a cynicism regarding frequently repeated statements emanating from whatever quarter. It is not merely that repetition can be counterproductive. The sad fact would seem to be that the churches have been learning the same kind of lesson that the producers of documentary programmes have done. No matter how well researched and objective a programme is, more frequently than not it had tended to reinforce rather than to remove prejudices. Too often the reaction to church statements had been to pick out and emphasize the element in the statement that is acceptable and to deplore the absence of something else, which, if it had been included, would almost certainly have been ignored.[11]

As Gallagher and Worrall point out, the joint Protestant communique on internment of 9 August 1971 was a poignant example of this.

To bring the political narrative up to date, Mr Callaghan's reform programme pushed ahead from the autumn of 1969 but did not avert a winter of discontent and rioting. Northern Ireland in the two years between the arrival on the streets of British troops and the introduction of internment had lurched from one crisis to another. At first the main threat to the peace being precariously held by the troops seemed likely to come from the loyalist community where bitterness and resentment at the reforms being promoted by Mr Callaghan simmered and occasionally boiled over. By early 1970, however, the first policemen had died and the

Unionist government of Major James Chichester-Clark was putting pressure on the military authorities to take a more aggressive line against nationalists, especially in the so-called 'no-go areas' of Derry and West Belfast.

So long as a Labour government remained in power at Westminster, political advances seemed likely to prevail over the 'military solution' to the problem of Northern Ireland favoured by so many within the Protestant community. However, in June 1970 the government of Mr Harold Wilson was defeated in the United Kingdom general election and Mr Edward Heath's Conservatives came to power. It was no surprise when British troops moved forcefully into the Bogside in Derry and into nationalist areas of West Belfast in the weeks following the Conservative election victory.

It is now clear that the events of June 1970 were pivotal in bringing into existence as the most violent and most enduring of republican paramilitary forces the Provisional I.R.A. Their grip on the Roman Catholic communities of Derry and West Belfast tightened during the autumn and winter and the number of confrontations with the army increased steadily.

In March 1971 Major Chichester-Clark resigned and Mr Brian Faulkner became Prime Minister of Northern Ireland. Although he made some notable conciliatory gestures, he was expected to take a more hard-line stance and he favoured a policy of internment. In August the decision was taken to round up and intern those suspected of sedition. However, when the decision was implemented on 9 August, it was only suspects from the Catholic community who were rounded up; Protestant paramilitaries remained at large.

The time of the introduction of internment was the worst in Dr Simms' life. Cardinal Conway made an immediate response to the news, abhorring internment but appealing to Roman Catholics to stay calm. As Dr Simms and the President of the Methodist Church were on holiday no immediate response was made by them but the government, through the Ministry for Community Relations, was pressing for church support for its ban on loyalist marches, which was imposed as a counterbalance to internment. Accordingly, the appointed substitutes of the Protestant leaders issued a statement on their behalf, urging loyalist acceptance of the ban and giving qualified support for internment. It was difficult to accept the principle of internment, for it was an infringement of human rights but it was recognised that it was aimed at the paramilitaries who were destroying the human rights of Roman Catholics and Protestants alike. Dr Simms would have had the opportunity to consider the statement before its appearance had not the telephones to Portnoo been jammed. As time wore on, it seemed necessary to proceed and so it appeared on the evening of 9 August.

To make matters worse an early morning news bulletin on 10 August confused the two main points of the statement — 'We regret the necessity for the introduction of internment', and 'We welcome the acceptance of the Government's decision by those planning the march proposed for Thursday next', giving the erroneous impression that the leaders welcomed internment. The statement was pounced on by one side as evidence of favouring repression, by the other as inadequate support for authority. Dr Simms returned in haste from Portnoo. Had he been in residence at Armagh he would have done everything possible to avoid making any statement on internment which did not emanate from all four leaders but it was unthinkable that he would try to ease his own position by disclaiming responsibility. Instead he tried to speak on television in terms of the lesser of two evils and of the need for monitoring its operation. Inevitably this was not very convincing and some of his friends tried to relieve the anger in some quarters at his apparent support for internment by making it clear that he had been away when the statement was drawn up. Now he was under fire from both sides; those who had approved of the statement were furious at the implication that he did not subscribe to it.[12]

Many of his close friends and associates say that the only time they have seen Dr Simms really upset was then. He would not discuss the issue off the record with anyone but he suffered intensely. In those agonising weeks he practised what Bonhoeffer had taught in *The Cost of Discipleship*. Christ's disciples 'renounce all self-assertion and quietly suffer in the face of hatred and wrong. In so doing they overcome evil with good, and establish the peace of God in the midst of a world of war and hate.'[13] Despite the ridicule and hatred he continued to love and never despaired. No one ever heard him complain or saw him indulge in self-pity.

Another incident which demonstrates his understanding of discipleship occurred at an ecumenical service to mark the establishment of the new town of Craigavon. A crude opposition was in attendance, with the intention of disrupting the worship. When a Roman Catholic priest came forward to read a lesson, some of them up-ended the lectern. Dr Simms quietly went and put it upright again. Mercifully his attitude prevailed and the service continued after the congregation had clapped in approval.

There were other bridge-building initiatives in which Archbishop

Simms was always in the vanguard, the chief of which were the Ballymascanlon Conferences. These, the first official conferences between the Roman Catholic Church and the other churches, arose from an Irish Council of Churches request to Cardinal Conway for a working party on joint pastoral problems in Ireland. Eighty delegates from all the main churches attended the first Conference on 26 September 1973. Chaired jointly by Cardinal Conway and Dr Simms (as Chairman of the Irish Council of Churches), it established working parties to consider vital issues. Afterwards the Cardinal was reported as saying that 'nobody who had attended yesterday's inter-church talks . . . would ever be the same again'.[14] While he was right in implying that it marked a significant new departure, it brought far less change than was generally anticipated. Dr Simms, who looks back on the Conferences as the great religious breakthrough of his time as primate, was nevertheless, careful to stress from the outset that the 1973 Conference was only the beginning of a long process towards mutual understanding.

He faced a lot of sharp questioning over his leadership of the Church of Ireland delegation to Ballymascanlon. His diocesan synod, following shortly upon the Conference, gave him an opportunity to explain it to his people. As always he sought to highlight the positive and acceptable; 'The areas of agreement included our common human concern for the suffering of people in the present violence prevailing as well as the urgent world need of aiding the hungry in the underdeveloped countries.' He went on to reassure: 'There was no question of a "sell-out", as may have been mistakenly supposed by those not present.' . . . (but) 'there was a welcome opportunity to make clear the sincerely held convictions of one church, so that another could appreciate the points of difference and could respect the sincerity of them'.[15] Knowing that the mixed marriages question would be uppermost in the minds of many of his listeners, he went on to express the hope that it could be discussed constructively at subsequent Conferences.

By 1976 there was a marked degree of disillusionment among the Protestant members, most noticeably within the Church of Ireland. A statement by the Role of the Church Committee best illustrates the reasons:

The churches must engage in an open, honest and courageous examination of issues such as church/state relations, law and morality, mixed marriages, experience in integrated education, freedom of conscience and basic human rights. We are bound to say that the unreality of inter-church dialogue hitherto e.g. the Ballymascanlon meetings, is illustrated by an apparent inability to come to grips with these moral, social and practical issues which affect the lives of ordinary people and contribute to the maintenance of divisions based on suspicion and fear.[16]

Disappointment with the lack of concession in the 1976 *Directory on Ecumenism* issued by the Roman Catholic hierarchy, concern over the continued troubles in the North and the controversy over developments within the World Council of Churches, all added to dissatisfaction over Ballymascanlon but Dr Simms used his influence to foster all the positive aspects of the Conference. Undoubtedly he was frequently disappointed at the slow rate of progress but his experience of worldwide ecumenism had already taught him how much patience is required. Disappointment never gave way to despair; he could criticise and still go forward in hope and that was a very important part of his leadership.

While he was wholehearted about developing dialogue, what he said at Ballymascanlon in 1977 illustrates his own approach: 'We cannot solve the problems of this country sitting around tables . . . There is more than one way of a bishop saying a thing. He can have more effect than his words if he goes places — to a trouble spot, a school, a meeting of minds. That is a form of leadership. It is not so much what is said, as what is done that counts.'[17]

To return briefly to the World Council of Churches, anxiety within the Protestant churches in Ulster about the Council's speed in developing relations with the Roman Catholic Church, was manifest before Dr Simms went to Armagh as primate. However, the 1970s grants from the Programme to Combat Racism Fund to organisations such as the Patriotic Front in Rhodesia gave rise to grave concern and finally led to the secession of the Presbyterian Church in Ireland. Dr Simms, always well-informed about international developments and trends within the World Council of Churches, argued cogently against Church of Ireland withdrawal. While he shared the widespread concern, he believed that it was only by continued membership that the Church of Ireland could exert any influence within the Council. He was quick to point out that the grants were only one aspect of the Council's work and that the Church of Ireland had not contributed to them, as they came from a special fund. He felt it necessary, when speaking on the subject at his diocesan synod, to confirm support for the World Council of Churches' opposition to racialism, if not to its methods of combating it. 'As a church,' he stated unequivocally, 'we are opposed to racialism and regimes that promote an apartheid policy'.[18]

Dr Simms was instrumental in dissuading the Council from

sending a joint World Council of Churches-Vatican delegation to investigate the Northern Ireland situation in 1973. Mooted as a 'crisis intervention ministry', the archbishop was convinced that it could not achieve anything at that time and persuaded the other church leaders to write jointly to the Council and the Vatican. Their letter pointed out the inappropriate timing, just as the first Ballymascanlon Conference was about to be held. It also stressed that ultimately the people of Northern Ireland would have to solve their own problem but did not close the door on a possible future visit.

When Dr Simms communicated with the World Council of Churches on Northern Ireland affairs he saw himself not only as primate of the Church of Ireland but as a representative of all who sought a peaceful and just solution. He was often asked to speak in Britain and abroad on the problem and whenever possible he undertook such engagements. He appreciated how shallow the understanding of the Northern conflict was and hoped that he could deepen it. For instance, in 1977 he was invited to Düsseldorf by the Evangelische Kirche to address an ecumenical gathering. Having spoken (in German) for an hour to an audience of 2,000, he was encouraged by the ensuing questions to believe that he had conveyed some of the complexities of the situation and was pleased to receive a promise of support for inter-church and community effort in Northern Ireland.

No one in the province was better equipped to speak on inter-church and community efforts than he. His 'bridge-building' extended to support for the various peace movements and to a large number of community efforts, whether by groups or courageous individuals. Among these were PACE (Protestant and Catholic Encounter), the Corrymeela Community (an ecumenical body with a multi-faceted programme for rapprochement) the Christian Renewal Centre in Rostrevor (the object of which is to work through charismatic renewal to breakdown religious barriers) the Northern Ireland Children's Holiday Scheme (which provides an opportunity for young people of both communities to meet away from Northern Ireland) and the Irish Association for Cultural, Economic and Social Relations.

Archbishop Simms and Cardinal Conway walked together in Armagh at peace marches, the first organised by Women Together.[19] In the early 1970s it required courage to join in such demonstrations and tension frequently ran high. At the beginning of one march the two archbishops encountered a hostile ambulance driver. Dr Simms went to talk to the driver who spat derisively on the primate's shoes. Nothing daunted, Dr Simms continued to talk and after a few more spittings, the driver got out of the ambulance and joined in the march. The easing of tension was palpable. Sadly, like all the other peace movements, Women Together proved ephemeral. The Peace People, which emerged in 1976 enjoyed phenomenal support for a time. It had no direct church links but Dr Simms repeatedly commended its work and the four church leaders were present at a great meeting on the banks of the Boyne in December 1976. Before long it too faded into insignificance but the combined effect of the various movements was to enlist more people on the side of peace. Dr Simms, in supporting such endeavours, did not necessarily expect them to provide a solution or to become permanent forces for good in the province, but he always brought Christian hope to bear in each case.

The two archbishops launched initiatives of their own, in the form of united vigils of prayer in the city and in December 1974 the four church leaders mounted a joint peace campaign, timed to draw inspiration from the Christmas season of goodwill. They appeared together on television, placed full-page advertisements in the papers, held rallies and issued car stickers, in order to mobilise support among the people and hoped that the politicians would use the opportunity for an advance. On the day when they launched their campaign (12 December) the world at large was astonished to hear that the Gardaí had broken up a meeting in Feakle between Protestant churchmen and leaders of the Provisional I.R.A.[20]

Despite the opprobrium visited on the Feakle group for meeting the terrorists, their initiative and that of the church leaders bore some fruit in the winter of 1974–75. Once again hopes were raised and dashed, no permanent solution emerged and it was necessary to try again. When he retired in 1980, Dr Simms regretted that none of the efforts in which he had a part had brought about a lasting peace. No-one could reproach him for lack of effort, however, for he never gave up trying. His constant striving for peace was important for the Church of Ireland and for the Northern community as a whole during the years of his primacy.

How did Dr Simms' stance compare with that of other responsible church leaders in the North and with the four Church of Ireland bishops? In general their pronouncements were similar, in that they were directed at Christian reconciliation, peace and justice. Thus the *Presbyterian Herald* stated that all were sinners and 'it is not possible to justify the claim that either side is taking a Christian way',[21] while Bishop Edward Daly condemned bombers as immoral, saying, 'How can anyone who professes to be a Christian continue to do this sort of thing?'[22] Of course there were instances of a different perspective. For instance in 1972 when Britain introduced direct rule and abolished the Stormont parliament, the Methodist President (the Rev. C. H. Bain) and Archbishop Simms urged upon people the necessity of accepting legitimate authority and of using the new system constructively; the government committee of the Presbyterian Church interpreted it as British concession to the demands of the Provisional I.R.A. and attacked it as a denial of the democratic rights of the majority, while Cardinal Conway reflected Roman Catholic belief that Westminster would be fairer than Stormont and raised Protestant hackles by expressing the hope that it would open the way to eventual agreement on reunification!

There was another difference. Because of the authoritarian structure of the Roman Catholic Church, prelates expect to be able to speak to and command the attention of their people (though the paramilitaries all along ignored their strictures). The Protestant churches, on the other hand, are to a large extent democratic institutions, where major decisions are made by elected clerical and lay representatives. This poses a problem for Protestant church leaders of whatever denomination; as Gallagher and Worrall put it, 'Does the leader speak for or to his people? Does he follow the light of his own insight and hope that he can convince his membership? Or does he put his ear to the ground and give voice to the murmurings he hears?'[23]

It needs to be stated that Christian leadership is radically different from leadership in the secular world, for its prototype is 'the good shepherd' who calls his flock, leads them out and goes before them (John 10. 3–4). Thus the Christian leader's chief purpose is not to devise political solutions or to spearhead social initiatives but to lead people to God. His 'going on before' allows for a prophetic role, and certainly does not suggest that he should limit himself to reflecting the views of the people.[24]

However, a prophet runs the risk of so alienating the people that he can no longer minister to them effectively. Dr Simms, in common with many other Protestant leaders, was acutely aware of the dilemma and trod carefully. They had to judge just how far they could try to lead their people, how much they could say. Thus when Dean C. I. Peacocke became Bishop of Derry he resigned from the Orange Order. Bishop Butler in 1971 attended the requiem mass for Fr Hugh Mullen, a Roman Catholic priest shot dead in the aftermath of internment while giving the last rites to a wounded man, and was one of the Protestant clergymen at Feakle in 1974.

In so doing they ran the risk of alienating their people, but usually managed to walk on the tight-rope. Sadly, however, in Clogher Bishop R. P. C. Hanson was too outspoken to be accepted. His was an appointment made by the House of Bishops in 1970 after the electoral college had failed to reach consensus. An Anglo-Irish theologian, he returned to Ireland from Nottingham and soon found that his liberal views, modern biblical criticism and outspoken denunciation of the Orange Order caused mounting hostility in his diocese.

Although Bishop Hanson was outspoken, and decisive, he did not criticise Dr Simms for his approach. 'Some might have thought he was weak,' he recalled, 'but I gradually came to the conclusion that I must not and could not criticise him but that I must let him do what he wanted in his own undemanding way.'[25] Bishop Hanson could not tolerate the 'barbaric attacks' on the primate and castigated the fanatics in his presidential address to the Clogher Diocesan Synod in 1971.

There were always some on the look-out for a stray word or a sin of commission or omission. The impossibility of 'doing the right thing' is evidenced by the rumours which spread about Dr Simms' whereabouts on the day of de Valera's funeral, 2 September 1975. The funeral of a murdered policeman took place that afternoon in Newtownhamilton and some who heard that the archbishop had gone to Dublin for de Valera's funeral assumed that he had therefore not been at the policeman's funeral and made disparaging remarks to the effect that he had his priorities wrong. The events of that day show his determination to do his utmost: he drove straight from Dublin to Newtownhamilton after de Valera's funeral to preside and preach at the funeral of the policeman. While he was there he heard of a multiple shooting near Newry and doubled back to see what he could do. He visited each injured man in hospital and then drove to Armagh for a routine meeting of the Diocesan Board of Mission.

While considering the difficulty of saying and doing the right thing one should take cognisance of the pronouncements of Ian Paisley and his newspaper, *The Protestant Telegraph*, which was described by Gallagher and Worrall as 'the vehicle for what seemed to many to be scurrility and scandal-mongering against all who sought any degree of reconciliation between the communities.'[26] On 10 January 1970 it carried a typical stream of anti-ecumenical invective:

There is every reason to believe that Jesuit infiltrators have wormed their way into positions of prominence in the ecumenical movement, especially in the Church of England, and have been largely instrumental in the sell-out of Protestantism. One of these Jesuits is the present Archbishop of Canterbury, Dr Michael Ramsey. Dr Ramsey has demonstrated to the world that he is an idolator, a liar who had repudiated his ordination vows.

It even goes on to suggest that he had recently been made a cardinal by the Pope! Archbishop Ramsey was far enough away from the Ulster scene to discount such nonsense but as Gallagher and Worrall point out, 'At first it was possible to laugh at these attacks, but later, as violence increased, it was no longer a joke to be named in a periodical which was widely read by Protestant paramilitaries and assassination gangs'.[27]

In his years as primate the only people who issued threats to Dr Simms were Paisleyites. Typically he did not worry about them but he did worry about the extent to which Ian Paisley fed the fears of Northern Protestants in order to block political initiatives and ecumenical progress. Dr Simms always endeavoured to develop a dialogue on the few occasions on which they met; he also preached to Paisley over three coffins but his words of reconciliation fell on deaf ears.

Dr Simms showed no concern about his personal safety and drove across the border and through difficult areas at night as the need arose. He refused a police escort although one was occasionally provided in sensitive areas at points of high tension whether he liked it or not. When a political murder or tragic incident occurred in the Church of Ireland community within his diocese, the archbishop always visited the family concerned and attended the funeral if at all possible. The political implications lurked menacingly in a situation which was primarily pastoral. His purpose was to convey the comfort of the Gospel, to show his compassion as chief pastor, the difficulty was that the media were at hand to relay his words across the world and private anguish could so easily be turned into a public spectacle. For one who entered so fully into other people's suffering, it was difficult to control his feelings on such occasions but he never failed to do so.

The strain of constant political traumas told on him even during the first year and increasingly during his primacy. He never spoke about it but those who were close to him observed it. Many tried to ease his burden, among them the three archdeacons who served him, T. D. D. Mayes, J. R. M. Crooks and F. W. Gowing. As a result of the troubles the archbishop constantly had to incorporate the abnormal into his normal routine. It meant fitting more into the day, frequent trips outside Ireland as a church 'ambassador' and consequently the archdeacon's job in the diocesan sphere became more onerous. Their attitude was expressed by Archdeacon Gowing: 'You loved the man — anything you could do to help him was a pleasure.'[28]

Most of all the archbishop relied on Mrs Simms, who made a point of staying home as much as possible to provide support. She found life in the North difficult. Appreciating the delicacy of the situation and knowing that she was suspected by some of being a nationalist, she determined to choose her words very carefully and to live as normally as possible. Thus she cycled into Armagh to do her shopping, joined local societies, attended evening classes and kept open house. She went to the North full of constructive ideas (in an attempt to share them, she wrote to Ian Paisley and Bernadette Devlin, neither of whom replied), but soon discovered that they were almost impossible to implement and concentrated more and more on prayer.

She derived strength from her membership of the Irish Association, an organisation which aimed to increase North-South, Catholic-Protestant understanding, and, in the later years, from an ecumenical prayer group which emanated from the renewal movement. Almost all her public involvements were open to misinterpretation; when she was appointed to the Southern Area Health and Social Service Board, her nomination was attacked in the press on the grounds that she did not represent any group or sector in the community, while her proven interest and experience in social action were ignored.

It was at once an advantage and a disadvantage that their children were not at home much; an advantage in that they were not subject to the strains which their parents experienced, a disadvantage in that the presence of young people would have made the atmosphere in the palace more relaxed. Although the palace was a vast mansion in a lonely position in its own grounds, Mrs Simms never minded being alone there. She made it as homely as possible, softening the awesome vastness of the rooms, with their enormous items of furniture and sombre portraits of former primates, by intermingling family possessions. She spent long hours polishing the chapel pews and tended the garden with care. She and Dr Simms were in some ways sad to move to the new see house in the cathedral close in 1975 but were hopeful that the old palace would enjoy a secure future as the district council offices.

It was very important to the archbishop that Mrs Simms was at home when he returned from a tragic funeral or a difficult interview. She often bore the brunt of the abusive phone calls, which, with similar letters, intruded on them. However, they generally avoided talking about the troubles when they were alone, for the archbishop spent so much of his time in discussion of them. The inter-action between Dr and Mrs Simms was such that there was no short-age of topics in the discussion of which a couple of hours would pass and the archbishop could relax. By her supportive presence, in the sharing of her interest in the work of the church, in current affairs and social issues, Mrs Simms was an invaluable help-meet. In an inter-view for the *Armagh Guardian* in 1977 the archbishop paid tribute to her; 'Mercy has been a real tower of strength to me'.[29]

When he went to Dublin there was always a bed available in the Divinity Hostel. Canon Brown knew that he needed a retreat after a day's meetings and ensured that he was not disturbed. Frequently meetings took place in the Hostel and this afforded the primate the opportunity to enter the room just before the beginning, thus avoiding any danger of being canvassed. A letter to Canon Brown thanking him for his hospitality during the week of the General Synod in 1970 refers to the 'haven of peace and calm'[30] provided, a line which suggests that he found it difficult to preside over General Synod when he was so beleaguered in his daily ministry.

However difficult the Northern situation was, Archbishop Simms could not let it consume his entire energies. As Primate of All-Ireland he had great responsibility in the administration of the national church and as diocesan he had a demanding routine. The appalling pressures of the time militated against strong initiatives, clear thinking and good preaching. Weaknesses, scarcely noticed in Dublin, were accentuated in the abnormal conditions prevailing in Armagh in the seventies.

His peculiarly passive style of leadership was very clear at Synod, where he rarely took the initiative and where strong leadership might often have been helpful. Undoubtedly he would have been more innovative as primate had it not been for the Northern conflict, yet quite a number of developments were directly influenced by him. These include the establishment of the Role of the Church Com-mittee to relate the work of the church more closely to problems in society, a communications committee, the appointment of a national press officer, and the Bishops' Appeal for Overseas Aid. Less definable but discernible nevertheless was a change in the leadership of the church towards a more open, more democratic government.

It has already been suggested that the presidency of the General Synod was an onerous burden, given the daily traumas with which he grappled. Even in the best circumstances the presidency is exhausting, demanding on stamina, concentration and patience. Dr Simms was scrupulously fair, if anything overcareful in allowing everyone who wished to speak an opportunity to do so. Some were exasperated that he was not a firmer chairman but many realised that he exercised his leadership at Synod precisely by permitting a debate to run long enough to obtain a unanimous decision. All without exception were impressed by his ability to greet each speaker by name; it made a large assembly much less formidable. No less impressive was his command of the complex workings of Synod and his ability to prevent rancour in the debate. He had a gift for creating a positive atmosphere, a gift well illustrated by an incident in his first diocesan synod in Armagh. During the debate on a contentious issue there was a certain amount of drumming of feet, at which point Dr Simms beamed benignly at the assembled synodsmen and remarked, 'I see this is a participatory synod!'

As primate he chaired meetings of the House of Bishops, the Representative Body, the Standing Committee, the Finance Committee in turn and many other important bodies. All of this committee work required meticulous preparation in which he never failed. Before a meeting of the Standing Committee, for instance, he would meet with the secretariat to draft resolutions for each item on the agenda. His wisdom and his skill as a tactician came to bear at this stage, in choosing suitable wording and often in suggesting a nominee for a particular task. Likewise, there were many opportunities at the meeting for subtle guidance on his part. His seemingly innocent (even naïve) questions often enabled him to probe a topic and steer the discussion; his knowledge of the constitution and traditions of the Church of Ireland and his memory of previous deliberations and decisions, his skill at putting into neat phrases the ideas which a committee was trying to express, proved valuable. Timing was very important too; Dr Simms was able to sense the stage of discussion at which a specific motion would bring the desired action. As a result of this skill and of his consummate tact he received a high degree of co-operation and achieved consensus more readily; the veteran administrator, J. L. B. Deane, asserts that Dr Simms got every policy decision he wanted and never asked the Finance Committee for money in vain. The disadvantage of this was that when he made an error of judgment few opposed him and their trust in him led to some questionable decisions.

There was real difficulty in keeping the political situation out of his mind long enough in order to give measured consideration to church strategy and other matters. With regard to appointments a weakness had been apparent in his episcopate in Dublin, albeit an endearing weakness: his rare capacity for seeing the best in everyone predisposed him to misjudging their abilities and placing more trust in them than was warranted. Within his diocese, difficulties were accentuated by hard-line pressure on boards of nomination for the appointment of men of fundamentalist outlook. Dr Simms, ever optimistic, rarely made an issue of it, thus missing the opportunity to achieve a broader churchmanship among his clergy.

People may criticise him for some of the decisions he influenced but all praise him for his Christian witness at every meeting. Bishop Butler writes, 'Never once did I see George get short-tempered, lose patience or say a harsh thing, despite some harsh things being said to him. Always he remained calm and serene and even the most obstreperous would say afterwards, "What a remarkable Christian he is." '[31] Even meetings of the House of Bishops could be difficult, for, as Dr Simms once remarked, 'Our problem is that all bishops are themselves chairmen.' Because he appreciated this, he steered his colleagues carefully, allowing scope for the most vocal to have their say and readily delegating as much work as possible.

Among the committees was the Board of Education. As chairman he exercised responsibility for little national schools in isolated parishes with the same care as for the Church of Ireland Training College. The Representative Body report for 1980 testified to this: 'Through big issues involving delicate, shrewd and very highly informed negotiation, and lesser ones which might have seemed tedious by comparison, he skilfully guided the Board.'[32] From one committee to another it was the same; he hardly missed a meeting and was always prepared.

Throughout his primacy the work of the Liturgical Advisory Committee continued. Progress was aided by various developments, internal, inter-Anglican and ecumenical. Three Committee members were appointed to a committee established in 1971 by the General Synod to review the Canons Ecclesiastical of the 1870s, under the vigorous chairmanship of Bishop Hanson. Some of the Canons were unduly restrictive and needed to be modified; others, being totally ignored, merited repeal. (The Canon forbidding a cross on the communion table had already been repealed by the General Synod in 1964.)

The revised Canons, passed by the Synod in 1974, incorporated many changes of import for liturgical revision; they permitted variations in the liturgy and the use of prayers and hymns from other sources, provided that they conformed to the church's teaching. The tone of the Canons became more positive as some were redrafted to state what the minister and congregation might do, rather than what they were forbidden to do.[33] The effect was to bring the practice of the Church of Ireland into line with other parts of the Anglican Communion, while permission for visiting clergy of churches not in communion with the Church of Ireland to perform a wider range of functions reflected the improving ecumenical climate. Dr Simms was well pleased with the revision of the Canons.

The Partners-in-Mission consultation held in Ireland in 1977 helped the home church to realise more of its Anglican heritage, while the doctrinal discussions and reports of the Anglican-Roman Catholic International Commission brought some understanding of what is held in common. From the local viewpoint it was important that Ireland was so fully involved through the co-chairmanship of Dr McAdoo (who succeeded Dr Buchanan as Archbishop of Dublin in 1977) and, in the context of the Liturgical Advisory Committee, his experience on ARCIC was most valuable. Another ecumenical dimension influenced the revision; a second member of the Liturgical Advisory Committee Dean Gilbert Mayes, Dean Mayes was a member of the interdenominational International Commission on English texts, which produced a number of liturgical texts for the universal church and these were adopted by the Church of Ireland.

When Dr Simms retired in 1980 *The Alternative Prayer Book* had taken shape, although it was not in use as a whole until 1984. Although he continued to love *The Book of Common Prayer*, he was deeply committed to the production of *The Alternative Prayer Book* and was pleased to know that it would reflect contemporary theological understanding, would be in the mainstream of ecumenical agreement and would be both Anglican and Irish, 'catholic' and 'evangelical'. He acted as chief proof-reader and has remained a consultant to the Liturgical Advisory Committee to date.

As has been suggested preaching was not his forte; during his primacy his sermons tended towards allusion and word-picture as some internal inhibition prevented him from being direct and precise. It meant that sometimes he stood up with a lot to say and said little. This flaw hindered his effectiveness on other occasions too and it seems fair to attribute much of it to the pressures he endured. Understandably it was not evident when he gave a lecture on *The Book of Kells* or a devotional talk. With *The Book of Kells* he was 'on his own ground', while a devotional talk derived from the deep springs of his personal spirituality. In both cases he had a sureness of touch which he never had in the Northern situation *per se*.

If aspects of his primacy revealed weaknesses, his pastoral
ministry was, if anything, stronger than ever. Apart from the crisis
management occasioned by the political situation (when he heard
of the news of a murder in an area of his diocese, he would ring
the rector to see if the victim was a parishioner and thus set in train
the care of the family and ordering of the funeral), he strove to
maintain a purely pastoral ministry to clergy and people alike. He
continued to appear unannounced at the hospital beds of the sick,
he always had time for the children at confirmations, everywhere
he went he reached out to people in the same fashion which had
made him beloved in Cork and Dublin. He was as accessible as
possible, given the fact that he was often besieged by the media; if
a clergyman or lay person telephoned the palace, Dr Simms would
come to the phone if available and frequently an invitation to call
was issued. In a determined attempt at normality he held Bible
classes in the palace.

He knew that his clergy needed even more support than in his
previous dioceses and was also aware of the necessity of maintaining discipline in the church, surrounded as it was by a society
which seemed to be falling apart. This he sought to do through the
formal channels of synod and diocesan council as well as in personal contact with the clergy. He also saw the need to develop an
infrastructure of people to do the groundwork within the diocese:
he always saw himself as part of a team and enjoyed having groups
at the palace to work on various projects.

As *pastor pastorum* he enjoyed the complete trust of his clergy,
who knew that they could approach him in confidence, confess
their weaknesses, air their personal problems, that they would
receive an empathetic hearing, counselling and comfort, and that
none of it would ever be remembered against them. Not all clergy
enjoy that confidence in their bishop.

Frequently his clergy learned a great deal from his counselling
which they in turn could apply to their own pastoral ministry.
While some required more directive counselling, others learnt from
him the paramount importance of being a good listener, of coming
alongside people in their misery and resisting the temptation to
offer advice. Some of them discovered for the first time that he who
would listen to people should first listen to God and realised that
the strength derived from their visit to their diocesan came because
his study or chapel had been quiet with the presence of God. Many
of the clergy were devastated when he retired and several speak of
it as a loss similar to bereavement. They did not always agree with
him but they did love and revere him.

Turning to the everyday life of the church at the time, Dr Simms became primate one hundred years after the Disestablishment of the Church of Ireland. He devoted part of his enthronement sermon to the centenary, placing the faith of those who rebuilt a church stripped of state support and prestige in the context of his text 'They continued steadfastly'. Mention has already been made of his being chief speaker at the centenary conferences in his own diocese. In the commemoration he saw an opportunity for a positive review of the previous hundred years, leading to inspired planning for the future. He was quick to point out the distinctive aspects of the disestablished Church of Ireland, such as synodical government, the opportunity afforded for lay participation in church affairs, and the impetus to reassessment and renewal.

It was Fr Michael Hurley who mooted the idea of a volume of essays written by churchmen of the differing traditions to mark the centenary.[35] Archbishop Simms took up the idea enthusiastically and asked Dr Kenneth Milne to act as advisor to the contributors. The archbishop accepted the volume on behalf of the Church of Ireland at an ecumenical service in the chapel of Gonzaga College, Dublin, on 15 April 1970.

The archbishop believed that writings such as these were valuable, even if read only by an educated minority. This belief explains why he was prepared to spare time to head the editorial committee of the Church of Ireland's own theological journals, *New Divinity*, first published in 1970, and its successor *Search*.

Dr Simms himself contributed to the centenary literature. The subtitle 'Years of Spiritual Maturing in the Church of Ireland' of his article on Disestablishment in *New Divinity* makes his attitude clear; as he wrote in that article 'the calamity turned into a spiritual opportunity'.[36] The mood at the time of Disestablishment was one of anger and bitterness; inter-church relations were virtually non-existent and the Church of Ireland itself was engaged in unhealthy introspection. As Dr Simms said in another essay 'spirituality was quite evidently scanty in the ordinary expression of the faith; there was rarity in the celebration of holy communion.'[37] His essays on Disestablishment concentrated on figures within the church who led it to a more mature spirituality; men like J. H. Bernard, R. M. Gwynn and M. L. Ferrar, great teachers of prayer, who built on the Irish love of psalms and Celtic hymns as well as the glories of *The Book of Common Prayer*. This was a necessary development, for the Church of Ireland in Disestablishment days 'was reluctant to be caught praying. . . The fear of ostentation was strongly felt in a church known for its padlocked doors and its three-decker-pulpits and its once-a-week usage'.[38] Likewise he admired the creative vigour seen in the Church of Ireland in church building, as at St Fin Barre's Cathedral and in hymn writing such as that of Mrs C. F. Alexander.

Dr Simms' own brand of Irish spirituality speaks clearly in these articles; in his desire to see a praying church, one where the sacramental life is highly valued, where the church building is a centre for seven-day activity. His broad churchmanship, catholic and evangelical, made him glad that the post-Disestablishment drive for revision of liturgy and canons in accordance with evangelical precepts was checked by men like Archbishops Plunket and Bernard.[39]

Understandably his writings were attenuated during the years of his primacy but he did find time to write articles of ecumenical import for a wide range of publications. One should not be dismissive of the value of hopeful, positive articles like 'Studying Scripture Together' and 'Ecumenism in Ireland During the Seventies'.[40] Nor should one underestimate the importance of lectures on *The Book of Kells* given across Northern Ireland to community audiences of every political and religious outlook. Some criticised these as irrelevant in the tragic prevailing situation but Dr Simms knew that they served at least two purposes; continuing a sense of normality and sharing a part of the common heritage. They were part of his work as a bridge-builder.

It is a great pity that these years so drained his energy that he could not then or subsequently produce a major work on spirituality. His most important writing during his primacy was a Lenten book for 1975. With a foreword by Cardinal Conway, *Christ Within Me* was a meditation on St Patrick's Breastplate with ready application to any Christian but with special relevance to Christians of all denominations in Northern Ireland.

His reference to 'the prayer at barricades, the existence of a peace line at the intersection of city streets in times of riot' as things which 'underline with a special poignancy the reality of the "one in Christ" '[41] is one of the few specific allusions to the Northern situation. Many of his references are applicable to difficult situations across the world: thus,

those who seek settlements and happy relationships among churches, between sections of the community and political groupings, must seek for the triumph of Christ over all the differences and points of contention. The individual Christian is called upon to surrender, to give up things and to deny himself.[42]

As in Dublin much of Dr Simms' work was carried on in the

sphere of the wider church. As chairman of the Irish Council of Churches he frequently chaired meetings of the tripartite Church of Ireland, Presbyterian, Methodist talks.[43] One of the chief problems which hindered their progress was that of constantly changing personnel; Archbishop Simms was 'a continuity man', one of the few long-term participants, and this gave him a pivotal role. A declaration of intent was produced but Dr Simms was disappointed that it did not lead to further steps; theological molehills assumed the appearance of mountains, while the non-conformist view of the episcopacy was a veritable problem for the Church of Ireland members. Having had a share in the anguish of the Anglican-Methodist reunion talks in England, Dr Simms was not unduly hopeful but still, when he retired, he was sad not to have seen more achieved.

The work of the Anglican-Roman Catholic Commission on the Theology of Marriage,[44] begun while Dr Simms was Archbishop of Dublin, continued until 1975. As the members came to know and trust one another their discussions prospered. In the chair, Archbishop Simms made few pronouncements but his presence was felt, nevertheless. When he was not in the chair, he felt free to contribute to the discussion. He followed his usual policy as chairman, to allow full and frank discussion, to keep the peace and steer the meeting towards a positive conclusion. Professor Dunstan recalls his style in words which could apply to his chairmanship of many another body. 'His gentleness and courtesy always prevailed. He never had to reduce us to order because we never fell into disorder.'[45] Likewise Monsignor Cremin sums up Dr Simms' contribution in succinct classical terms as 'eirenic'.[46]

The Commission achieved a remarkable degree of agreement, discovering on examination that differences which had been considered fundamental were merely differences of emphasis or of practice. It found that despite the fact that Roman Catholics look on marriage as a sacrament and Anglicans consider it sacramental but not a sacrament in the strict sense, the two churches were much closer on the question of marital breakdown and divorce than had been supposed. The problem of mixed marriages was much more difficult. The crux of the matter was the promises as to the upbringing of the children. At the second meeting (in Rome in November 1968) the Commission had progressed far enough to recommend that 'no more be asked of the Anglican party than was proposed by the Synod of Bishops in Rome on 24 October 1967, namely that he knows of the obligation in conscience of the Roman Catholic party and at least does not rule out

the Roman Catholic baptism and education of the children'.[47]
In the final report the Commission put forward an alternative
that was far less demanding; simply that the priest involved would
give written confirmation to his bishop that he had put the couple
in mind of the Roman Catholic partner's obligations. Moreover,
the Commission also felt able to recommend that, after joint
pastoral preparation, the marriage take place before either a
Roman Catholic or an Anglican priest.

The sticking point, past which the Commission could not go,
was not the promise itself but the underlying 'doctrine of the church
which Roman Catholics cannot abandon and which Anglicans cannot accept',[48] the doctrine that the Roman Catholic Church is the
one true church and that all other churches lack the fullness of
truth. Although they knew it sounded anti-ecumenical and
unhelpful, the Roman Catholic members had to enunciate their
belief: unacceptable as the Anglicans found it, the doctrine explains
many of the remaining theological difficulties between the two.

At its final meeting in Venice in June 1975, however, the Commission managed to give unanimous approval to the report. It is a
great disappointment to Dr Simms that it has never been formally
adopted by either church. In common with other members he finds
it hard today to assess its impact but he feels it has influenced combined counselling and co-operation between the respective clergy.
There has been some relaxation of the rules but how much is due
to the work of the Commission is uncertain and the position varies
not only from country to country but from diocese to diocese. In
accordance with Paul VI's *Matrimonia Mixta* (1970) the Protestant
partner no longer makes any promise, while the Roman Catholic
partner does: it may be a written promise or merely an oral
assurance. In some dioceses dispensation is given for a mixed marriage to take place in an Anglican church by an Anglican priest, in
others it will only be allowed in a Roman Catholic church but an
Anglican priest is welcome to take part, yet in some dioceses no
leeway is given.[49] In Ireland a mixed marriage is in the early 1990s
more often solemnised in a Church of Ireland church than was the
case in the 1950s, and the children are more likely to be baptised
and educated in the Church of Ireland. One sad aspect of the snail-
like progress of the churches, recognised by Dr Simms, is that
many couples drift away from both churches. The most hopeful
aspect is the growing number of inter-church families, who see their
'mixed marriage' as a positive opportunity for growing together in
the faith.

The Commission's modest claims to success need to be viewed in the context of the progress made by the main Anglican-Roman Catholic International Commission. Between 1970 and 1981 when its final report was drawn up, the meetings achieved a considerable degree of consensus in the three main areas of controversy; the doctrine of the eucharist, ministry and ordination, and authority.[50] One of the Anglican members, the Rev. Julian Charley, retrospectively called it 'a ground-clearing exercise',[51] an apt description, as its work involved the identification and examination of barriers, the removal of obstacles and the restatement of dogmatic positions. All of these were necessary preliminaries if the churches were to proceed further towards unity. It was found that barriers were often psychological rather than theological, that dogmas were elastic enough to permit of development, that theologians' views converged on many subjects. The most intractable subject was that of universal jurisdiction: the Commission did manage to agree that a form of universal primacy based on Rome might be a planned feature of any future unity.

The members believed that enough progress had been made to allow a new relationship to develop between the two churches, while 'some difficulties will not be wholly resolved until a practical initiative has been taken and our two churches have lived together more visibly in one *koinonia.*'[52] Here lay one of the difficulties: the Commission, whose work had to be done by specialists, had gone far ahead of the ordinary church members, whom it represented. Organic unity was still a long way off but a great amount had been achieved in a dozen years and ARCIC II was established immediately so that the momentum would not be lost. Dr Simms was not directly involved in the work of ARCIC but took a close interest in it, for its work was of enormous importance in the ecumenical endeavour. In common with other Anglicans he was sad that the Roman Catholic Church made no move to ratify its report.

Another of Dr Simms' external commitments was as president of the International Leprosy Mission, a post which he had accepted in 1964 in succession to Archbishop Fisher. In choosing him the Mission reverted to the policy of having an Irish president, to stress its Irish origins: the Mission, founded in 1874 by an Abbeyleix man, Wellesley C. Bailey, had been the first mission to leprosy sufferers in India. It has developed into an international and interdenominational organisation, running hospitals in some thirty-five countries round the world. In addition to its medical work, the Mission is concerned for the social and spiritual welfare of its patients and is involved in education and the promotion of peace and racial harmony.

The centenary tour which he undertook in 1974 provided a

welcome change for Dr Simms, although it was no holiday. For five weeks a schedule of mammoth proportions took him and Mrs Simms to hospital visits, preaching engagements and civic functions in five countries. Virtually every day was programmed down to each quarter of an hour, leaving little time for rest, despite the heat. For instance, within hours of arriving in Madras via Bombay from London he had to preach at a thanksgiving service in the cathedral. Many engagements were immediately preceded by lengthy journeys by road or rail. Fortunately with his abundant energy and a strong constitution, Dr Simms was able to fulfil all his engagements. In the hospitals he sat beside patients and talked with them, not finding them at all untouchable. In Calcutta he enjoyed meeting Mother Teresa and learning from her understanding of the needs of the poor in India. In Delhi he also met with government officials and encouraged them to develop the interest taken under President Giri in the work of the Mission. Soon the government started an education and treatment programme, which was welcomed by the Mission. As a gifted linguist he readily picked up a few words in the local languages; altogether he managed to say a grace and a blessing in six languages, knowing that it would be taken as a great compliment by the people.

The tour was not an easy undertaking, considering the burden of the primacy in the difficult early 1970s and the considerable preparation in paper work and research which was necessary. Dr Simms worked consistently over the years for the Mission and remained as president after his retirement in 1980.

Once again Dr Simms was a member of the steering committee of the Lambeth Conference of 1978. In the previous year, feeling that it might be better to allow a new primate to lead the Irish bishops to the Conference, he took soundings about retiring but was urged not to consider it at that time. There was a strong conviction that no Irish bishop was as well qualified to answer questions which might arise at Lambeth as to the Northern situation; Dr Simms, while feeling that there were others who could speak better than he, accepted that he was the chosen spokesman.

The eleventh Lambeth Conference was held in the University of Kent at Canterbury. This new departure made possible the first residential conference and in consequence, a much greater degree of fellowship than any previous Conference. The overall theme was 'Today's Church and Today's World': given a mere three weeks in which to work, there was no time to produce long reports and debate a large number of resolutions. In any case, it was the policy of the Steering Committee that most of the Conference was spent in small groups, in which individual bishops could more readily voice their opinions. The conference divided into three sections and thirty-four small groups, to which bishops had been allocated nine months earlier in order to allow time for preparation. The main sections were 'What is the Church for?', 'The people of God and Ministry' and 'the Anglican Communion in the Church'. Bishop Desmond Tutu was chairman of Section 1 and Dr Simms vice-chairman.

Bishop Tutu was at the time an assistant bishop of only two years' standing in the Province of Southern Africa and had recently been appointed General Secretary of the South African Council of Churches. His country was beginning to hit the headlines in the world press and the role of the church was emerging as a significant factor. Given Bishop Tutu's personality and position, he was destined soon to become an international quasi-political figure. He came to Lambeth XI as the rising voice of anti-apartheid and there was a danger that under his chairmanship section I might become over-politicised, had it not been for the calming influence of Archbishop Simms.

That the section produced such strong statements on Christian ethics, Christianity and politics and human rights was in large part due to Bishop Tutu's urgent and dynamic leadership but he himself asserts that 'any good that may have come out of that section which might have been thought to be due to the leadership . . . must be attributed to George Simms.' His recollections of their work together illustrates clearly the quiet way in which Dr Simms worked:

He was such a tremendous help and support for a maverick such as I was, utterly inexperienced, not knowing from one moment to the next what I was supposed to be doing and he would be there by my side, an encouraging presence and influence. I am enormously grateful for what I learned from my association with him. He did not speak a great deal but whenever he did quietly, unobtrusively and unassumingly. It was to make a very telling contribution to the meetings of leaders of the sections when we were assessing how the conference was doing and what things needed to be done or done differently. . . I am wonderfully enriched, truly blessed to have been touched by him, for I know myself to owe so much to so many people and he is one of them, now that I look back, who has made a tremendous impression although we met only for about three weeks.[53]

The Most Rev. R. H. A. Eames, then Bishop of Derry and Raphoe, and now Archbishop of Armagh, was a member of section 1. In the intervening years he and Archbishop Tutu have become close friends and at Lambeth XII in 1988 both were involved in another, painful, debate on violence in the light of the Gospel. Looking back on Lambeth XI, Archbishop Eames believes that Dr Simms, the eirenic and experienced archbishop, added a dimension to Bishop Tutu's work which no one else at the Conference could have done.[54] Black and white, African and Celt, extrovert and contemplative, they presented as they worked together in theological debate a wonderful visual example of the conflict and yet the unity of the Anglican ethos.

The views of section 1 were substantially expressed in the resolutions of the Conference but it was pointed out that the Conference as a whole was responsible only for the resolutions adopted by it. In referring to the need for a new economic order, international peace, urban planning, fulfilment through work and leisure, there was constant stress on human rights. For instance it was maintained that, where development schemes conflicted with the interests of minorities, consideration should be given 'to the needs of persons rather than to economic advantage'.[55] The Conference also specifically stated that it 'regards the matter of human rights and dignity as of capital and universal importance. . . We deplore and condemn the evils of racism and tribalism, economic exploitation and social injustices, torture, detention without trial and the taking of human lives as contrary to the teaching and example of our Lord in the Gospel.' It went on to 'urge all Anglicans to seek positive ways of educating themselves about the liberation struggle of people in many parts of the world.' Appealing for support from all Christians for 'those who struggle for human freedom', it stated 'we should not abandon them even if the struggle becomes violent'.[56]

The last statement did not imply that the conference supported violence as a means of achieving reform but the Section 1 report came nearer to accepting it than the conference as a whole. The relevant part of its report reads

We have drawn back from advocating as a political instrument the way of violence, either by a government or by those opposing the government. Violence begets violence and human life is devalued. We recognise, however, that in situations where injustice has been built into political structures, threatening people with perpetual suppression, Christians may feel that non-violence is no longer the appropriate response and physical violence is the only way to intervene on behalf of the oppressed.[57]

The conference resolutions were more cautious: they condemned the use of violence and called on Christians everywhere 'to engage themselves in non-violent action for justice and peace and to support others so engaged'.[58]

In avoiding the full force of the words of Section 1's reports, the Conference stepped back from the controversial position in which the World Council of Churches found itself. In the section on ecumenism Resolution 29 urged the World Council of Churches to look again at Christ's teaching 'against all violence in human relationships'.[59] It nevertheless made a very strong statement, one which showed a remarkable development in sensibility since Lambeth X ten years before had declared that 'the Christian commitment is generally to the maintenance of law and order'.[60]

Although Bishop Tutu's influence was clearly felt, he was only one, albeit the most vociferous, of the South African bishops who were desperately concerned about human rights in their land, while there were many bishops from other provinces, who were, with good reason, anxious. These included first and foremost the bishops of Uganda, a country suffering terribly under the iniquitous regime of President Idi Amin. The Primate of the Ugandan church, Archbishop Janani Luwum, had been murdered by Amin's agents, a tragic loss which sent waves of shock reverberations round the civilised world. It was an achievement for the Ugandan bishops to get to the Lambeth Conference, for they lived in great danger and their movements were being monitored. S. G. Wani had succeeded Archbishop Luwum but in the international Anglican Communion the best known bishops were W. B. Herd, the Irish-born Bishop of Karamoja, soon afterwards exiled by Amin, and Festo Kivengere, bishop of Kigezi who brought himself to write a book entitled '*I Love Idi Amin*'.[61] Among many other bishops who expressed their anxiety about human rights were Dr Simms himself with almost daily experience of violence in Northern Ireland, J. T. Walker, Bishop of Washington, Trevor Huddleston, metropolitan of the Province of the Indian Ocean and H. B. Dehqani-Tafti, President Bishop of Jerusalem and the Middle East and Bishop of Iran.[62]

Ten years later Lambeth XII's resolution on violence prompted Dr Eames, to make an emergency statement on behalf of the Irish bishops, dissenting from the body of the Conference. The 1988 resolution, which caused such outrage, did not represent a substantial change from the section 1 report of 1978 but there were two significant differences; firstly, by expressing understanding of those who resorted to 'armed struggle' in conditions of extreme repression, it used words imbued with sinister connotations in the Irish context, for the Provisional I.R.A. attempts to justify its murderous campaigns in exactly those terms; secondly the 1988 resolution was not merely the finding of a Section but had the consent of the entire Conference.

It should not be supposed that section 1 restricted itself to human rights issues; it had much to say about openness to the power of the Spirit, family life and sexuality. Other issues, raised in sections 2 and 3, led to commitment to tithing as a 'guide for normal Christian living', and to a review of lifestyles so that they became 'related to necessities rather than affluence and consumerism'.[63]

The newly-found social and political awareness of the bishops found expression too in the resolution on the public ministry of the bishop. In talking about a bishop's 'concern for the well-being of the whole community (especially of those at a disadvantage)' it identified the need for him to be involved in secular situations on the side of 'justice, mercy and truth'.[64] Gone was any idea that a bishop's job was to exercise a pastoral ministry exclusive to his own flock, in a somewhat rarified ecclesiastical atmosphere.

With reference to the other forms of ministry, the Conference recommended that member churches which had not begun to ordain women as deacons should take steps to do so. It also declared its acceptance of members who had gone ahead with the ordination of women to the priesthood and of those who had not, acknowledging the pain involved and encouraging all to remain within the Anglican communion.

Apart from the working sessions of the Conference, one of the highlights was the award of honorary degrees by the University of Kent to three of the Anglican bishops: they were Desmond Tutu, J. B. Coburn, Bishop of Massachusetts and, representing the elder statesmen, George Simms.

In the later years of his primacy honours were heaped on him, all of which he received with genuine humility. Characteristically, he chose to receive them as honour paid to the historic office which he held rather than to him personally. In some instances this was at least partly true but his election as an honorary Fellow of Trinity College, Dublin (F.T.C.D.) in 1978 was a tribute to his scholarship and personal service to the university. That he was Archbishop of Armagh was incidental, just as had been his tenure of the see of Dublin when he was elected a member of the Royal Irish Academy.

Although he had been dissuaded from retiring before the Lambeth Conference of 1978, Dr Simms determined to retire in his seventieth year. The announcement that he would retire in February 1980 caused widespread regret but the primate was convinced that he should allow a younger man to assume the leadership of the Church of Ireland in the 1980s. It was the right decision, for the traumas of the seventies had taken their toll of his energy and the job was too demanding for a septuagenarian.

One of the last events of his primacy was the visit to Ireland of Pope John Paul II. Huge crowds attended the masses which he celebrated across the country and the rest of the population followed his progress closely on television or by radio. Archbishop Simms introduced the Church of Ireland bishops and the secretaries of the General Synod to the Pope at a special meeting in Dublin, during which the pontiff spoke about the ecumenical movement. Dr Simms hoped and prayed that the Pope's message of peace in Ireland would bear fruit but had to face the fact that the ears of the paramilitaries were as deaf to papal entreaties as to any others. At the end of his primacy Archbishop Simms' chief regret was that peace had not been achieved in Northern Ireland.

Dr Simms' farewell address to the diocesan synod was one of encouragement, urging them to remain faithful and loving. His final exhortation was characteristically positive: 'Christ *will* triumph'. There was a final service of thanksgiving in the cathedral in Armagh on 10 February, after which, true to form, the archbishop stood at the door to shake hands with each member of the congregation. He thanked many of them for their help and support during his primacy; this was something he valued greatly and he said at the time that his most lasting impression of those years was of the power of faith.

On his retirement the daily newspapers paid handsome tributes. The *Irish Times* editorial[65] picked up Bishop Hanson's criticism that all the major denominations in Northern Ireland had bartered their integrity in return for the support of their people to make the point that Dr Simms absolutely refused to take on the semi-political role in which bishops tend to be cast. It continued

Some of his own flock did at times demur at his quiescence, as they thought, and contrasted him with 'more outspoken' prelates. He was criticised at times as being too much on the establishment side; he was mistrusted by others for his Irish cultural leanings and his devotion to the ecumenical movement. But George Simms went his way. The words of Isaiah might typify his approach: 'in quietness and confidence shall be your strength.'

Within the church retirement tributes are *de rigueur* but there was nothing 'routine' in the nature of those paid to Dr Simms: Archdeacon Gowing, in his farewell speech said 'He has peace in himself. He brings the reconciling spirit wherever he goes. You find peace in his presence.'[66] At the farewell service in the cathedral Dean J. R. M. Crooks spoke of his 'goodness' which 'shines like a beacon leading us by the light of his own life through the morass of evil deeds and hateful words by which we have been surrounded'.[67] Archbishop McAdoo, at Dr Simms' final meeting of the Standing Committee, spoke of his response in the troubled days of his primacy as one 'in which love had dominated and in which firmness of purpose in principles had always combined with a deep concern for individuals and their rights'.[68] The vast majority of tributes focused on the person rather than his deeds and on his qualities of love, joy and peace. What comes across clearly is how much people loved him.

In the course of history attempts will be made to assess the success of Dr Simms' primacy in the light of events in Northern Ireland. Political historians will judge him by the world's standards, in terms of the impact of his leadership. It is too early to attempt an assessment at this stage; in any case the writer of spiritual biography works on different criteria. As Richard Harries says 'the only success is that which counts as success with God',[69] reminding us that 'the wisdom of this world is foolishness in God's sight'.[70]

As far as Dr Simms' ministry was concerned, it was a great pity that he had to leave Dublin for Armagh at such a troubled time. He never won acceptance in the North comparable to that which he enjoyed in the Republic; just as Northerners failed to plumb the depths of his personality, they thought he did not fully understand them. As an ecumenist and liturgist of vision he generally knew what would be the right development in those spheres but was unable to implement them, so unpropitious were the times.

Whatever the flaws in his primacy, his spiritual leadership was unfailing. He never forgot the fundamental role of the bishop as chief shepherd, leading his people closer to God. As Bishop Butler wrote, 'he was always in every situation a faithful servant of his Lord and Master and that above all else was what he was ordained and consecrated for'.[71]

VIII

WRITINGS

Consideration of Dr Simms' writings must be based on the knowledge that none of them was undertaken spontaneously but only by specific request. Despite his academic prowess and facility with words, his attitude has always been 'Who am I to write on the subject?' Notwithstanding his genuine humility, there were several subjects where his particular scholarship and talents led to repeated invitations for him to write books or articles. His study of *The Book of Kells* for the facsimile edition of 1950 and his ability to explain the complexities of the gospel book in layman's terms, his firm grasp of the history of the church and of the Church of Ireland in particular, his profound spirituality, glimpsed at conferences and quiet days, and manifest in his daily life, constituted three areas where he had a particular contribution to make. It would be a mistake rigidly to categorise these into 'early Christian manuscripts', 'devotional' and 'church history', for there is a frequent blend of all three and a devotional aspect is present in virtually all his writings.

Dr Simms has made a unique contribution to the study of Irish illuminated manuscripts. The painstaking task of collation frequently attracts a scholar who, like the original scribe, is content to spend his time in seclusion with his manuscripts. Dr Simms, however, having studied the texts, proceeded to share the fruits of his scholarship with the general public, seeking to make this part of the Irish heritage accessible and comprehensible. In doing so he has demonstrated rare gifts.

Much of the magic of his presentation lies in his realisation of the spiritual dimensions of the scribe's labour and his understanding of the artistic details. On the one hand the work is 'of the nature of worship',[1] on the other he has a great sense of 'the rollicking fun of the monk's scattered imaginings, the grotesque touches, the close marriage of ornament and text'.[2] Thus his interpretation often brings out the thrust of the text and the collator's attention to detail prompts him to highlight tiny features which might otherwise escape notice. No one who has heard him lecture on *The Book of Kells* could forget the boyish delight with which he picked out the two mice nibbling a communion wafer at the bottom of the Chi-Rho page at the beginning of St Matthew's Gospel,[3] nor his imaginative reconstruction of an incident in the monastery which might have given rise to the drawing. There was considerable entertainment value in unravelling the details of a full-page illustration but Dr Simms directed the reader and listener beyond a mere appreciation of the artistry to an understanding of its inspiration. Thus he pointed out that the two cats peaceably watching the mice, while another two mice are besporting themselves on the cats' backs, is considered to be a Celtic interpretation of Isaiah's prophecy of a Messianic age when the wolf will dwell with the lamb and the leopard lie down with the kid.[4] The portraits of two pairs of bearded men are similarly interpreted as illustrating Christ, the Prince of Peace. Their 'antagonisms and arguments are brought beneath the judgment of the Saviour's name. Reconciliation does its work and the beards clutched in strife are ready to be loosed'.[5]

He shows us how the figures concealed in the lozenge-shaped intersection of the 'X' remind us that 'where Christ is . . . there is also creation . . . There lie hid in subjection, acknowledging as it were, the authority of the creative word, four human figures, four reptiles, four quadrupeds and no fewer than twelve winged birds. As Adam named the animals, so nothing in creation is outside the influence of the second Adam'. He continues, 'The page teems with life. Even the dead letters of the manuscript spring into life. The curve of the [Greek] "R" of Christ's monogram becomes a human head. If the Word was God, then the Word was life: if the Word became flesh, then we perceive why, under the artist's hand, his letters sprout hands and feet'.[6]

Dr Simms sees movement in the tall 'X', which, although it dominates the page, 'dances lightly with its sweeping, graceful cross'.[7] He interprets the geometric design of circles, frames, whorls and interlacing as enhancing the mystery of Christ's birth; 'perhaps the point is that the profane should not have ready access to this news which must not be blatantly noised abroad, lest what is sacred for the faithful should be vilified or mischievously distorted'.[8]

Obviously his lectures on *The Book of Kells* had an extra dimension. His delivery has a dynamism which cannot be conveyed in print. In his lectures even the pauses are significant, as Canon John

Barry recalls. 'How one waited for him to arrive at the picture of Jesus in the garden! To experience the long pause that followed the pointing out of "the great, deep pool of suffering in the eyes". That long, long pause.'[9]

His eye for colour and line is a great advantage, as is his poetic English. His descriptions reflect the grandeur of the artistry and his knowledge of the Celtic heritage, spiritual and artistic, is brought to bear as he places the manuscripts in the context of the Columban tradition and draws comparison with the great stone crosses and with decorative metalwork.

Even his examination of textual errors and correctors' additions is made interesting as he seeks to show how interpolation and plain error affect the ancient text. One Friday evening in 1982 as I was driving along a leafy lane in County Meath I turned on the radio to listen to 'Pick of the Week' on BBC Radio 4. I joined the programme in the middle of an item which was unmistakable: the lines from the Pangur Bán poem, depicting the copyist watching his white cat and writing in the margin of his manuscript,

> I and Pangur Bán, my cat,
> 'Tis a like task we are at;
> Hunting mice is his delight,
> Hunting words I sit all night,

recited in Dr Simms' rich voice, were being used to explain the exacting nature of the scribe's task, the difficulties of concentrating for hours on copying a text.[10]

Dr Simms extended his interest to other manuscripts of the early Christian period, both of Irish and continental origin[11] but his name was so much associated with *The Book of Kells* that it was jokingly suggested that in retirement he could have taken the title 'Lord Simms of Kells' to parallel the peerages of retiring English primates! Most of the writings on the subject are simple but he has written articles for publications such as *Hermathena* on the more academic aspects of studying the texts and producing the facsimiles.[12] One of his general introductions to *The Book of Kells* has been translated into French, German and Irish, in response to demand in the tourist trade.

This aspect of his life's work has made him a well-known figure far beyond the Church of Ireland. By his writings and lecturing he has reached a wide public in Ireland and elsewhere and has become an acknowledged authority on Irish illuminated manuscripts.

Dr Simms' most significant devotional books are of a type: *Christ Within Me* has already been mentioned as a Lenten book having particular significance in Northern Ireland. His meditation on the prayer from 'St Patrick's Breastplate' offers guidance on the different aspects of prayer, on spiritual emptiness, coping with fear, and much more. Anglican in tone, the book presents the truth in a quiet way, at once scholarly and devotional, with no attempt to drive home the message. While it contains many quotations from the collects or other parts of the liturgy of *The Book of Common Prayer*, it has a wide appeal. Dr Simms draws on the psalms, the early church, the Irish saints and on modern thinkers of many traditions such as Bonhoeffer, Tillich and Quoist, to achieve a universality of reference. He uses his historical and classical scholarship, teasing out the meaning of key words, yet he succeeds in presenting profound truths in simple, non-theological terms.

St Patrick's prayer focuses on Christ in every aspect of our living; Dr Simms opens new perspectives for his reader into each line of the 'Breastplate'. When he leads the reader into Holy Week his presentation is of Christ who took the initiative on Palm Sunday and 'begins things in us still', of a cross which 'lights up our hearts and minds'[13] and a resurrection which enables disciples then and now to live together in Christ. Like so much in this little book, it issues a fresh challenge to the Christian. In his foreword Cardinal Conway wrote of the book's 'gentle persuasiveness'. What is most persuasive is the profound spirituality which underpins it, the sense of peace and security in God's love.

The prayer from 'St Patrick's Breastplate' provided a highly appropriate theme for a Lenten book aimed at Christians of all traditions in Ireland. Like *The Book of Kells* it was part of an ancient common heritage and could be explored as a unifying factor. His words were aimed not only at bringing reconciliation between the divided communities in the North but also at nurturing the ecumenical spirit. The section on 'Christ in hearts of all that love me' draws a message of hope and love from our Lord's prayer for unity in John 17; although the implications for Northern Ireland are obvious he refrains from spelling them out, opting instead for universality of application.

Having asserted firmly that 'Divisions among Christians cannot be healed without prayer',[14] he goes on to advise on the nature of such intercession. 'In prayers that breathe unity we are right perhaps to refrain from harping all the time on the subject of unity itself to the exclusion of any searching after the conditions of life and behaviour that make for unity. We should also be praying for tolerance, for a willingness to change, for friendship, for courtesy, for an honest review of our beliefs and attitudes.'[15]

Because the book was based on St Patrick's prayer Dr Simms had ample scope to demonstrate the vital importance of prayer in the Christian life. Prayer is the predominant theme of the meditation. Some of what he says is very simple but he says it, nevertheless, because he is aware that people who complain that they are unable to pray have often ignored the basics. Thus he states 'The only way to learn how to pray is to pray',[16] and 'ultimately we pray for people because Christ died for them'.[17] In contrast, the reality of some of his suggestions can only be realised by seasoned practitioners of prayer. When he writes 'Prayer is a means of linking a moment of time with timelessness, eternity and God's presence; it lifts us out of this world and yet adds to our life in this world a dimension at once inspiring and fulfilling,'[18] he is not addressing the beginner. One of the strengths of the book is his ability to enlighten and inspire Christians whose experience ranges from little to great. In common with much devotional literature, *Christ Within Me* is inspirational rather than didactic; it contains little that is new or original in terms of scholarship or style but it is full of creative thinking and thus offers a fresh application of old themes to the needs of his time. Many of the clergy of the Church of Ireland had heard Dr Simms say much the same things on prayer before, whether as students in Trinity College or at quiet days but they were delighted to see his words in print. Many treasured his insights on prayer, indeed many had been greatly influenced by them.

There was likewise a warm welcome for *In My Understanding*, when it was published two years after his retirement in 1982. It appeared in response to a request from Michael Gill of Gill and Macmillan for another devotional book.[19] On this occasion he chose to build on a series of retreat addresses which he had given for the diocese of St Alban, on the famous prayer *In the Sarum Primer*. His extended meditation on the doublets closely parallels his treatment of St Patrick's prayer but this second guide to prayer packs so much into each section that it requires discipline to stop after a couple of paragraphs and ponder their contents. Some of the points on the basics of prayer are exactly the same as in *Christ Within Me* but here he has space to expand them more fully. At the end of the book he reaches an arresting conclusion: 'Ultimately, to pray is to express love for God. . . Perseveringly and unceasingly the selfishness of that constant inclination to claim "My will be done," has to be transformed into "Thy will be done." This is a life work, yet not a life sentence.'[20]

Again his concern for Christian unity is given repeated

expression. His words are those of a veteran ecumenist, undaunted
by the particular problems of Ireland; 'we ask that God may be in
our thinking . . . to build up trust among the churches, to plant
fresh seeds of understanding, to point to areas of common action,
that we may be open to change, and ready for the kind of compromise which combines apparently opposing views, without
betraying convictions.'[21] He writes with enthusiasm about
dialogue at Ballymascanlon, the Irish School of Ecumenics, about
every positive venture. A reference to William Temple — 'it was
said that he rarely brought an inter-church debate to a conclusion
without a statement which included several opposing doctrinal
positions in a balanced synthesis',[22] — makes it clear what Dr
Simms would have liked to achieve in this sphere. In the
autobiographical nuances lies some of the importance of this book,
for they afford glimpses of a Christian leader who had preserved
his integrity and retained his hopefulness by cultivating the inner
life of prayer.

Dr Simms' other devotional writings are mostly very short. Some
are not writings in the strict sense, being printed sermons or addresses,[23] while others were written for diocesan or parish magazines.
A typical piece was 'Lenten Patience', which was printed in Lenten
books in the U.S.A., and England, an American diocesan magazine
and a Dublin parish magazine.[24] In a tender but strong study of the
text, 'In your patience possess ye your souls' (Luke 21.19), he discusses
our need for patience, as our lives 'are for the most part marked by
a fair measure of monotony and uneventful routine', and reminds
us that 'those who live in the faith of Christ learn gradually to use their
days, not caring in the long run whether they are times of excitement
or drab routine.' He examines the patience which Christ showed in
his earthly ministry, likening it to 'a weapon which he unsheathed.' He
looks at the words with which Christ repelled Satan's temptations
(Matthew 4.1–11), remarking that they may 'sound
impatient, but in reality are deeply patient. Patience does not mean
docility and meekness but steady purposefulness and resolution to live
to the end, faithful and unflinching'.[25] The careful reader, seeking
strength to endure the forty days of Lent, would find much to ponder
in this miniature. Like his two devotional books it is revealing of the
archbishop's own faith.

These writings are based on theological orthodoxy and up-to-date
reading but are devotional rather than theological works. Leaving
exegesis and hermeneutics to the professional theologian, Dr Simms
concentrated on the devotional, historical and liturgical. Most of his
historical and liturgical studies have a strong devotional aspect:

this is clear in the articles on disestablishment,[26] as it is in his selection of the addresses and papers of Michael Ferrar and his accompanying memoir,[27] in his articles on the litany and the marriage service according to *The Book of Common Prayer*.

His objective in writing was not merely to increase the reader's understanding but thereby to deepen his devotion to God; hence the title of his article on four hundred years of the litany is 'Let the people pray'.[28] Likewise *For Better, for Worse* does more than explain the structure of the marriage service, it sets it in the context of a God-given institution, in which 'by loving each other' a couple 'learned more of the love which God had to give them and more of the love which they could return to God'.[29] The didactic and devotional are woven together inextricably here as in his other writings. Aware that few couples had holy communion at their marriage service, he points out the good reasons for including it, most significantly that the bride and groom 'cease to be the central figures of the drama and at the communion join with all worshippers on earth and in heaven'.[30]

In 1946 he wrote two unsigned booklets for the A.P.C.K., *Preparing for a Mission* and *Following up a Parish Mission*. These guides for parish clergy have all the marks of being written by an older man with a lifetime of experience. While they have clear practical application they aim to build up the clergyman in his parish, to inspire him with new vision. Practical details of good planning are included but are put firmly in their spiritual context; 'If possible, before the mission, make use of a refresher course or quiet day, if available; for it is by self-dedication and special prayer that the difficult and rather unspectacular work of building on another's foundation is faced'.[31]

In these booklets George Simms anticipated developments which are only partly achieved forty years later: he urged clergy to plan for what he called 'cells', made up of people who wanted to share in the 'building work' of the parish. He laid stress on the importance of Bible study groups, sternly saying that 'many of our staunch church members have remained infantile in their thought about the profundities of the faith', adding 'if the rector is the leader of the group he must beware of lecturing or speaking in animated monologue'.[32] What he envisaged was 'ministry for all'.

Most of his writings pertaining to the history of the Church of Ireland are biographical. His only full-length history is the history of the parish of Tullow,[33] in addition to which he has made two other forays into parochial history. In 1985 he and Raymond Jenkins produced a twenty-nine-page booklet, *Pioneers and*

Partners, the story of the parish of All Saints', Grangegorman, Dublin in the days of William Maturin and Henry Hogan. Short it may be, slight it is not, for it contains two meticulously researched essays, written in scholarly fashion with copious footnotes. In 1987 his edited version of Kathleen Turner's history of Rathmichael parish was published.[34] This was a delicate undertaking; Kathleen Turner had devoted many years of research to the subject and had completed much of the writing before she died in 1985. After her death Dr Simms was asked to take it over. Thanks to his sympathetic treatment a handsome book appeared in her name and its format resembles that of the Tullow history but, with consummate grace, Dr Simms has preserved her style and kept his contribution in the shade.

In his foreword to *Tullow's Story* Dr Simms provides the justification of parish histories — 'parish histories fill in the details of our island's story' — but the particular reason for his interest is that ultimately a parish history is about people.[35] The nearer the narrative gets to the present day, the greater the scope; he includes pen portraits of all incumbents since 1863, records gifts and memorials, traces the contribution of parishioners both to parish and community life. The life of Tullow Church is set in context from the first Christian foundation at Tully, through all the vicissitudes of history, with the comment 'Changes of the severest kind may take place, governments may rise and fall, revolutions may disrupt, but the parish never dies'.[36]

In his ministry Dr Simms had seen enough parochialism to make him include an explanation of the parish system given in Raymond Jenkins' sermon at T.N.D.C. Salmon's institution in 1950:

The clergyman is a local official; but he is the local official of a supra-local society. He is instituted to his cure by the bishop and exercises his parochial ministry by the bishop's authority. But the bishop is at once the centre of unity of the parishes of the diocese and their link with the church universal. So each local parson, delegated by the bishop, points to a church life far beyond parochial boundaries. . . So the parochial system properly understood is the enemy of a narrow and petty parochialism. Yet there is . . . something much deeper than this. This fellowship is not . . . only horizontal, it is also vertical, it comes down from Heaven and has its source in the perfect fellowship of the Holy Trinity.[37]

In a tightly-written history such as this there is no room for expanded comment but with this quotation, mention of the church being open every day, the involvement of the congregation in the

Above: Visit to Bielefeld, West Germany in 1973 to thank the Evangelische Kirche for funding peace projects in Northern Ireland, G.O.S. and M.F.S. with President Thimme.
Below: Lambeth Conference 1978, concelebration at the nave altar of Canterbury Cathedral. Facing, left to right: M.Loane, G.O.S., J. Sepeku, H.Dehqani-Tafti, T.Huddleston.

Above: Lambeth Conference, 1978, University of Kent, conferring of honorary degrees in Canterbury Cathedral: the Vice-Chancellor, Archbishop Coggan, the Chancellor (Rt Hon J.Grimond), G.O.S. D.M.Tutu, J.B.Coburn. Below: primates' meeting at Ely in 1979. *Back row:* J.Howe, R.Runcie (then Archbishop designate of Canterbury), M.Kahurananga, C.Woodroffe, E.Ngalamu, F.D.Coggan, T.Huddleston, S.Wani, B.Ndahura, D.Hand, E.Scott, A.H.Johnstone, M.Loane, A.Haggart, A.Kratz, M.Scott. Front row: G.Hha Gyaw, T.Nakamichi, G.O.S., N.Palmer, T.Olufosoye, H.Dahqani-Tafti, C.Bazley. Photo, courtesy Canon Degwell Thomas.

Above: On Pope John Paul II's visit to Ireland, September, 1979. Below: Cardinal O Fiaich, Archbishop Eames, G.O.S., and Bishop Poyntz at the Ballymascanlon Conference, 1987.

The Book of Kells, folio 34r, 'the Chi-Rho page'. Courtesy Trinity College Library.

new liturgy, Dr Simms encourages the reader to cultivate the best in parish life.

To a large extent his writings reflect both the stages of his ministry and developments within the Church of Ireland. In the 1940s the Anglican Communion marked the quatercentenary of the compilation of *The Book of Common Prayer*, hence his contribution on the litany and marriage service. It has already been mentioned that the Church of Ireland had not yet recovered its confidence after the trauma it suffered in the establishment of independence. The article 'Your Faith', in *Christ, Youth and the Conflict of Life*, was a printed version of his address to diocesan youth conference in 1943, in which he sought to give a clear and positive statement of what membership of the Church of Ireland involved. 'The Church of Ireland, which guards and expresses our faith, does not at her best expound middle-class morality or reflect a West-British ethos. Republican, imperialist, West African, pacifist, socialist, may all belong to the Church of Ireland.'[38] He goes on to ask for repentance for any snobbery or exclusiveness within the church, and to urge members to endure with faith their sense of frustration and helplessness, rather than to leave the country.

Likewise, in the same year, the thrust of his contribution to *The Country Shepherd, Pastoral Work in Country Parishes of the Church of Ireland*, was to strengthen the vision of the clergy, to enable them to withstand the pressures brought about by uncertainty about the future. Typically, having given advice as to the choice of sermon themes, their lay out and presentation, he concludes 'What the preacher is counts more than what he says or how he says it.'[39]

Just as these writings reflect the situation in the forties, many articles derive from the ecumenical progress of the late sixties and seventies. An article on 'Ecumenism in Ireland during the 70s'[40] is a positive review of developments, with frank admission of the barriers. He links Irish ecumenism to that in the international scene, reminding readers that the World Council of Churches assembly of 1968 had stated that the only possible victory in the process was that of Christ over our divisions and not of one church over another. He takes the same approach in 'What about the World Council of Churches?'[41]

In contrast, other articles, such as *The Role of Protestants*,[42] were written to explain the Church of Ireland and the other Protestant Churches to the majority population. That article dealt with difficulties in community relations since independence, firmly but charitably stating the grievance felt over mixed marriages. His article on 'Some Insights from the Churches of the Reformation' in *Irish Spirituality*,[43] traces the divisions since the sixteenth century and the spiritual contribution of the reformed churches. He is at pains to make it clear that the Church of Ireland at the Reformation did not see itself as a new church, but sought to recapture the primitive practice of the early church. He demonstrates the desire of churchmen through the centuries for the unity of all believers, the importance of the Bible in the reformed tradition, both as it is read at services and in private use. Commending the unchanging practice of saying the psalms on a daily basis throughout the month, he deftly explains the stages of development by which hymn-singing became such an important element of worship. As he traces the emergence of the Presbyterian and Methodist churches, with their particular contributions to worship, he opens up the heritage of the metrical psalms and Wesleyan hymns for his Roman Catholic readership. He also sets in context the role of the great intellectual churchmen like Berkeley and Swift, of the famous preachers and of the sermon itself and moves forward to a consideration of modern spiritual writing within the reformed tradition. His aim is to make the writings of thinkers such as C. S. Lewis and Helen Waddell more accessible to Roman Catholics, to make the heritage comprehensible. There is no hint of condescension but a patent longing to share what is best. Dr Simms has always shown himself ready to borrow prayers from the Roman Catholic tradition and to read the works of Roman Catholic theologians. One so steeped in Celtic spirituality, so sensitive to differing traditions and so well-informed about them was the obvious choice to write on the Protestant contribution to Irish spirituality. Unfortunately all of these are minor writings, which leave one wishing that he had undertaken a major work on the theory and practice of ecumenism.

Over the years he has gained a reputation as a writer of potted biographies. This is based on his numerous retrospective articles on such figures as J. A. F. Gregg, J. H. Todd and M. L. Ferrar, and on memorial sermons, many of which were subsequently printed. He has a rare gift for encapsulating the personality of whom he is treating. His masterly study of M. L. Ferrar is a timeless portrait of a much-loved friend, whose full stature was appreciated only by those who could penetrate the barriers of reserve. His appreciation of J. A. F. Gregg likewise, reveals an insight into the private person behind the formidable primate. Dr Simms well knew Gregg's reputation for sternness and attempted to balance this with the following view; 'When minds to match his intellect met him, then there was a casting away of reticence, a flow of conversation, and witty repartee from a personality delightfully relaxed'.[44]

Skilfully he attunes the article to the personality of whom he is writing, as in the classical restraint and eloquence of his tribute to that eloquent classicist, W. B. Stanford, on his retirement in 1980.[45] Often he unconsciously holds up for admiration characteristics which others admire in him. This is not surprising in one who has prayerfully cultivated the Christian virtues over half a century as a priest but it is striking that he illustrates his point with the same details as others instance when talking about him. In talking of Bishop Hearn's humility he says that he was 'loath even to let another carry his bag'.[46] His appreciation of J. E. L. Oulton makes mention of his meticulous accuracy as a scholar,[47] the article on Gregg recalls how 'he examined and caressed words', and 'found the exact word for the current topic with an unerring flair for a phrase'.[48]

Whether writing an article for a learned magazine, or a loving tribute to a friend, he always seeks to place the subject's work and achievements in their historical context. Thus the three teachers of prayer of whom he writes in 'On Irish spirituality' for *Theology*, are portrayed 'not as isolated individuals or exceptional eccentrics but as teachers of proved influence [whose lives] throw light on the marks of the disestablished church'.[49]

This chapter would not be complete without mention of his weekly Saturday column in *The Irish Times*.[50] Year after year, decade after decade, it has appeared under the simple signature 'S'. Generally linked to the theme of the Sunday it precedes, what he writes comprises a series of impressions and hints, an individual yet impersonal 'third-person' view. Considering the long number of years that he has been writing and the fact that he never looks back to see what he has written previously, it is amazing that there is so little repetition. Some are bland, mundane, especially where he gives in to the temptation to play around with words. Others are minor masterpieces. A meditation on Advent[51] gives insight into the reason why so many readers look forward to the column every week:

DARKNESS INTO LIGHT

The strong and solemn music of Advent prepares the heart and mind for the coming festival. The lights are lowered and the worshippers sense the mystery of the message of prophecy and promise. Nothing is too clear; we are encouraged to search out a way ahead. The season of early darkness and shortening days reminds us of our needs and deficiencies. Artificial light, brightly blazing, cannot dispel every kind of gloom and dark shadow surrounding us. There is the true light to look forward to; Advent urges us to make sure that our wants and our needs genuinely coincide.

Darkness has a part to play in our spiritual development. We cannot expect to see and understand every issue and problem with an equal clarity. We close our eyes when we pray; not to escape nor to wish away unpleasant distractions but to concentrate upon Him who is invisible. Shutting out the light we symbolise our helplessness and our dependence upon God. Some, in their maturity, remain open-eyed, casting off prejudices and hates, removing the blinkers that shield the wider view, focussing where we can with care and concern on others' needs. Such are the preliminaries to the putting on of the armour of light.

There are many kinds of darkness. The gross darkness of cruelty and greed obviously appals us. Yet there are also twilight regions, less black but subtly misleading, in which apathy, carelessness, and self-pity darken counsel and blind our judgment. We think we can get by with bluff and fudge; this semi-darkness is light enough.

Out of such darknesses, we begin to be shaped, with lessons learnt and pain endured. We benefit when, in addition to going through the motions of the Advent ceremonies, we discern, not without some humbling and agonising, how our lives should be directed.

With God the darkness is no darkness. The night is as clear as the day. So sang the psalmist, when at first he thought he could hide from life's realities and mused 'peradventure the darkness shall cover me'. In the darkness, willingly faced and accepted, discoveries are made. The wisest among us are not know-alls; on the contrary, they are the sort who recognise human limitations. A modern poet has shared some of his wisdom with us in the lines he wrote:

> 'O Lord of hidden light
> Forgive us who despise
> The things that lie beyond our sight
> And give us eyes.'

Another, inspired by a view from his beloved Portnoo, is less substantial but has its own power.[52]

AN ISLAND'S STORY

There is a small island off the north-west coast which has a life and a charm all its own. At low-tide, a sandy corridor, left dry and viable by the ebbing waters, invites the stranger, the searcher after crabs hidden among the creviced rocks, the historian and the pilgrim, too, with a welcome and a warning.

The visit must be short for the waters at the tide's turn will soon flow again, often silently but always rapidly, to leave the island on its own once more. Although approachable, this Iniskeel, for all its nearness to the shore, preserves an atmosphere of isolation and quiet serenity unimpaired.

No dwelling has survived, no traffic apart from the movement of cattle to and from the rich green pasturage that crowns the firm and rocky foundation constantly hammered by the waves.

The silence and security of this fragment of land set in the ever-changing sea, the moods of whose waters can be watched from the high cliffs of the shore, less than a mile distant, with a fascination that never tires.

From such a height, the island seems to lie peacefully like some flat fish basking in the waters. At its eastern end, the mouth, as it were, opens to shape a harbour; the jaws enclose a pool where ships can anchor in water that continues deep, unaffected by the movements of the tide. Above the pool on this eastern promontory, the grey ruins of churches and grave-slabs tell the story of an island-faith sustained through many centuries.

At the western end, less than a mile away, the 'fish's tail' is constantly lashed by the white foam as the sea, more actively swelling at this end of the island which faces the wider, more open expanse of wave and water.

The fins of the fish withstand the splendour and the rage of the frothing swell, as it rises upon the rock and then withdraws, sucking and gurgling, before the next assault. The small island, measured in yards, not in miles, preserves a dignity and a large-hearted personality amid this chafing of the waves.

It has assuredly survived the wildest of storms, for traces of shipwreck and stranded sailors are here also. Yet even on the calmest of days, there is always movement at the island's tip, a stirring that highlights the role of sentinel as well as host in which this island-sanctuary is cast.

For all its scenic beauty, this Donegal island, with the name of a saint from more than a 1,000 years ago, has been a spiritual centre of no mean significance.

Today the history and the eloquent stones remaining, some of them most beautifully carved and designed, still carry a message from a life of faith and discipline of long ago.

The site of a monastic community, near the shore, yet at certain regular times withdrawn in a place apart, tells of the link between two worlds. The locality still speaks in this kind of language in which words belonging to this world's practical problems are intertwined with insights upon eternal values and the meaning of all that has to be endured and suffered.

A calm life amid storms; a simple and controlled rule of life marked the choosing of this ideal site for prayer, study, and the dedicated work of fine craftsmanship. Both the sea-lashed, rugged rocks and the finely sculptured stones figure in this island's story.

This type of article has been most aptly described by Canon R. P. S. Richey as 'like a little piece of music'.[53] As such it offers a pleasant interlude in the fast pace of a daily newspaper, harmony amidst the disharmony of the world; for a brief time it lifts the mind and soul unto a higher plane.

Dr Simms became a frequent broadcaster, giving many series of daily devotional talks on radio and television for the BBC and RTE. His excellent diction made him easy to listen to, his voice commanded attention and he had no mannerisms which could distract viewers on television. In the days before the clergy received training in media techniques producers were grateful that his fluency obviated the need for constant retakes. He received a great number of personal letters of thanks, mostly from Roman Catholics, in joyful reponse to his warm spirituality.

He has also contributed to numerous programmes on Irish illuminated manuscripts, ranging from a schools programme which he scripted and presented for BBC Northern Ireland in 1972 to a small but significant part in major series like Malcolm Billings' 'They showed us the past' for the BBC World Service in 1982 and 'The Celts' by Professor Barry Cunliffe in 1985. His most major undertaking was a three-part series, 'Scribes, Scholars and Saints, The Art of Celtic Manuscripts', which he scripted and presented for UTV in 1987. Filmed over a period of some eight weeks, it involved lengthy trips across the country and made considerable demands on the stamina of a seventy-six-year-old but his presentation was as fresh as ever, if somewhat slower in pace. Although it was a UTV production it was networked across the United Kingdom on ITV and received an enthusiastic response. One letter of appreciation summed up his artistry very well. Professor Ronald Fletcher, a sociologist responsible for several television series on social history, wrote

your own voice and manner of presentation exactly suited the subject-matter. There was a perfect precision of language, articulation and expression, without the slightest trace of the 'academic' in any pretentious sense, and your commentary — personal and direct — carried no touch of 'ego-intrusion'.[54]

Many producers and many viewers have realised that the compelling power of the programmes which he scripted and presented over the years derived from his love of the subject. Likewise love of God and of people show through in his devotional talks and made them compelling.

During his primacy he was often interviewed for news programmes and regularly broadcast Christmas messages on radio and television. The combined effect of these media appearances was to make his even more a household name throughout the land than it had been when he was Archbishop of Dublin. The reaction to the retirement tributes to him on RTE and UTV in February 1980 makes it clear in what high esteem he was held by the viewing public. The controller of local programmes at UTV, J. B. Waddell, wrote to say 'we have been overwhelmed with the reception that [the programme] received throughout Northern Ireland',[55] while one of many other letters illustrates the eagerness of Roman Catholics in the Republic to see Kevin O'Kelly's interview. Fr Gerry Reynolds wrote to say that the whole Redemptorist community in Athenry had gathered in the common room to watch the programme. 'This spontaneous gathering underlined for me an aspect of your achievement as Archbishop — we all felt close to you in your gentle witness to the Gospel of Jesus.'[56]

Broadcasting did not end with his retirement; a number of devotional series followed, as well as contributions to programmes on Irish manuscripts and an evocative biographical talk on Radio Éireann in 1981, under the title 'In my time'. Retirement brought a bonus in that there was more time available for preparation for such programmes, as there was for his writing.

Consideration of Dr Simms as a broadcaster is a side-issue to that of him as a writer. Cardinal Newman is reputed to have said that 'the true life of man is in his letters'; while this may be correct with reference to the single-minded scholar it is too academic a view of George Simms' writings. Although they reflect the man he is, his love of God and his warmth of personality, George Simms is much more than his writings.

Whether because of his onerous episcopate or his belief that writing was for him a sideline, he did not write a major spiritual work. It was never a priority to devote the time and effort which would have been necessary, as ministry was always more compelling for him. The strain of the primacy during such troubled years drained him of energy that no *magnum opus* could be expected in retirement; in its absence the Church of Ireland is the poorer.

IX

RETIREMENT

Retirement constituted a major break: one month Dr Simms was fulfilling a hectic schedule of official engagements, church committees, meetings of church leaders, press interviews, pastoral visits, special services; the next he was free to discard all formal responsibilities if he so chose.

He and Mrs Simms moved to a small, semi-detached house in Dublin, where they were centrally placed for the many involvements of an active retirement. The cumulative pressures of the primacy left Dr Simms tired and worn, as is evidenced by Basil Blackshaw's portrait, painted in 1979.[1] It successfully conveys several aspects of his personality, the quiet dignity of his erect bearing, the sensitivity, shown in the long, slender fingers, most of all the artist captures the soft, compassionate lines of the face, a face aged by the strains and suffering of eleven tragic years in Armagh. It could well be the face of one who had given his all and had no more to give but rest brought rejuvenation and he soon embarked on a new phase of ministry.

Regular commitments, such as a celebration of holy communion in Rathfarnham Parish Church on Sunday morning and another for the residents in St Mary's Home, Ballsbridge, on Friday morning provided a framework of routine. It was important to him to have opportunities to celebrate the eucharist and it gave him pleasure that in so doing he lightened the load for some of the parochial clergy. Gradually he added other voluntary tasks such as a day's duty on the monthly roster in St Ann's Church, Dawson Street; this ministry to the city is dependent on clergy who volunteer as counsellors and who celebrate the daily lunch-time communion as part of their duty.

For Dr Simms ministry was as compelling as ever. Frequent invitations to lead retreats and quiet days and to deliver devotional talks were a source of delight to him, while there was always a welcome for the individuals who sought a hearing. When he was archbishop many people who would have liked to confide in him refrained from doing so for fear of adding to his workload; in his retirement those constraints disappeared.

Strange as it may seem, retired bishops of the Church of Ireland are rarely asked to retain positions of responsibility: that suits some but others, like Dr Simms, are very willing to continue to serve in this way and to relieve their erstwhile colleagues of some of the burden of committee work. Dr Simms continued to work with enthusiasm in many areas, as president of the Sunday School Society, chairman of the A.P.C.K, of the board of *Search* and, from 1986, of the Religious Education Curriculum Committee of the General Synod Board of Education.[2] In October 1983 he was invited to 'come back' for a conference organised by the Standing Committee on the church's role in national life and was touched to be appointed chairman of a cultural section. As already mentioned, he also remained International President of the Leprosy Mission.

Other interesting assignments were offered and accepted; for instance, in 1981, he shared the talks on a Swan Hellenic tour with W. B. Stanford, in 1983 he was asked to represent the Irish Council of Churches at the Lutheran quincentennial celebrations at Eisleben and Leipzig. Each special invitation came because of his experience or expertise in a particular sphere; in this instance his lengthy spell as chairman of the Irish Council of Churches, his long-established ecumenical contacts on the continent and his fluency in German made him an obvious choice.

He now had an opportunity to concentrate on his own writing but with typical generosity he devoted much time to helping other scholars, both in research and proof-reading. As chief proofreader of *The Alternative Prayer Book* he pored over the text for many hours, with the same attention to detail which he had shown as a collator of manuscripts. Many academically-minded bishops devote most of their retirement to a *magnum opus*. It has already been remarked that the strains of the primacy in the seventies made this unlikely but Dr Simms might not have wished to devote the time to this anyway, as he would have had to curtail many of his pastoral duties. As it was, he was content to write in response to specific requests. Thus there appeared a steady stream of books and articles, including his second devotional book, *In My Understanding*, his children's guide to *The Book of Kells* and his history of Tullow parish, to name a few. Likewise he has continued to give talks on *The Book of Kells* and on *The Book of Durrow* all over the country and beyond.

Having relinquished the primacy, Dr Simms revelled in the time afforded for private prayer. His devotional life has changed little over the years, his preference being for a liturgical framework allowing ample space for silence and meditation. On a personal level he understands prayer as 'bringing your thinking into line with God's will' and so it has always been a mainspring of his actions. He sees intercession as part of the work of a Christian, and in retirement he has devoted himself to it to an extent which was impossible during his episcopate. There is a formal aspect in that he follows the prayer pattern suggested by the Anglican Cycle of Prayer and the Leprosy Mission, for example, and an informal aspect in that he intercedes for innumerable individuals often unknown to them. On the other hand, many people, fellow students, members of his flock, bishops, friends, have said 'I often knew George had been praying for me'.[1]

At last Dr and Mrs Simms had leisure for each other, their family and friends; they enjoyed babysitting for their younger grand-children and entertained a succession of visitors to lunch. He even revived a much-loved practice of reading aloud; on holidays in Portnoo he could frequently be found reading Austen, Trollope or another of the English authors, rendering each climax and pause for any member of the family who would sit and listen!

Writing this in 1990, one is aware that, with the passing of a decade since retirement, Dr Simms walks and works more slowly but there has been no reduction in the amount of work he is prepared to take on. Apart from one short bout of illness he has continued to enjoy exceptional health and retains his zest for life.

It seemed appropriate to ask his view of developments over more than fifty years of ministry. As it happened he was asked to give a review of ecumenism in the annual London lecture of the Irish School of Ecumenics in November 1988. His title, 'Continuing Dialogue', gave him scope for a wide-ranging review of ecumenical endeavour, national and international, during his ministry. He eschewed a chronological treatment of developments, neatly avoiding a step-by-step assessment of progress. His borrowing of Hilaire Belloc's phrase 'small beginnings, out to undiscovered ends', illustrated his hope for the future along the lines of St John's assertion, 'what we will be has not yet been made known.'[3]

Among the small beginnings he highlighted conferences, inter-national and Irish, pointing out that 'the conference supplies what reading and writing cannot offer' for there 'mind meets mind, dif-ferent points of view receive an airing with openness, in debate, in informal discussion, in friendships made where disagreements can be expressed in an agreeable (and charitable) manner! There is no doubt in Dr Simms' mind that the Ballymascanlon Conferences still constitute the greatest step in inter-church relations in Ireland during his life-time.

He dwelt at length on improved communication, and on the achievement of the International Commission on English Texts in producing common sections of the liturgy. On the developments of inter-church communication in the violent days of his primacy, he began on the cautionary premise that 'words can kill':

Half truths also could do much damage. Wrily, it was observed in the stone-throwing areas that a half-truth was not unlike half-a-brick; when you throw it up in the air it goes further than the whole article. Statements made by those who would be reconcilers and peace-makers sought to be balanced and were at times neglected or scoffed at as merely bland. Church leaders soon ensured that what they said together indicated their common stance, not becoming party-political, though of course, seeking to influence right thinking among individuals, communities, and all the citizens. Statements were necessary; important also that the reporting of them should be in full, set in their proper context. Counter-productive were headlines that only singled out isolated phrases and unfortunately misled. Communications which emerged from discussion, scripture study and prayer became more coherent and consistent. There was gradually less artificiality and more genuinely combined thinking in the Christmas messages, the pointers towards peace.

Gradually it became clear that simple condemnation of a fatal explosion or a street riot or any act of violence was not enough. Yet if opposition to such methods was not expressed, controversy and adverse criticism of the churches ensued. Ways of overcoming the evil with good are not easily expressed in words. Visits to the bereaved, prayers for a change of heart, encouragement of political activity, rather than the violence of shooting, ambush, and raiding made us realise the limitations of verbal communication.

Other small beginnings were commended, particularly those directly involved in peacemaking. The Renewal Centre in Rostrevor was singled out for its treatment of the whole person, for 'peace is very like healing — correcting prejudices, killing the pains of fear, real fears or the equally imaginary fears, the fears of fears, draining the poisons of hates and instinctive dislikes. Unexamined bigotries are gently but firmly diagnosed and wonderfully dispelled.'

A long-time friend of the School of Ecumenics, he rejoices not only in its continued work of dialogue and study but also, with particular feeling, in its introduction of courses in Peace Studies. It is from the depths of his own experience that he said, 'Too often history seems to imprison the hearts and minds of those who have not had the desire or the inclination to examine the whole story and the complexity of the issues.'

Characteristically it was an optimistic lecture in which Dr Simms chose to highlight 'our joyful fellowship' rather than 'our unhappy divisions.'[4] Although he admits privately the difficulty of remaining optimistic while inter-church talks (even between the reformed churches) progress slowly, he is full of hope for the future. Specifically he hopes for more sharing of churches between denominations, for congregations from different churches to engage in joint projects, for intercommunion at inter-church marriages, aspirations which focus on the actions of the people rather than the deliberations of the theologians. He is also in favour of intercommunion without examination of orders, although he fully realises how controversial an issue it is.

When asked where he envisages renewal for the church he points to the ecumenical process as one source, the development of the ministry of the laity as another; not surprisingly, however, he refers to the prayer, 'Lord, renew your church and begin with me', stressing once again the vital importance of faithful prayer, individual and corporate.

Dr Simms, aware that he is no longer among the church's decision-makers, is increasingly cautious about giving his own opinion on contentious issues such as the ordination of women to the priesthood and episcopate. Knowing how easy it is to offer facile solutions from the sidelines, he refuses to be drawn on the issue. One may criticise his reticence as fence-sitting, but one must respect it, emanating as it does from a humble spirit.

As to liturgical revision, Dr Simms professes himself pleased with *The Alternative Prayer Book*, particularly with the holy communion service which he feels will prove to be durable. He prefers to use the new rite except where circumstances dictate otherwise, and it makes him sad that some congregations have refused to use it. Although he loves the language of *The Book of Common Prayer* his answer to those who attack the modernity of *The Alternative Prayer Book* is that Cranmer's English was modern in 1549 and that revision has been going on for a very long time.

While some argue for *The Book of Common Prayer* as a bond of unity, he is not convinced that uniformity is of value and thinks more in terms of unity in diversity. While he admits that there is some difficulty in defining Anglican worship, he points to the lectionary, participation of the people and the stress on the eucharist as being the distinguishing festures. He would very much like to see a celebration of the eucharist in every Church of Ireland church every Sunday.

His view of ministry has changed little over the years since he was ordained: 'original thinking is not nearly as important as being there at the right moment.' Ministry for him is serving people in God's name and he cites the text of Michael Ramsey's favourite confirmation address; 'O God, my heart is ready, my heart is ready; now I will sing and give thanks'.[5] Retirement and advancing years have in no way diminished his readiness and availability to serve. Far from regretting that that service is no longer of the type which hits the headlines, he rejoices that since 1980 he has had time for the minutiae. He has always believed it very important to be reliable, to attend to detail and has observed again and again that trivial things often turn out to be important.

As ministry is so inextricably bound up with people, he knows that 'you couldn't do much without loving people, even the unlovables, and seeing how much they have to give you.' He has never tired of people and refuses to write anyone off; on the contrary, he determinedly keeps in touch with difficult people, trying to encourage and help them. He perseveres in the sure conviction that God does achieve in our encounters.

One of the striking aspects of Dr Simms' character is the rare combination of consistency and flexibility. He has always been ready to consider new ideas and has read avidly in order to keep abreast of developments but nothing has changed the basics of his faith and outlook, grounded as they are on God who is the same yesterday, today and forever.

This is exemplified by his advice on coping with spiritual dryness; it was written in 1954 but could equally have been written thirty-six years later, when it would have been no less appropriate. In advising the priest about helping the young man in question (who was totally unknown to Dr Simms) he suggests that he should be encouraged to consider the communicant life 'from rock bottom.' He continues;

Ultimately — as Francis de Sales often said — he has got to see the point of loving God. He sees the point and place of love in life (presumably) — loving neighbour, wife, fellow-workers, enemies — can he go on logically to loving a personal God (Creator and preserver of all mankind) and see that if he doesn't do this, he is not running his life on as many cylinders as he should?

The great choice must ultimately be between self-centredness and *God*-centredness. Is he satisfied suddenly to relapse into a self-centred position (not feeling the reality of things) or can he, by brushing up his rule of life and making an effort of will, wait still upon God, offering calmly and unemotionally, often without any feeling, all that is best in his thought, desire and activity to the right end. If he doesn't do this 'offering' regularly his life will get disordered, his energies will be dissipated, he will be partaking of much of the fruit of Christianity but the root will not be in him and he'll dry up.[6]

This is George Simms at his most directive!

In conclusion, it is far too early to attempt an historical assessment of George Simms as a leader of the Church of Ireland. Time alone lends perspective and the contemporary biography must needs be tentative. Whether or not history judges him to have been a great leader, it can now be stated that he will stand as one of the few outstanding figures in the Church of Ireland in the twentieth century.

One inevitably asks what makes a great church leader: the qualities generally pinpointed in spiritual biographies are vision, theological prowess, administrative flair, compelling delivery from the pulpit, but there are two indispensable attributes which are sometimes taken for granted: a deep personal spirituality and an ability to draw others to enter upon or maintain a Christian commitment. The adage that faith is 'caught not taught' is correct in that a radiant spirituality, which might be called charisma, is far more compelling than fine words.

Greatness in leadership remains difficult to define; it is possible to possess all the qualities mentioned without being a great leader. Moreover, there are many styles of leadership, each having validity: John Gregg may be deemed to have been a great leader of the Church of Ireland; without doubt his leadership was quite different from that of George Simms. Likewise Michael Ramsey may enter the ranks of great Archbishops of Canterbury and his style of leadership was different again. Labels are dangerous too; labels for Gregg run along the lines of 'guardian of the faith', for Ramsey 'the saintly scholar' but therein lies the danger of distortion, even of caricature. George Simms could easily be labelled 'the people's bishop', a term which has some veracity but is dangerously misleading.

Whatever the historical verdict on George Simms, bishop, ecumenist, scholar, he will undoubtedly be remembered as a remarkable Christian. In his dealings with people he is marked out by his interest in them (from which stems his phenomenal memory for names), his understanding and compassion. He himself admits that William Temple whom he admired so much, failed to understand many of the weaknesses and problems of the human condition;

no such criticism could be levelled at him. Two other aspects of his inter-personal relationships are noteworthy; he is a Barnabas, someone who encourages and enables, and he backs this up with sustained intercession.

For the most part George Simms has always known his friends better than they have known him. He is not a self-revealing person and is adept at turning the conversation away from his own concerns to those of his companion. Friends have told the author of their repeated resolve, when meeting him for a meal, to talk of his affairs and their subsequent chagrin at spending almost all the time together telling him about their own! This arises not from any desire to be secretive but from an overflowing interest in people, behind which lies a natural reticence. On the other hand, all his friends can tell anecdotes which are extremely revealing: the fact that if he is held up at traffic lights by a person whose car doesn't move he says 'God bless you', instead of honking his horn, speaks volumes, as does the following; on holiday in Portnoo in 1986 one day he went in mufti to the Northern Ireland Children's Holiday Scheme house and struck up a conversation with a group of teenagers, one of whom came from County Armagh. They were discussing the town where the girl lived when the question came 'How do you know Armagh?' and the answer 'Oh, I used to work there'. The conversation flowed on and it was obvious that none of the teenagers realised they were talking with a former Archbishop of Armagh. One of the endearing things about George Simms is that he wears even his humility lightly.

Dr Simms is possessed of the psalmist's sense of awe and reverence and his awareness of the rhythm of each day. His faith makes him ever ready for God to take an initiative, expectant of God in every situation. While he sees God in the splendours of nature, he equally sees him in the most excruciating suffering and in the people encountered in the course of a day. Prayer and work are closely intertwined.

While constantly practising the presence of God, he never loses awareness of the realities of the world. The conundrum of being 'in the world but not of the world' poses no problems for him, for he has the eternal perspective. Worldly wealth has no attraction for him and the most basic comforts suffice. Simple living is matched by a simple, ageless, theology.

In all this he is very much a churchman of the Celtic tradition; his Celtic spirituality was partly derived from his experience of the Donegal seaboard but its chief sources were his study of Celtic manuscripts and the repeated use of early Irish hymns in the daily services at the Training College during the forties. (Not only does he share the Celtic vision of God and his created world but his descriptive writing and word-pictures have much in common with Irish Christian poetry of the monastic period in medieval Ireland.) His is not the robust missionary spirit of Columba nor the solitary spirit of the hermit in his cell but that of the 'quiet pilgrim'.[7] For all his gregariousness and sense of fun, all his love of people, one of the most noticeable aspects of his character is the inner quiet, a creative quiet which is consonant with someone whose life is a journey into God.

The words with which Eric Abbott introduced him as bishop to the people of Cork and those with which, four years later, Archdeacon Royse bade him farewell encapsulate George Simms: an intimate of Jesus Christ, a man greatly loved.

NOTES

CHAPTER I

1 'The 1920s in Donegal', in Sharon Gmelch (ed.), *Irish Life*, Dublin, 1979, p. 117.
2 Ibid., p. 127.
3 Ibid., p. 118.
4 In 1971 the Prior School, already amalgamated with The Royal School, Raphoe, became the Royal and Prior Comprehensive School, Raphoe. The original building was converted into a military barracks.
5 On occasion, Gerald walked the land stretches home from Oxford and George walked home from Trinity College, Dublin. The tradition has been maintained; Patrick Simms, Harry's eldest son, has written the Donegal section of *Irish Walk Guides, The North West, Donegal/Sligo*, Dublin, 1979.
6 See Jonathan Fryer, *A Biography of Christopher Isherwood*, London, 1977, pp. 38–39.
7 Some boys, such as W. H. Auden, were oppressed. See Humphrey Carpenter's *W. H. Auden, a biography*, London, 1987, pp. 16–23.
8 Auden's recollections of his time in St Edmund's quoted in Carpenter, op. cit., p. 17.
9 An older old boy, recalls being 'liturgically overborne, paralysed by repetitive psalms . . . exhausted in Lent by cod-fish and the Miserere. . .' R. C. Robertson-Glasgow, *46 Not Out*, London, 1948, p. 29.
10 Summer report 1924.
11 Letter to J. F. A. Simms, 28 March 1924.
12 Letter to author, 24 October 1986.
13 'In my time' radio broadcast on R.T.E. November 1981.
14 Ronald Prain — *Reflections on an Era*, Letchworth, 1981.
15 Letter to the author, 7 October 1986.
16 Letter to the author, 14 October 1986.

CHAPTER II

1 In the statutes students had been divided into four classes, corresponding to the four years of study for a B.A. degree. One entered as a junior freshman and passed through the ranks of senior freshman, junior sophister, finally to senior sophister. Entrance in the Hilary Term was not exceptional then.

2   In Oxford the first five terms were given to the study of classical texts, leading to 'Mods', the final seven terms, leading to 'Greats' covered the literature, history and philosophy of classical civilisation. Gerald's chief publications are *The Williamite Confiscation in Ireland, 1690–1703*, London, 1956 (Studies in Irish History, vol. VII), *Jacobite Ireland, 1685–91*, London, 1969 (Studies in Irish History, 2nd series vol. V) and a section of *A New History of Ireland*, vol. III, Oxford, 1976, on the Restoration, 1660–85.

3   Letter to parents, 19 October 1932.

4   Women's clubs had to acquire a male representative as DUCAC was a male establishment.

5   Bishop Holmes was George's former rector in Lifford. Bishops of the Church of Ireland who were Trinity graduates used to receive a D.D. *jure dignitatis* from Dublin University.

6   Lecturer in theology in the University of Durham, 1963–1980. His writings were few but included a significant article, 'An Anglican's Reflections on Priesthood', in Nicholas Lash and Joseph Rhymer, (eds), *The Christian Priesthood*, London and New Jersey, 1970.

7   He was ordained in 1937 while assistant master in Eton College. After the war he returned to Ireland as headmaster of Portora Royal School, Enniskillen, whence he went to Dean Close as headmaster.

8   Letter, 20 July 1987.

9   Where his father was rector.

10 Letter, 20 July 1987.

11 Interview, 8 August 1986.

12 His own inquiry into George's suitability was very thorough. He even imposed a voice test in the empty church and followed this with a request to preach an extempore sermon across the vacant pews.

13 Many of the practices condemned, such as the singing of hymns during the communion, have since become accepted and the Canons have been altered to permit them.

14 In 1937 S. R. S. Colquhoun, vicar of St John's, Sandymount, was suspended for his ecclesiastical practices and Simpson and George helped by taking the services for him.

15 The talks were based on addresses given in Oxford in 1931, printed in *Christian Faith and Life*, London, 1931.

16 Ibid., pp. 19–20.

17 Ibid., p. 137.

18 Ibid., p. 126.

19 E. S. Abbott, *Escape or Freedom*, London, 1939.

20 Letter, 26 November 1934.

CHAPTER III

1 At the same time the organist, W. H. Vipond Barry, and his wife taught George to sing the service.
2 He took his first three-hours'-service on Good Friday 1937. Sometimes he was given an unusual task, such as acting as chaplain to the hereditary head of the Assyrian Church when he visited Dublin in 1935.
3 A. G. Hebert, *Liturgy and Society, the Function of the Church in the Modern World*, London, 1936. Later, G. Dix's *The Shape of the Liturgy*, London, 1945, also influenced him.
4 It is indicative of his confidentiality that, half a century later, he would not grant access to this journal but read censored excerpts on request.
5 Letter, 30 April 1939.
6 Letter, 11 May 1937.
7 Letter, 21 July 1941.
8 From a printed excerpt in Dr Simms' papers. Provenance unknown, possibly from a parish circular inviting subscriptions to a farewell presentation.
9 E. S. Abbott and others, *A History of Lincoln Theological College, 1874–1974*, Lincoln, 1974.
10 Letter, 14 February 1938.
11 Letter, 20 February 1938.
12 J. Ford, letter, 26 September 1940.
13 Letter, 1 July 1986.
14 R. C. D. Jasper, *George Bell, Bishop of Chichester*, London, 1967, gives an illuminating account of Bell's pre-war and war-time international work.
15 Letter, 17 January 1987.
16 A. M. Ramsey, *The Gospel and the Catholic Church*, London, 1936, W. Temple, *Nature, Man and God*, London, 1931, E. L. Mascall. *He Who Is*, London, 1943, V. A. Demant, *The Religious Prospect*, London, 1939.
17 Ramsey, op. cit., p. vi.
18 Ibid., pp. 223–224.

CHAPTER IV

1 The appointment was made by the Board of Trinity College, on the recommendation of the House of Bishops. Four years earlier his salary as a priest in St Bartholomew's had been £300.
2 He was assistant lecturer to the Archbishop King's Professor of Divinity, R. R. Hartford.

3 He had to pay for 'Commons', however. Since the earliest times lecturers and resident students dined 'on Commons'. The term refers to the evening meal, eaten in the formal setting of the Dining Hall.

4 Roman Catholics in Ireland had always been discouraged by their bishops from attending Trinity College or any college not under Roman Catholic management. Archbishop J. C. McQuaid, appointed to the archdiocese in 1940, continued the formal ban.

5 On occasion he recommended students to spend a term or two of further training in England or abroad after their divinity testimonium. Several went to Lincoln Theological College for this purpose. Bishop King Irwin of Connor was the first of the bishops to appreciate George's wisdom and to see the difference it made in ordinands.

6 Originally the Fellows' Common Room, with its clubrooms and lunch-room situated in the Dining Hall, it was the chief meeting place for staff.

7 Interview, 2 March 1987.

8 These conferences, attended by students from all over the British Isles, replaced the well-known Swanwick conferences during the war.

9 This maintained houses in Grenville Street and ran camps for boys from poor houses.

10 The late evening office, a reflective service with monastic origins.

11 These ranged from George Berkeley (by the vice provost) to Studdert Kennedy (by R. M. Gwynn).

12 Miller was a Presbyterian from the Iona community. Vidler was editor of *Theology* at the time. His visit led to George's first article for that publication. 'Let the people pray, four hundred years of Litany', *Theology* xlvii, no. 288, June 1944.

13 Letter, 13 February 1987.

14 *St Mark's, Portadown, Parish Magazine*, January 1980.

15 Reading parties were part of the Oxford tradition, organised because Oxford students were not allowed to stay in College during vacations. Another precedent was Bishop Gore's reading parties at Babington and Radley.

16 *Church and State in Fascist Italy*, Oxford, 1941.

17 W. B. Stanford, *A Recognised Church* (Dublin, 1944). H. R. McAdoo, *No New Church* (Dublin, 1945).

18 I am grateful to Canon W. C. G. Proctor for detailed information on inter-church relations. See also L. O. Broin, *Frank Duff, a Biography*, Dublin, 1982, pp. 62–67. Miss G. FitzGerald, librarian of the R.C.B., was also a member.

19 'In my time,' interview broadcast by Radio Éireann, 1981.

20 An aunt, Miss Lucy Gwynn, had been the first lady registrar of Trinity College.

21 Susan M. Parkes, Kildare Place. *The History of the Church of Ireland Training College, 1811–1969*, Dublin 1984, p. 178.

22 Apart from the short-lived journal of his early curacy, the only diaries he has ever kept were engagement diaries devoid of any comment.

23 G. O. Simms with R. W. Jackson and H. M. Harriss, *The Country Shepherd*, Dundalk, 1943.
24 *For Better, for Worse*, Dublin and Belfast, 1946.
25 *Christ, Youth and the Conflict of Life*, Dublin, 1943.
26 680 in all.
27 'In the manuscript room, a cold collation', unpublished talk among Dr Simms' papers.
28 E. H. Alton, Peter Meyer and G. O. Simms (eds), *Evangeliorum Quattuor Codex Cenannensis*, Berne, 1950–51.
29 By the Dublin University Press.
30 In 1949 and again in 1950 a committee was appointed to consider the revision of the baptismal service but the resultant bills both failed. In 1952 Archbishop Barton proposed a bill to revise the Confirmation service, a committee was established but no legislation was forthcoming.
31 He was appointed to represent the needs of the young people of the Church of Ireland.
32 As Warden of the Divinity Hostel.
33. *Addresses and Papers of Michael Lloyd Ferrar, 1909–1960*, London 1962.
34 Op. cit., p. 20.
35 Op. cit., p. 18.
36 Op. cit., p. 21.
37 'In my time', op. cit.

CHAPTER V

1 G. O. Simms, *The Cathedral Church of St Fin Barre, Cork, A Short Guide* (Cork, 1952).
2 The clergy conference which he had planned with the bishop went ahead in September and gave all the clergy of the diocese an opportunity to see him at work.
3 See above, p. 26.
4 An account of the proceedings appears in the *Church of Ireland Gazette*, 10 October 1952.
5 Letter to Dr Simms, 2 October 1952. A lengthy list of candidates was formed by the synod, of whom Dr Simms, Dean Elliott of Belfast and Dean de Pauley of St Patrick's were nominated by the Standing Committee.
6 There is a printed copy in the R.C.B. Library, with no indication of date or place of publication.
7 Interview, 24 March 1987.
8 Population levels fell for all sectors of the Irish population in those years but the Protestant decline was far more than proportional.

9   Stanford, op. cit., p. 17.
10   Ibid., p. 18.
11   Ibid., p. 28.
12   McAdoo, op. cit., p. 11.
13   Ibid., pp. 31–32.
14   Ibid., p. 34.
15   Dr Evans was then fellow lecturer at Corpus Christi College, Oxford, and Dr Hanson lecturer in theology at Nottingham University.
16   To say thousands of names is no exaggeration. As bishop and archbishop he has confirmed more than 20,000 candidates.
17   *Into the Ministry*, Dublin, n.d. (1940s).
18   *Which Way? This Calls for an Answer*, Dublin, 1954.
19   The others were Major C. W. Roberts, the Rev. R. B. Pike, Bishop R. G. Perdue, Archdeacon G. McKinley, J. L. B. Deane, J. F. Eustace and Major S. H. Pakenham-Mahon.
20   Interview, 10 July 1986.
21   *Which Way?* op. cit., not paginated (p. 22).
22   Strictly, the Incorporated Society for Promoting Protestant Schools in Ireland.
23   *Cork Examiner*, 7 December 1956.
24   Resolution 41.
25   Founded in 1923 as the United Council of Christian Churches and Religious Communions in Ireland.
26   A. A. Luce, G. O. Simms, P. Meyer and L. Bieler (eds), *Evangeliorum Quattuor Codex* Durmachensis, Olten, Lausanne, Fribourg, 1960.
27   Letter to R. G. F. Jenkins, 27 September 1955.
28   Later Bishop of Tuam, translated to Connor.

CHAPTER VI

1   The Archbishop of Armagh is Primate of All Ireland.
2   The synod elected Dr Simms on the third vote, in preference to three other men — Bishops McCann and Mitchell, and Professor R. R. Hartford.
3   Article by James H. Reidy for Friday Focus, *Irish Independent*, 14 October 1966.
4   Letter, 10 February 1987.
5   *Focus*, August 1964, vii (a monthly review).
6   *First of All, Report by the Priorities Committee to the Representative Body of the Church of Ireland*, Dublin, 1979, 4,6.
7   *Into the Ministry*, n.d. (1940s) Dublin, not paginated.
8   *Following up a Parish Mission*, Dublin and Belfast 1946, p. 7.
9   *Thoughts after Lambeth*, in *Studies* lvii, winter 1968. A small number of Celtic studies appeared, including *The Psalms in the Days of St Columba*, Dublin, 1960. When he moved to Dublin he was still completing his work for the facsimile edition of the Book of Durrow, which was published in 1960.
10   See above, p. 45.

11 Ibid., p. 25.
12 Ibid., p. 21.
13 London, 1963. Dr Simms showed no alarm in his review for *Anglican World*, issue 17, iii, no. 3, May/June 1963.
14 *The New Essence of Christianity*, New York, 1961, *The Gospel of Christian Atheism*, Philadelphia, 1966..
15 *God, Christ and the World*, London, 1969.
16 Ibid., p, 8.
17 Ibid., p. 98.
18 *Understanding the Trinity*, Eastbourne, 1987, p. 12.
19 Letter to R. G. F. Jenkins, 17 July 1958.
20 *Lambeth Conference, Encyclical Letter, Resolutions and Reports*, London, 1958 2.93.
21 Bishop Bell was quoted in R. C. D. Jasper, *George Bell, Bishop of Chichester*, London, 1967, p. 384. Archbishop Simms was asked to contribute an article on 'New Ways of Worship' for the popular report of the Conference. F. N. Davey (ed.) *Lambeth and You*, London, 1958.
22 Vatican II, Document on Ecumenism, paragraph 13, translation by W. M. Abbott, S.J., *The Documents of Vatican II*, London, 1967, p. 356.
23 Printed in ARCIC final report, London, 1982, pp. 117–118.
24 The Instruction, *Matrimonii Sacramentum*, 1966.
25 Those who completed the Anglican team were Bishop D. H. Y. Hallock of Milwaukee and Bishop R. S. Dean of Cariboo. They both resigned in 1974 on retirement and were replaced by the Rev. L. M. Knox, a theologian from Wisconsin, and the Rev. Barnabas Lindars, S.S.F. of Cambridge University. Those who completed the Roman Catholic team were Bishop L. D. Fox of Menevia, North Wales and Bishop F. J. Spence, auxiliary bishop to the Canadian Forces, later Bishop of Charlottetown, Prince Edward Island.
26 Eugene R. Fairweather (ed.), *Anglican Congress 1963, Report of Proceedings*, Toronto, London, New York, 1963, p. 15.
27 Ibid., p. 122.
28 *Sunday Press*, 8 September 1963.
29 'Toronto Reflections' in *Church of Ireland Gazette*, 25 October 1963.
30 'Looking back on Toronto', in *All Saints' Grangegorman, Parish Paper*, xiii, no. 4, All Saints' tide, 1963.
31 On the Conference see N. Goodall (ed.) *The Uppsala Report*, Geneva, 1968, K. Slack, *Uppsala Report*, London, 1968.
32 Michael Viney, *The Five Per Cent*, Dublin, 1965, p. 36.
33 *The Lambeth Conference, 1968, Resolutions and Reports*, London, 1968, Resolution 22.

34 Ibid., Reports p. 74. See also James B. Simpson and Edward M. Story, *The Long Shadows of Lambeth X*, New York and London, 1969, p. 128.
35 Resolution 34.
36 'The Lambeth Conference, an Appraisal', in the *Church Observer*, Winter 1968, p. 20. The actual quotations come from Dr Simms' original manuscript, which is fuller.
37 Simpson and Story, op. cit., p. 230.
38 Reports, p. 138.
39 Quoted in Alan M. G. Stephenson, *Anglicanism and the Lambeth Conferences*, London, 1978, p. 249.
40 These quotations from the debate are given in Stephenson, op. cit., p. 250.
41 *Church Times*, 13 September 1968.
42 'The Lambeth Conference, an Appraisal', op. cit., p. 19.
43 Letter, 30 August 1964.
44 See for example John Feeney, *John Charles McQuaid, The Man and the Mask*, Cork and Dublin, 1974.
45 *Rome and Canterbury*, London, 1967.
46 Jack White, *Minority report*, Dublin, 1975, p. 131. His study of the Protestant position since the founding of the Irish state affords many valuable insights.
47 *The Irish Times*, 31 July 1952.
48 Desmond M. Clarke, *Church and State, Essays in Political Philosophy*, Cork, 1984, p. 89. Infallibility is claimed only for *ex cathedra* statements. See also V. G. B. Griffin, *Pluralism and Ecumenism, State and Church*, Dublin, 1983.
49 Reported in the *Irish Times*, 20 December 1973.
50 The *Times*, 18 July 1969.
51 *The Irish Times*, 11 February 1980.
52 Interview, 24 March 1987.
53 Formerly the United Council of Christian Churches and Religious Communions in Ireland. For reunion negotiations in the 1930s, see above, pp. 36–37.
54 Letter, 16 October 1987.
55 Susan M. Parkes, *Kildare Place: the history of the Church of Ireland Training College, 1811–1969*, Dublin, 1984, p. 183.
56 My thanks to Mrs Jill Stevens for access to her unpublished thesis (Master of Letters, N.U.I.) September 1984, 'The Marriage Counselling Service, a study of its origin and development'.
57 Interview, 10 July 1986.
58 Interview, 26 October 1986.
59 The beneficed and licensed clergy of the diocese and double their number of laity, under the presidency of the metropolitan.
60 No change was planned in the appointment of the Archbishop of Armagh. This remained the prerogative of the House of Bishops.
61 Letter to Archbishop Simms, 23 May 1959.

62   *Church of England Newspaper*, 12 March 1965.
63   For a thorough treatment of the subject see M. C. Kennedy's Ph.D. thesis (1987), 'The Theological Implications of Recent Liturgical Revision in the Church of Ireland', Open University, 1987. Unpublished, there is a copy in the R.C.B. Library. The minutes and papers of the Liturgical Advisory Committee are also in the Library.
64   The Rev. T. W. E. Drury spoke on 'Prayer Book Revision: The Last and the Next', to the Clerical Association in 1945. Reproduced in the *Church of Ireland Gazette*, 27 April and 4 May 1945. The I.P.P. minutes are in the R.C.B. Library. See also J. E. L. Oulton, 'The Parish and People Movement' in H. M. Harriss (ed.), *Fundamentals of the Faith*, London, 1958.
65   J. Jagger, *A history of the Parish and People Movement*, Leighton Buzzard, 1978. The Rev. K. G. Packard was rector of Fenny Compton, in the diocese of Coventry. De Candole's early writings included *The Sacraments and the Church, a Study in the Corporate Nature of Christianity*, London, 1935. *The Church's Offering, a Brief Study of Eucharistic Worship*, London, 1935. A. G. Hebert, *Liturgy and Society*, London, 1936. *The Parish Communion*, London, 1937. G. Dix, *The Shape of the Liturgy*, London, 1945. The writings of the last two scholars had influenced Dr Simms greatly. See above pp. 21–22.
66   Archdeacon H. W. Rennison of Armagh, Dr A. T. Hanson, Canon R. R. Hartford, the Revs. C. Gray-Stack, G. Mayes, R. E. Turner, J. S. Brown and Major R. Garratt.
67   *Pan-Anglican*, xiv, no. 1, Spring 1968, p. 23.
68   Several members of the Committee have provided information. My particular thanks to Dean Mayes, who has been its secretary since 1976.
69   *Report of the Advisory Committee on Administration to the General Synod 1967*, Dublin 1967.
70   Ibid., p. 38.
71   Dr Simms had been among the speakers who urged the necessity of proper training in order to enable laymen and women to fulfil their ministry.
72   *Report*, p. 6.
73   Ibid., p. 61.
74   Ibid., p. 25. All cathedrals would retain their historic names, whether or not they kept their status.
75   Ibid., pp. 28–29.
76   Ibid., pp. 36–37.
77   Interview, 9 October 1986.
78   Op. cit., p. 21.
79   Ibid., p. 24. Meath and Kildare emerged as a new diocesan combination in 1976.
80   15 July 1969.
81   *The Irish Times*, 18 July 1969.
82   Soon to be appointed Bishop of Kerry.

CHAPTER VII

1 See above, pp. 118–119.
2 London and Oxford, 1972. David Bleakley, a former Labour M.P. at Stormont and prominent member of the Church of Ireland, established a pioneering peace committee in Belfast during the August crisis. His commitment to reconciliation was recognised by Mr Brian Faulkner in 1971, in appointing him as Minister of Community Relations.
3 Ibid., pp. 44–45.
4 Interview, 9 October 1986.
5 Letter, 25 August 1987.
6 Reported in *Ulster Gazette*, 14 October 1971.
7 *The Irish Times*, 18 July 1969.
8 The first time the four leaders made a joint appearance on television was after Mr Callaghan's first visit in 1969, the first joint statement by them was issued in May 1970. Cardinal Conway presented Dr Simms with a typed and bound copy of personal and joint statements made in the 1968–72 period.
9 *Violence in Ireland, A Report to the Churches*, Belfast and Dublin, 1976.
10 Eric Gallagher and Stanley Worrall, *Christians in Ulster 1968–1980*, Oxford and London, 1982. Anyone seeking understanding of the conflict should read their book.
11 Ibid., pp. 203–204.
12 The leading article in *The Irish Times* of 8 September made it public knowledge that he had not signed the statement. The fury of supporters of internment was exacerbated by his later support for an inquiry called for by Cardinal Conway into the working of internment and particularly the allegations of torture. Many of his fellow bishops rallied to his support. Archbishop Buchanan wrote in *Our Church Review*, that month, 'I wish to be identified with him in good days or bad. My trust in him is absolute. I speak, I think, for Dublin'.
13 *The Cost of Discipleship*, revised edition, London, 1959, p. 102.
14 *Belfast Newsletter*, 27 September 1973.
15 *Journal of the Synod of Armagh, 1973*, Armagh, 1974, pp. 7–8.
16 Printed in the *Church of Ireland Gazette*, 11 February 1977.
17 See also C. B. Daly and A. S. Worrall, *Ballymascanlon, An Irish venture in Inter-Church Dialogue*, Belfast and Dublin, 1978.
18 *Journal of the Synod of Armagh, 1978*, Armagh, 1979, p. 13.
19 See D. Bleakley, *Peace in Ulster*, pp. 82–88.
20 Gallagher and Worrall, both members of the Feakle group, give a vivid account in their book; op. cit., pp. 1–2.
21 *Presbyterian Herald*, November 1969.
22 Reported in *Belfast Newsletter*, 8 April 1974.
23 Op. cit., p. 207.
24 H. R. McAdoo gave a clear statement of the nature of episcopal

leadership when he preached at the consecration of the Rt. Rev. R. A. Warke as Bishop of Cork on 1 February 1988. The text is printed in the *Church of Ireland Gazette*, 12 February 1988, pp. 2–3.

25 Letter, 7 June 1987.
26 Op. cit., p. 19.
27 Ibid., p. 19. In the autumn of 1969 Archbishop Buchanan wrote an open letter to Paisley but his charitable approach received an intemperate verbal reply.
28 Interview, 6 March 1987.
29 10 November 1977.
30 Letter, 16 May 1970.
31 Letter, 17 February 1987.
32 *General Synod Reports 1980*, p. 137.
33 The ban on coloured stoles, on making the sign of the cross and bowing, except in the baptismal service and the Nicene Creed respectively, and on carrying a cross in procession was removed.
34 Dr McAdoo was chairman of the sub-committee which produced the Holy Communion 1972 rite.
35 Michael Hurley (ed.), *Irish Anglicanism 1869–1969, Essays on the Role of Anglicanism in Irish Life*, Dublin, 1974.
36 'After Disestablishment', in *New Divinity*, vol. 1, no. 1, April 1970, p. 3.
37 'On Irish Spirituality, the Influence of Three Teachers of Prayer in the Church of Ireland', in *Theology* lxxiii, no. 599, May 1970, p. 195. That number was devoted to the disestablishment theme.
38 Ibid., p. 198.
39 See also his article, 'In Retrospect, Archbishop Plunket', in *Search*, v no. 2, Winter 1982, pp. 28–31.
40 'Studying Scripture Together', in *Petrus* 1977, the magazine of St Peter's College, Wexford and 'Ecumenism in Ireland During the Seventies', in *Aquila*, no. 22, 1980.
41 Belfast 1975, p. 52. The book was based on a series of devotional talks at Mirfield for the Community of the Resurrection.
42 Ibid., p. 63.
43 See above, p. 102.
44 See above, pp. 83–84.
45 Letter, 15 October 1987.
46 Interview, 3 November 1987.
47 This was, in fact, embodied in the new legislation issued by Pope Paul VI in 1970.
48 *Report*, London, 1975, p. 6.
49 In the diocese of Ferns significant progress has been achieved by a joint approach to what are carefully called 'inter-church marriages'. A scheme for joint pastoral care of such marriages was prepared for and endorsed by the bishops, the Rt. Rev. N. V. Willoughby and the Most Rev. Brendan Comiskey in 1986.
50 *Final Report*, London, 1982.
51 Julian Charley, *Rome, Canterbury and the Future*, Bramcote, 1982, p. 21.

52 *Final report*, p. 98.
53 Letter, 30 January 1987.
54 Interview, 7 March 1989.
55 *Report*, London, 1978, p. 30, Resolution 2.3.2.
56 Ibid., p. 37, Resolution 3.
57 Ibid., p. 69.
58 Ibid., p. 39.
59 Ibid., p. 49.
60 See above, p. 89.
61 *I love Idi Amin*, New Jersey, c. 1977.
62 Dehqani-Tafti's son was later assassinated and he and his wife had to flee to exile.
63 *Report*, p. 40.
64 Resolution 18, p. 44.
65 *The Irish Times*, 11 February 1980.
66 Printed in the *Armagh Diocesan Magazine*, February 1980, p. 1.
67 Reported in the *Armagh Guardian*, 14 February 1980.
68 Reported in the *Church of Ireland Gazette*, 15 February 1980.
69 *Prayer and the Pursuit of Happiness*, London, 1985, p. 99.
70 1 Cor. 3.19.
71 Letter, 17 February 1987.

CHAPTER VIII

1 'Between the Lines in the *Book of Kells*' in *The Crane Bag*, ii, nos. 1–2, 1978, p. 104.
2 'Codex Cenannensis', in *Friends of the Library Bulletin*, T.C.D., 1950, pp. 16–17.
3 Folio 34r. The term 'lecture' is really too dry a word to describe the talks he has given. Recent scholarship suggests that the mice may be kittens.
4 Isaiah 11.
5 *Leaves from the Book of Kells*, Dublin, 1962, p. 16.
6 Ibid., pp. 15–16.
7 *Irish Illuminated Manuscripts*, Irish Heritage Series, 29, Dublin, 1980, not paginated.
8 *Leaves from the Book of Kells*, p. 15.
9 Letter, 18 December 1988.
10 Malcolm Billings, 'They showed us the past', BBC World Service.
11 'Early Christian Manuscripts', in Peter Fox (ed.), *Treasures of the Library, Trinity College, Dublin*, Dublin 1986; *Irish Illuminated manuscripts*, Irish Heritage Series 29, Dublin, 1980. 'Scribes, Scholars and Saints', 'The Art of Celtic Manuscripts', a three-part series for Ulster Television in 1987.
12 'Some Notes on the Text of the Book of Kells', in *Hermathena* lxxiv, 1949. 'The Doublet Readings in the Book of Kells', in *Hermathena*

xciv, 1960. For a full list, see Bibliography. Dr Simms has always been a generous scholar, going to endless trouble to provide references, verifications and advice to all who approach him with a query.

13 Op. cit., p. 102.
14 Ibid., p. 51.
15 Ibid., p. 91.
16 Ibid., p. 25.
17 Ibid., p. 53.
18 Ibid., p. 46.
19 A hardback edition, by the Fortress Press, appeared in the U.S.A. and Canada.
20 *In my Understanding*, p. 149.
21 Ibid., p. 120.
22 Ibid., p. 24.
23 For example, 'The Temptation of Our Lord', a sermon preached at Harrow School on 2 March 1961, published as a supplement in the *Harrovian*, lxxiv, no. 16, 1961.
24 *Those Forty Days*, New York, 1961. In *Lenten Counsellors*, a catena of sermons, London, 1962; The *North-East*, Diocese of Maine, vol. xc, no. 1, February 1963; *All Saints' Parish, Grangegorman*, Parish Paper, Lent 1963.
25 *Lenten Counsellors*, pp. 59–60.
26 See above, pp. 145–146.
27 See above, pp. 76–77.
28 'Let the people pray', in *Theology*, xlvii, no. 28, June 1944.
29 *Op. cit., p. 10*.
30 Ibid., p. 6.
31 *Following up a Parish Mission*, Dublin and Belfast, 1946, p. 2.
32 Ibid., pp. 7, 10, 12.
33 *Tullow's Story, A portrait of a County Dublin Parish*, Dublin, 1983.
34 *Rathmichael, A Parish History*, Dublin, 1987.
35 *Tullow's Story*, p. 14.
36 Ibid., p. 32.
37 Ibid., pp. 69–70, Dean Salmon used the same extract when he returned to preach at W. W. L. Rooke's institution in 1971.
38 *Christ, Youth and the Conflict of Life*, Dublin, 1943, p. 18.
39 Op. cit., p. 21.
40 Op. cit.
41 A printed version of a sermon given in the Church of the Resurrection, Queen's University, Belfast, 24 January 1971, Belfast, 1971.
42 In *Everyman*, no. 2 (annual review from the Servite Priory, Benburb) 1969, pp. 121–23.
43 Michael Maher (ed.), Dublin, 1981.
44 'John Allen Fitzgerald Gregg, 1873–1961', in *New Divinity* iv, no. 1, Summer 1974, p. 16.

45 *Trinity Trust News*, v, no. 2, October 1980.
46 *Robert Thomas Hearn, 1875–1952*, memorial sermon preached in St Fin Barre's Cathedral, 20 July 1952, Cork, 1952, not paginated.
47 John Ernest Leonard Oulton, *Trinity*, an annual record, ix, 1957.
48 Op. cit., p. 14.
49 Op. cit., p. 195.
50 See above, p. 66.
51 *The Irish Times*, 12 December 1987. Some of these have been reprinted in *PACE* and in modified form in *Angels and Saints*, Dublin, 1988.
52 *The Irish Times*, 10 August 1985.
53 Interview, 25 July 1986.
54 Letter, 1 September 1987.
55 Letter, 18 February 1980.
56 Letter, 18 February 1980.

CHAPTER IX

1 It hangs in the Alexander Synod Hall in Armagh.
2 Other commitments included the chairmanship of the Incorporated Society, membership of the board of the Church of Ireland College of Education (formerly the Training College), visitor of St Columba's College, governor of The King's Hospital, member of the committee of various charitable institutions such as the Molyneux and Northbrook Homes.
3 1 John 3.2.
4 All the quotations come from a copy of the lecture among Dr Simms' papers.
5 Psalm 108.1.
6 G. O. Simms, letter to J. S. Brown, 18 April, 1954.
7 Canon James Hartin, in interview, 2 October 1986.

SELECT BIBLIOGRAPHY

MANUSCRIPT SOURCES

Dr. Simms' papers, which include:
Correspondence, diaries, sermons, and speeches.
Letters to J. S. Brown, D. L. Graham, R. G. F. Jenkins.
Liturgical Advisory Committee of the Church of Ireland, minutes and papers, 1962-1979 (in R.C.B. Library).

PRINTED SOURCES

Abbott, E. S., *Escape or Freedom*, London, 1939.

Abbott, E. S. and others, *A History of Lincoln Theological College*, 1874-1974, Lincoln, 1974.

Abbott, E. S., *The Little Flock* (sermon preached at consecration of G.O.S. as bishop, 28 October 1952), N.D., N.P.

Advisory Committee on Administration, Report to the General Synod, 1967, Dublin, 1967.

Anglican-Roman Catholic International Commission, final report, London, 1982.

Anglican-Roman Catholic International Commission on the Theology of Marriage and its Application to Mixed Marriages, report, London, 1975.

Bayne, S. F., junior, (ed.), *Mutual Responsibility and Interdependence in the Body of Christ*, London, Toronto, New York 1963.

Bleakley, D., *Peace in Ulster*, London and Oxford, 1972.

Bowen, K., *Protestants in a Catholic State*, Dublin, 1983.

Carpenter, Humphrey, *W. H. Auden, a Biography*, London, 1981.

Chadwick, Owen, *Michael Ramsey, a life*, London and New York, 1990.

Chandlee, H. E., 'The Liturgical Movement', in a *Dictionary of Liturgy and Worship*, ed. J. G. Davies, London, 1972.

Church of Ireland Gazette

Clarke, Desmond M., *Church and State, Essays in Political Philosophy*, Cork, 1984.

Daly, C. B., and Worrall, A. S., *Ballymascanlon, An Irish Venture in Inter-Church Dialogue*, Belfast and Dublin, 1978.

de Candole, H., *Being the Church Today*, Leighton Buzzard, 1974.

Dix, Gregory, *The Shape of the Liturgy*, London, 1945.

Drury, T. W. E., 'Prayer Book revision: the last and the next', in *Church of Ireland Gazette*, 27 April and 4 May 1945.

Fairweather, Eugene R. (ed.), *Anglican Congress, 1963, Report of Proceedings*, Toronto, London and New York, 1963.

Feeney, J., *John Charles McQuaid, the Man and the Mask*, Cork and Dublin, 1974.

First of All, report of the Priorities Committee to the Representative Body of the Church of Ireland, Dublin, 1979.

Fryer, Jonathan, *A Biography of Christopher Isherwood*, London, 1977.

Gallagher, R. D. E., and Worrall, A. S., *Christians in Ulster, 1968–1980*, Oxford and London, 1982.

General Synod of the Church of Ireland Reports, 1930–80.

Goodall, N., *The Uppsala Report*, Geneva, 1968.

Griffin, V. G. B., *Anglican and Irish, What We Believe*, Dublin and Belfast, 1976.

Griffin, V. G. B., *Pluralism and Ecumenism, State and Church*, Dublin, 1983.

Hebert, A. G., *Liturgy and Society, the Function of the Church in the Modern World*, London, 1936.

Hebert, A. G., *The Parish Communion*, London, 1937.

Hurley, M., (ed.), *Irish Anglicanism 1869–1969, Essays on the Role of Anglicanism in Irish Life*, Dublin, 1974.

Iremonger, F. A, *William Temple, Archbishop of Canterbury, His Life and Letters*, London, New York, Toronto, 1948.

The Irish Times.

Jagger, P. J., *A History of the Parish and People Movement*, Leighton Buzzard, 1978.

Jameson, F. C., 'The Church of Ireland and the Irish Experimental Liturgy', chapter 14 of C. O. Buchanan (ed.), *Modern Anglican Liturgies, 1958–1968*, London, 1968. 'The Church of Ireland and the Irish Experimental Liturgy, 1974', in *Further Anglican Liturgies 1968–1975*, Bramcote, 1975.

Jasper, Ronald C. D., *George Bell, Bishop of Chichester*, London, 1967.

Joint Group on Social Questions, *Violence in Ireland*, (report under joint chairmanship of C. B. Daly and A. S. Worrall,) Belfast and Dublin, 1976.

Journal of the Synod of Armagh 1969–1980, Armagh.

Lambeth Conference, Encyclical Letter, Resolutions and Reports, London, 1958.

Lambeth Conference, 1968, Resolutions and Reports, London, 1968.

Lambeth Conference, 1978, Resolutions and Reports, London, 1978.

McAdoo, H. R., *No New Church*, Dublin, 1945.

McAdoo, H. R., *The Unity of Anglicanism, Catholic and Reformed*, Connecticut, 1983.

McDermott, R. P., and Webb, D. A., *Irish Protestantism Today and Tomorrow, A Demographic Study*, Dublin, 1945.

McDowell, R. B., *The Church of Ireland, 1869–1969*, London and Boston, 1975.

Macquarrie, J., *God and Secularity*, Philadelphia and London, 1968.

Mascall, E. L., *Theology and the Gospel of Christ*, london, 1977.

Milne, Kenneth, *S. Bartholomew's, a History of the Dublin Parish*, Dublin, 1963.

Morgan, M. C., *Cheltenham College, the First Hundred Years*, Cheltonian Society, 1968.

Neill, S., *Anglicanism*, London, 1958.

O Broin, L., *Frank Duff, a Biography*, Dublin, 1982.

Oulton, J. E. L., 'The Parish and People Movement', in H M Harriss (ed.), *Fundamentals of the Faith*, London, 1958.

Parkes, Susan M., *Kildare Place, The History of the Church of Ireland Training College, 1811–1969*, Dublin, 1984.

Ramsey, A. M., *God, Christ and the World*, London, 1969.

Ramsey, A. M., *The Gospel and the Catholic Church*, London, 1936.

Ramsey, A. M., *Rome and Canterbury*, London, 1967.

Robertson-Glasgow, R. C., *46 Not Out*, London, 1948.

Robinson, J. A. T., *Honest to God*, London, 1963.

Seaver, G., *John Allen Fitzgerald Gregg*, Leighton Buzzard, 1963.

Simpson, J. B., and Story, E. M., *The Long Shadows of Lambeth X*, New York and London, 1969.

Slack, K., *Uppsala Report*, London, 1968.

Srawley, J. H., *The Liturgical Movement, its Origin and Growth*, Alcuin Club Tracts xxvii, 1954.

Stanford, W. B., *A Recognised Church, the Church of Ireland in Éire*, Dublin, 1944.
Stephenson, A. M. G., *Anglicanism and the Lambeth Conferences*, London, 1978.
Temple, W., *Nature, Man and God*, London, 1931.
Temple, W., *Christian Faith and Life*, London, 1931.
Turner, R. E., 'Revising the Prayer Book, How We Did it', in *Church of Ireland Gazette*, 26 October 1984.
Viney, M., *The Five Per Cent*, Dublin, 1965.
Webb D. A. (ed.), *T.C.D., An Anthology 1895–1945*, Extracts in Prose and Verse from *T.C.D.*, A College Miscellany, Dublin, 1944.
White, Jack, *Minority Report*, Dublin, 1975.
Whiteley, Peter, *Frontier Mission, An Account of the Toronto Congress*, London, Toronto, New York 1963.
Wilson, W. G., *The Faith of an Anglican*, Glasgow, 1980.

OTHER SPECIAL STUDIES

'Unpublished theses'

Kennedy, M. C., 'The Theological Implications of Recent Liturgical Revision in the Church of Ireland', Ph.D., O.U, 1987, (copy in R.C.B. Library).
Stevens, Jill, 'The Mar   riage Counselling Service, a Study of its Origin and Development',   M. Litt. N.U.I. (U.C.D.) 1984. (copy in M.C.S.)

PUBLICATIONS OF GEORGE OTTO SIMMS

This is not a full list; all the major writings are included but the minor writings are so extensive that only a representative selection is listed. They are listed chronologically.

The Country Shepherd, Pastoral Work in Country Parishes of the Church of Ireland, with R. W. Jackson and H. M. Harriss, Dundalk, 1943.
'Your Faith,' in *Christ, Youth and the Conflict of Life*, (report of a youth conference for the dioceses of Dublin, Glendalough and Kildare, held in Dublin 24–31 October 1943), Dublin, 1943.
'Let the People Pray. Four Hundred Years of Litany', in *Theology*, xlvii, no. 288, June, 1944.

For Better, For Worse. A short Introduction to the Marriage Service of The Book of Common Prayer, Dublin and Belfast, 1946.

Preparing for a Parish Mission, Dublin and Belfast, 1946.

Following up a Parish Mission, Dublin and Belfast, 1946.

'Some Notes on the Text of the Book of Kells', in *Hermathena*, lxxiv, 1949.

The Book of Kells, a Short Description, Dublin, 1st ed. 1949, 2nd ed. 1950, 52, 53, 54, 55 3rd ed. 1957, 58, 59, 60.

Into the Ministry, a Letter to Patrick, Dublin, n.d. (1940).

'To Love and to Cherish', in *At the Crossroads: Whither Youth?* (Report of youth conference of dioceses of Dublin, Glendalough and Kildare 1950), Dublin, Belfast and Limerick, 1951.

'The Clubs', in *Trinity, a college record*, ii, 1950.

'Codex Cenannensis', in *Friends of the Library Bulletin, T.C.D.*, 1950.

Evangeliorum Quattuor Codex Cenannensis, facsimile ed., E. H. Alton, P. Meyer and G. O. Simms, Berne, 1950–1951.

'Lent is Here', in *All Saints' Grangegorman Parish Paper*, Lent 1950.

A. E. N. Simms, Memorial Address (at St. Mary's Bryanston Square, London, 1 November 1952), London, n.d.

The Cathedral Church of St Fin Barre, Cork, a short guide, Cork, 1952.

Robert Thomas Hearn, 1875–1952, memorial sermon (in St Fin Barre's Cathedral, 21 July 1952), Cork, 1952.

'The Atmosphere of a Cathedral', extracts printed in *Calendar and Year Book of the United Dioceses of Cork, Cloyne and Ross, 1953*, Cork, 1953.

The Bible in Perspective, Dublin, 1954.

Which Way? This Calls for an Answer, with F. R. Mitchell, Dublin, 1954.

'A Militant Dean', (W. C. Magee) in *Year Book of United Dioceses of Cork, Cloyne and Ross and St Fin Barre's Cathedral, Cork, 1956*, Cork, 1956.

'John Ernest Leonard Oulton', in *Trinity*, ix, 1957.

'Bound in the Spirit, the Message of St Patrick's Confession' in *Theology*, lx no. 44, March 1957.

'Harvest Festivals', in J. C. Caley (ed.), *The Apostles' Doctrine and Fellowship*, California, 1958.

'New Ways of Worship', in F. N. Davey (ed.), *Lambeth and You*, London, 1958.

'The Doublet Readings in the Book of Kells', in *Hermathena*, xciv, 1960.

Evangeliorum Quattor Codex Durmachensis A. A. Luce, G. O. Simms, P. Meyer and L. Bieler, facsimile edition, Olten, Lausanne, Friburg, 1960.

The Book of Kells, a selection of pages reproduced with a description and notes, Dublin, 1961, with several impressions, new ed. 1968, again 1976 and 1988.

'They that wait on the Lord shall renew their strength' (Is. 40. 31) (sermon on the occasion of the College festival in Lincoln Cathedral, 30 May 1961).

'The Temptation of our Lord', (a Lent sermon, preached 2 March 1961) published in a supplement to *Harrovian*, lxxiv, no. 16, 1961.

'Lenten Patience' in

(i) *Those Forty Days*, New York, 1961.

(ii) *Lenten Counsellors*, a catena of Lent Sermons, London, 1962.

(iii) *The Northeast*, xc no. 1, February 1963 (magazine of the Diocese of Maine).

(iv) *All Saints' Grangegorman Parish Paper*, 2nd series xii, no. 1, Lent 1963.

Addresses and papers of Michael Lloyd Ferrar, 1909–1960, ed. with a memoir, London, 1962.

Leaves from the Book of Kells, Dublin, 1962.

'Robert Malcolm Gwynn', in *Trinity*, no. xiv, Michaelmas 1962.

'Be ye doers' (James 1:22) (sermon preached to the 63rd Annual Congress of the British Federation of Master Printers, 19 May 1963, printed in their monthly journal).

Das Buch von Kells, Trans. by Franz Lösel, Dublin, 1983.

'From Ireland to Iona', in *Church Observer*, no. xxi, July 1963.

'Looking Back on Toronto', in *All Saints' Grangegorman Parish Paper*, xiii, no. 4, All Saints Tide 1963.

The Psalms in the Days of Saint Columba, Dublin, 1963.

'Toronto Reflections', in *Church of Ireland Gazette*, 25 October 1963.

'The Appointment of a Bishop', in the *Church of England Newspaper*, 12 March 1965.

'Circa 1933 A.D.', article under the name of 'Outis' in *T.C.D.*, 29 January 1965.

'Israel Then and Now' (a talk on the Holy Land, given in Christ Church Cathedral, Dublin, 26 December 1964), in *Christ Church Year Book 1965*, Dublin, 1965.

Bible reading notes for the Feast of the Circumcision to the first

Sunday in Lent', in *Our response to God* and *Far and Near*, Canada, U.S.A. and London, 1966.

'Memorial Address for Dean Emerson', 22 January 1966, in *Christ Church Cathedral Dublin Year Book*, Dublin, 1966.

Sir Alfred Chester Beatty 1875–1968 (address at funeral service, 29 January 1968), Dublin, n.d.

'The Church of Ireland', in *Pan-Anglican* xiv no. 1, Spring 1968.

'The Lambeth Conference, an Appraisal', in the *Church Observer*, Winter 1968.

'Thoughts after Lambeth', in *Studies*, lvii, Winter 1968.

'James Henthorn Todd, Centenary Tribute', *Hermathena*, cix, 1969.

'The Role of Protestants in Ireland Tomorrow', in *Everyman* ii, (annual review from the Servite Priory, Benburb), 1969.

'After Disestablishment, Years of Spiritual Maturing in the Church of Ireland', in *New Divinity* i, no. 1, April 1970.

'On Irish Spirituality, the Influence of Three Teachers of Prayer in the Church of Ireland', in *Theology*, lxxiii, no. 599, May 1970.

'The Founder of Armagh's Public Library', in *Irish Book Lore*, i, no. 2, August 1971, and *Long Room*, Bulletin of the Friends of the Library, T.C.D., v, 1972.

'What about the World Council of Churches?' (sermon preached at Queen's University, Belfast, 24 January 1971). Belfast, n.d.

'John Allen Fitzgerald Gregg, 1873–1961', in *New Divinity* iv, no. 1, Summer 1974.

'As Others See Us', in *Presbyterian Herald*, July/August 1975.

Christ Within Me, Belfast, 1975.

'The Making of a Sermon', in *New Divinity* vii, no. 2, Winter 1976.

'Studying Scripture Together', in *Petrus*, 1977 (Magazine of St. Peter's College, Wexford).

'Between the Lines in the Book of Kells', in *The Crane Bag* ii, nos. 1–2, 1978.

'The 1920s in Donegal', in Sharon Gmelch (ed.), *Irish Life*, Dublin, 1979.

The Book of Kells, Symbols of the Four Evangelists, (Belleek Collectors' Society), Dublin, 1980.

'Ecumenism in Ireland During the 70's', in *Aquila*, xxii, 1980 (magazine of St. John's College, Waterford).

Irish Illuminated Manuscripts, (Irish Heritage Series 29), Dublin, 1980.

'Some Insights from the Churches of the Reformation', in Michael Maher (ed.), *Spirituality*, Dublin, 1981.

In my Understanding, Dublin, U.S.A. and Canada, 1982.

'In Retrospect: Archbishop Plunket', in *Search*, v, no. 2, Winter 1982.

Le Livre de Kells, translated by Evelyn Montague, Dublin, 1983.

Leabhar Cheanannais, translated by Seamus O Dugain, Dublin, 1983.

Tullow's Story, a Portrait of a County Dublin Parish, Dublin, 1983.

'Irish Spirituality', in M. McCarron (ed.), *Just a Thought*, (a selection from the series of the 1983–85 programmes on Radio Éireann), Cork and Dublin, 1985.

Pioneers and Partners, G. O. Simms with R. G. F. Jenkins, Dublin, 1985.

'The Book of Kells', in *Protext II, Proceedings of the Second International Conference on Text Processing Systems*, Dublin, 1986.

'Early Christian Manuscripts', in Peter Fox (ed.), *Treasures of the Library, Trinity College Dublin*, Dublin, 1986.

'The Book of Durrow', in *Protext III, Proceedings of the Third International Conference on Text Processing Systems*, Dublin, 1987.

Rathmichael, a parish history. Kathleen Turner, ed. G. O. Simms, Dublin, 1987.

Angels and Saints, (articles from *The Irish Times* in modified form), Dublin, 1988.

Exploring the Book of Kells, Dublin, 1988.

'In the News, The Book of Kells', in *P.S.A. News*, of (Past Students' Association of the Church of Ireland College of Education), May, 1988.

Brendan the Navigator, Exploring the Ancient World, Dublin, 1989.

INDEX